MW00612320

Dancing the Tightrope

What People Are Saying

Lynn is a *Master Storyteller.* But it's more than that. Yes, the stories are entertaining, but more importantly, they are both *metaphorical and applicational.* Lynn is able to take a story from her experience and relate it to ours. She is able to draw analogies that help us understand the principles. And given all of her years of experience, she is able to cut through the theory and focus us on what is really important to making our own improvement journeys. This book does all that and more.

" Kendall Lyman, Founder, The Highlands Group, a firm specializing in transformation at the individual, team, and organizational levels

As a rider/horse owner and with more than 45 years in the corporate world, I found that Lynn Carnes' book Dancing the Tightrope hit home. Her *relatable challenges* and experiences, personal fears, and struggle with perfectionism are things every rider and every driven adult in the working world experience. *There are helpful solutions/tools for all.* Thank you!

" Debra Faraone, Senior Account Manager, Target Marketing Group

Lynn is a *pioneer* who is truly multifaceted and gifted. Her strength is simply coaching and allowing YOU to identify your internal strengths. Her book demonstrates how she can take very complex concepts and feelings, and break them down into an *understandable and workable plan* of awareness and balance. Coaches who have "played" my sport, gain my ear. Lifetime advisor and friend!

" Roger Sipe, Healthcare Executive

This book is for anyone dealing with anxiety, wanting to find their passion and act on it, or anyone attempting to climb the corporate ladder. Culture can be brutal unless you have a plan to navigate it. Through a series of interesting and inspiring stories, Lynn does a wonderful job of *demonstrating how pressure can be used to your advantage* – if you learn how to use it! Lynn is one determined chick! She provides so many lessons in this book, with supporting diagrams that make it easy to understand the messages. You now have the tools and actions that can help you use pressure to your advantage too.

" Gail Morales, Former Strategy and Transformation Banking Executive

What a gift this book is! It hits the mark on so many levels – so much so that it is now on the list of books I point clients and colleagues toward as essential reading. You've actually done humanity a great favor by sharing the story of what the fall taught you and the lessons of dancing the tightrope. I have no doubt the benefits gained from that jarring moment will continue to come forward and ripple out as others open the book to find the *treasure trove of brilliant nuggets* you have gathered. Thank you.

“ Melissa McNair, Integrated Life Practices

It's amazing to see the parallel in Lynn's actual falling off a horse and my allegorical one. This connection completely drew me in to her story as I clearly visualized the many pictures she has created for the reader. I love how *Lynn has taken all the work she has done mentally and physically and turned it into something everyone can identify with.* A new co-worker of mine once said "prepare to get comfortable with being uncomfortable," and this work beautifully helps explain what she meant by that statement.

“ Stephanie Case, Workday Healthcare, Principal Managing Partner

In this book, Lynn Carnes creatively outlines through personal stories the different tools we develop as children to deal with stress and pressure, and how those tools are utilized for the rest of our lives. Lynn uses her personal and hard-learned life lessons to help readers grow out of their own locked-in structure of stress and pressure management. I really enjoyed the trip through time as we learn lessons side-by-side with Lynn from ages eight to present. *The stories were both fun and insightful.* Overall, I would give this book a *ten of ten,* and it is a *must read for any professional.*

“ Stephen Fusco, Senior Financial Advisor

In our current pressure-filled world, we can easily become paralyzed with fear and uncertainty. Instead of reacting by engaging in the "fight" or running and hiding, Lynn Carnes' *delightful and vulnerable storytelling* challenges the reader to learn the art and science of Dancing the Tightrope in order to be fully present, centered and balanced to respond wisely in each pressure-filled moment. Through a shift in mindset, the reader gains wisdom, encouragement and tools to solve problems by embracing the fear and allowing it to inform and guide instead of inspiring us to run and hide. I *highly recommend* Dancing the Tightrope to anyone interested in becoming more balanced and courageous in the face of fear and uncertainty.

“ Elizabeth Brooke, M.Div. Formation Director, Church of the Redeemer

Fear is a tremendous motivator. In Dancing the Tightrope, Lynn uses *personal vignettes to analyze the forces that come into play during stressful situations* and ways to channel those forces into something productive – allowing one to dance, not just walk, the tightropes of life.

“ John T. McElveen, Jr., M.D.

If you want to change and transform your life, this book is for you. Lynn's vulnerability highlights how fear can be your enemy or your teacher, leading you to inner freedom and inner confidence. When leaders overcome fear, they build resilient teams and high-performance culture. Overcoming fear and the impact of fear starts with self-awareness. But awareness only goes so far. Inner transformation and behavioral change are essential to a successful life. *Lynn provides examples and tools to help leaders transform and excel.*

“ Susan Robertson, Founder of Linceis Conscious Business and
Author of *Real Leadership: Waken to Wisdom*

Dancing the Tightrope is without question a *worthy read* by all accounts. From a personal perspective, I can naturally relate to many of the experiences, situations, and consequential outcomes that Lynn writes about. I feel certain that most who read this book will similarly, primarily because Lynn addresses Fear, Pressure, and Mistakes as inevitable factors in our lives. How we choose to manage through, find balance, or "Dance" with these elements essentially defines or determines who we ultimately become. It's important to be aware of, or recognize the impact and effects of fear on our lives, and to be able to apply the necessary tools and exercises to deal with it. Lynn does a *masterful job through storytelling* and chronicling some of her own experiences, of *providing perspective* as well as some clear and *digestible guidelines* to follow when we are faced with fear. I *highly recommend* this book to anyone who truly has the innate desire or drive to continually evolve and grow, be it professionally or personally.

“ Dwayne Hildreth, Storyteller and Consultant

No matter who you are, what you do, or what stage of your personal journey you are in, on some level, when under pressure, you may still be responding to some inner "tyrant" who is the total of all your past experiences. These responses are exacerbated as the pressure increases. In Lynn's earlier works, she shared the concept that we can say "no" (The Delicate Art) and survive, and that it works better to assume positive intent (The Elegant Pivot) rather than to always respond defensively. *Yet it took a simple, yet traumatic, event in Lynn's life to lead her to this next insight shared in Dancing the Tightrope.* We would like to believe that our complex, rapidly changing world is driven by technology. However, Lynn points out it remains driven by the natural world, that of relationship. Lynn posits the theory that instead of addressing our complex situations by our "rules" (learned behaviors from past experiences), we can with patience, curiosity, and courage develop new "tools" which are fluid and much better suited to achieve positive outcomes in today's complexity.

❝ Susan Kelly, Retired Corporate Executive

I have known Lynn since 2008. We met doing what we both love — water skiing. Lynn talks about her own experiences, actions, and what was driving those. *She analyzes clearly* her thinking and decision-making. Reading this helped me to analyze, reframe, and rethink my own actions, thoughts, and decisions or be satisfied and content with them. And it helped me to open my mind to understand and see what somebody else's drivers and motivations can be. It's almost as good as sitting with her in a room and talking it through.

❝ Heike Neumann, Marketing Executive

Lynn's book is a must read for anyone who has been faced with, is currently faced with, or will be faced with a challenge. Although not all of us have physically fallen off a horse, I am almost certain we have all had a similar metaphorical experience. Lynn's use of a personal experience to explain the process of turning what may appear as an unfortunate situation into a positive life change is laid out in a way that we can all grasp and understand, a truly *revolutionary feat* in the realm of coaching. *This book is a salient life tool* that should not be overlooked!

❝ Harley Smith, The Proper Group

Lynn Carnes' book Dancing the Tightrope is *wicked smart,* with many interesting stories that can *help you on your own journey of discovery* from perfectionism (not!) to personal strengths (yes!). Lynn and I met in Seth Godin's Akimbo Writing in Community during the pandemic. She has inspired many other writers and me with her *wit, candor, and fantastic business sense* as we muscled through our daily writing together, along with Zoom calls for accountability (cheerleading). Lynn masterfully turned thousands of words that need to be in the world into her books, like the one you are holding now. Thank you, Lynn!

❝ Terri Tomoff, author of *The Focused Fight A Childhood Cancer Journey: From Mayhem to Miracles*, and Chief Sewist of NeedleOnFull - Quilting and Long-Arm Sewing Services, dedicated to creating one-of-a-kind T-Shirt Quilts and more!

Carnes & Associates, Inc./Publishing Division
PO Box 127
Lake Lure, NC 28746

Paperback ISBN: 978-1-7332171-5-6
First Edition

Printed in the United States of America

Dancing the Tightrope

What Falling Off a Horse Taught Me About
Embracing Pressure, Fear, and Uncertainty

LYNN CARNES

Contents

FOREWORD

I first met Lynn Carnes and her husband Russ Pitts a decade ago when they were spearheading a campaign to fund a school for the community of Lake Lure. I was impressed with her energy and drive and organizational skills; Lynn and Russ and many other volunteers did indeed succeed in building what is now a flourishing charter school for all grades.

So, when a mutual friend suggested that Lynn wanted to get back into riding, I was delighted to invite her to share one of my three mature Kentucky Mountain horses, Mocha, for a trail ride in our Walnut Creek Preserve equestrian community, along with my sister-in-law Mary Kreider. As we were preparing to mount, I remember saying to her, "Use one rein at a time to walk him down a hill so he walks back and forth across the trail and not straight down." Of course, hearing and doing are two different skills, especially under pressure. I was last in the line of three when I rounded the curve and saw Lynn on the ground, with Mocha a few yards down the trail and Mary already off her horse, peering at Lynn with deep concern.

Lynn will tell you about the journey from that moment. What I want to convey is her extraordinary reaction to this traumatic event. Many would blame the horse, the horse's owner, or even the trail. Lynn did no blaming. She took total responsibility for her actions and decisions, and used this terrifying moment as a catalyst to seek training and to grow into a very capable rider who is today a true partner to whichever of my horses she is riding, including Mocha. My geldings show clearly that they like her, trust her and willingly submit to her direction now that she knows how to be their leader. She in turn has applied what she learned from this experience to other aspects of her life, and that is the inspiring story she tells here.

I too had experienced a version of Lynn's journey with horses. I bought a gentle older horse with my own savings when I was eleven. He only threw me once, when someone set off a firecracker and scared him. I lived in flat Florida then and didn't realize how much I didn't know until forty-five years later when I bought a green three-year-old Morgan to "get back into riding" on our farm in North Carolina. It quickly became obvious that I did not know how to work with a green three-year-old who spooked at everything, and that even with many lessons I would be better off trading for a more mature horse if I wanted to enjoy riding in my mid-fifties and beyond. Giving up a bad idea was a lesson in itself. I too am a dedicated achiever, and, like Lynn, I needed to learn to cut my losses and focus on my ultimate goal to enjoy riding again, using the new horse skills I had learned on the young horse to become a good partner to my new reliable horses.

Now I count Lynn as a good friend, a very fine riding companion and an inspiration in other unrelated areas of my life as I challenge myself to be the person I want to be. May this book inspire you as well.

Barbara (Babs) Suddath Strickland
Lake Lure, North Carolina

FOREWORD

I met Lynn several years ago. She was a friend of a client and she contacted us when she wanted to take a look at the work we do with horses as a possible tie-in to her coaching role with clients in the corporate world. The work I do is based on building and reinforcing your mental foundation through working with horses. The system that has developed over the years is called Natural Humanship™, because a true horseman (or horsewoman) can tell you, it is most often the human and not the horse that should build a foundation first. In other words, the "problem" usually isn't the horse but instead is the person when a conflict arises within that relationship. We can take that concept and apply it to other areas of life: relationships with our family members, friends, co-workers, etc. Through this work, the horse can become a metaphor for numerous aspects of your life, allowing you to work on your mental tools in a powerful way.

The first time Lynn came to work with us in the round pen, she came ready to work, to show what she already knew about horses and what she could do. I usually spend some time sitting on the back porch with new clients going over some of the key points in the system, but I could see that Lynn was really only interested in action. Her first task was to go into the field and pick a horse so we could get started, and it seemed to me that she was taking a very long time. Keep in mind we do sometimes stop and capture moments, so that does draw things out, but in this case, her actions weren't meshing with her talk. She wasn't as ready as she thought she was; in fact, she was almost paralyzed by her belief that she had to be able to complete an entire "picture" all at once. You might get away with that in "People's World," but in working with the horse, that attitude just doesn't work. We call it TyranT Mindset and the horse quickly realizes that if you're not in control, he/she will be. I believe that realization was a reality check for Lynn.

Whatever Lynn felt after that first session brought her back, realizing that if she was going to help her clients, she had to really experience the work for herself. As we built a working relationship, Lynn began to bring clients to us for workshops as part of their coaching sessions. Through these clients, she started to see that she wasn't really unique in her own personal growth journey. She began to realize that everyone's trauma could be addressed through the round pen, with the horse as a metaphor for their co-workers, supervisors, corporate environment, etc. She had already seen that the work was helping her, but when she saw that the work was also a powerful tool for helping others, it took her to another level of understanding. I believe that as the clients worked, she was working through them, to the extent that she was finally able to take her own mask off and deal with her original riding accident, the one that truly brought her to us in the first place. What she realized was the accident represented a multitude of other situations from her past that she hadn't dealt with. She thought the fall was the problem but finally found that it wasn't the fall, but the pressure created by the fall that continued to affect her. In working to get back on the horse, she started to deal with those other things. I believe her biggest takeaway has been the ability to deal with pressure. In working on getting back on the horse, she was really working on getting back to life, becoming her own.

It was actually the same with me in the beginning of my own journey. I thought I was going to help horses, but what I eventually realized is that horses didn't have problems; I was the problem. I represented the world we've created and that world was the problem for the horse through me. In the same way, Lynn's breakthroughs happened through the work because of the mirror the horse was offering. I can remember Lynn's major round pen meltdowns when she wasn't able to accomplish certain tasks. To see her now, when she struggles, it becomes an opportunity, not a mistake. She is able to let the situation tell her what to do, and when and how to do it. She doesn't get upset, well most of the time, anyway! To see that transformation within her, getting back to her own personal language and being in tune, is really a shift.

Over time, I've had to realize that I'm not selling anything; the work is what it is. I have to listen to the person and make connections so they can receive the message. In other words, I can't help those who aren't ready to help themselves. When you want to make a difference, when you want to make lasting change within yourself, your team, your company, this work is here. It's up to you. Over the years, Lynn has lived up to that challenge. To repeat an overused quote, she not only talks the talk, she is walking the walk.

Bruce Anderson
Nature's View, Camden, South Carolina

INTRODUCTION

Over the past 20 years, I've coached hundreds of corporate executives on dealing with pressure, uncertainty, and failure. Every one of them was more than capable of achieving any goal they set out to do – as long as they had full control. Not one of them had full control. None of us do.

We just like to think we do.

Nowhere does our lack of control become more evident than when the pressure is high.

Raise the pressure high enough, and your basic skills such as walking and even talking can suddenly seem out of reach. Tension fills our bodies. Muscles stop working. Brain cells quit connecting. We might "know" how to do something, yet under pressure, it's as if our knowledge is on the other side of an impassible canyon.

We all have a pressure gap, the space between the pressure in a situation and our mental tools. It's not about our skills. It's about our mental tools to bring those skills to bear under pressure. Even though we might have been talking our whole lives, giving a speech is not the same as talking to your neighbor across the fence. While we might all HAVE a pressure gap, we rarely if ever talk about it. For example, we might say we don't like giving speeches, but we don't say it's because there is a gap between my mental tools and the pressure in that situation.

The pressure gap can cause us to do illogical things, like use fear to fix fear. Or work incessantly to be free from work in some faraway future. Or use money to buy love and status and friendship. Or fall back on prior strategies when they are past their expiration date.

At some level, we know these things are illogical. For example, in all my years of coaching, not one client has ever asked me to help them figure out how to put more work into their work-life balance. We also realize that somehow, some way, we must address fear.

We also must work and make money, allow past strategies to inform us, and we have to balance thousands of other factors. During my corporate career, working in one of the mega-banks, it felt like I was always walking a tightrope, trying to balance SO MANY factors and walk the line to what I saw at the time as the path to success.

As leaders, we are walking tightropes all the time. We balance the short term with the long term. We balance the external forces of change with the internal ability to respond. We balance what is essential in our cultures with what is no longer serving us. We balance providing resources with delivering results. We balance our personal needs with the needs of the whole.

We value consistency, yet consistency overused is stagnation. We value flawless execution, yet flawlessness cheats innovation.

The balancing acts are endless.

Many of our most challenging balancing acts happen out of sight; the thoughts, inner beliefs, values, and emotions that drive our actions. We must balance the need to prove ourselves with the constant need to improve ourselves in an ever-changing world. We must balance what is good for ourselves with what is good for the people in our lives. In fact, many of our most delicate balancing acts happen around the question of what is good for the individual versus what is good for the whole.

These are the kinds of balancing acts that cause very smart, very capable executives to hire an executive coach. The pressure to perform, to align the many factors, and to sustain a high level of focus takes a toll. These same smart, capable executives second-guess themselves, put important areas of life such as family and health on the back burner, and lose their sense of purpose.

What clients ask me to do is help them find their power, restore their balance, and get a glimpse of peace of mind.

They want to change.

They want change.

You can't have one without the other.

There's a teeny, tiny problem with the need to change – or the act of leading change for that matter. You aren't going to get it "right" the first time. Or maybe the second time or third time.

In other words, changing something leads to mistakes. As a society, we talk a good game about mistakes. We say, "mistakes are learning opportunities," and "mistakes will make us better." If we really meant that, change would be easy. We would not obsess over the little things that go wrong when so much is going well.

Instead, we change what we know without changing how we behave.

My favorite way to change has always been to read a book. Gaining knowledge seemed like the key to everything. Once, one of my many coaches along my journey said something to the effect of, "Why don't you quit talking about being different and actually be different?" Another coach put me on a book moratorium. "Read no books for at least six months. Just DO the things you say you know how to do and see how that might actually work in real life."

Can you see how I might have a pattern there? My knowledge-gaining pattern was sort of like me learning to throw pottery. It looked so simple in the movie Ghost. "How hard can it be?" I thought.

All the knowledge I gained in books was pretty simple until I needed to do it in a real situation with real consequences. Rarely could I tolerate the feeling I got when trying something new, making mistakes, and being a beginner.

Eventually I learned to apply many methods as well as develop my own – effective methods – of creating change. My life was much better after practicing what I had learned, such as journaling, meditating, inner child work, exercise, and creating new habits to replace old ones.

These methods worked – to a point.

Then I fell off a horse.

It was a bad, hospital-inducing fall. My pressure gap had life-threatening consequences. Yet this "awful" event led to life-affirming insights and real change. Recovering would eventually raise my pressure threshold and lead me to the other side of fear.

Falling off a horse happens to someone, somewhere every day. So how could a fall off a horse lead me to the other side of fear? Especially when horses were not even part of my life, other than having a couple of friends who asked me to start trail riding with them? How could a simple accident turn into perhaps the most pivotal, powerful defining moment of my life?

I had many pivotal moments leading up to this, and I can break those moments into one of three journeys. First came my Career Journey. This one started in early adulthood when I got married at eighteen, finished college graduating summa cum laude, had a successful career in banking, and became a single mom. My career began to feel empty, my daughter struggled with drugs, and my marriage hit the rocks. Before my Career Journey killed me, I began to wake up to my Creative Journey. My Creative Journey was marked with meditation, self-awareness workshops, healing, painting, and pottery. It also correlated almost perfectly to my transition from being a cog in the corporate wheel to becoming an entrepreneur starting my own leadership development firm.

Dancing the Tightrope chronicles my Pressure Journey, covering a three-year period from the fateful fall to that pivotal test of my skills and confidence to get back on THE horse. (His name is Mocha by the way, and he's one of the most gentle, beautiful horses you could ever meet.)

This accident spiked my fear meter in ways I didn't even realize until I had a chance to get back on a different horse in a completely different setting. That's when I knew that I would either allow fear to own me or shape me. The first horse I mounted after my accident was a reining horse and a stallion to boot. My fear was tipping the scale at a solid 10. I was so flooded with adrenaline; I refused the reins to lead my own way. We just walked around the arena, the trainer leading me like a kid on a pony ride. In many ways, I WAS a kid on a pony ride.

A scared little girl with the opportunity to learn to use the tools that would help me grow up.

Fortunately for me, this accident conspired to put me in touch with different teachers, coaches, and mentors that, through varying levels of support, introduced me to a whole new plane than the one on which I had been operating. I had historically sought answers in the dimensions of knowledge, skills, rules, and effort. The horse trainers – and the horses – eventually helped me deepen my awareness, in real time and under pressure – that the root of the problems started with me, my beliefs, my thoughts, my emotions, my tools, and my energy. They taught me to recognize and be responsible for how I came to the situation or relationship and to actually DO something different – in the moment and under pressure.

It's easy to think that learning to perform under pressure is reserved for high-level athletes, public speakers, and daredevils. We often don't recognize the pressure we feel when the boss says, "Let's talk about that meeting," or when our spouse gets suddenly cold or when we realize that we might have made a mistake.

Early in my Creative Journey, I put enormous pressure on myself to make every painting a masterpiece. I had a personal rule that it was shameful to waste art paper. The pressure to paint a beautiful painting every time often froze me, brush in hand, even though nobody ever died from a bad painting.

This Pressure Journey showed me that we are all under pressure, and the pressure is often higher than we are aware (or care to acknowledge). It's almost as if we try to pretend the pressure away so we can keep up the illusion that we are mistake-free, in control, and all is well.

Pressure can feel like our own personal hell.

Yet, what if the pressure is a good thing? What if the control we crave is only available when we quit striving for it? What if missing the target leads to something that matters so much more than making the goal? What if we have it all backward? What if pressure is the catalyst to living in the moment?

Over this multi-faceted, three-year journey – and beyond – I've come to see that if I reverse the direction of energy from outside-in to inside-out, I have access to a much deeper set of resources that allows me to handle pressure, uncertainty, and failure in ways that expand me rather than crush me.

Reversing the order of what matters is much, much easier said than done.

You can't think your way out of a problem created by how you think, any more than you can lift a bucket up while standing in the bucket. You must find a way to get out of the bucket.

The deeper I've gone into this journey, the more I realize that our goals are the byproduct of the internal work that really matters. Society, schools and even our parents teach us that achieving goals is the point of life. This set of societal rules only makes sense if the purpose of our life is to build a resume.

But I don't believe we are here to build a resume, achieve goals, or make a bunch of money. We are each born with a unique spark, and our domestication designed to force fit us into "the way things are" has a way of dimming that spark as it forms us into socially acceptable humans. While society might prefer we be cogs in the wheel, the Divine unleashes us to be the light only we can bring.

The work that really matters – at least to me – is to become who the Creator made me to be, quirks and all. The most important journey of all is the one that only we can do, the journey back to our true selves.

As I was finishing this book, a friend texted the following to me:

"Know thyself," said Socrates. "Be thyself," said Plato. "Know the world of Nature, of which you are a part," said Aristotle, "and you will be yourself and know yourself without thought or effort. The things you see, you are."

There is no better teacher for us humans than Nature. Horses help bridge us to Nature. They are Nature. They show us our nature. They bring us back to who we really are.

Before I could understand any of this, first I had to deal with the big question: "Would I ever get back on the horse?"

A note to readers

I'm a huge fan of simplicity on the other side of complexity. My brain needs shortcuts to remember what really matters, especially under pressure. This book is going to take you through the complexity of my journey, including the false starts, denial, and the thinking that I already knew it all. During the process, I was introduced to new language, which I bring into this book, along with the stories and confusion I felt when I heard the words. Taking the reader through some of what I went through is the only way I can find to present incredibly complex information that is at the same time, very simple.

To that end, I'm going to go ahead and give you the secret to everything right here at the beginning of the book. When I'm under pressure, I can either reach for my Rules or reach for my Tools. Reaching for my Rules keeps me the same. Reaching for my Tools allows me to shed the armor that has kept me from accessing the spark the Creator gave me at birth.

Focusing on following the Rules perfectly causes us to over - or underreact, and that's where the book title comes from. Dancing the Tightrope simply means I'm in the moment, here and now, and that I've calibrated my balance point in such a way that I don't over - or undershoot in that moment. I'm only on the tightrope for moments at a time. Those moments are priceless, and anyone can have them. The side effect of all of those moments may hold the secret to a happy life. That's what this book is all about.

CHAPTER ONE

Too Much Pressure for Me

Just a Simple Trail Ride Through the Woods

As the three of us set out on the trail that day, I remember having the thought, steeped in ignorance, "This is sort of boring." This was my second time to ride with my friend Babs and her sister-in-law Mary. I was on Babs' horse Mocha. When she first asked me to come ride, I told her I knew how to ride horses and she confidently put us in the lead.

I might as well have claimed I knew how to do brain surgery because I successfully cleaned a fish once.

My definition of knowing how to ride horses was based on the false confidence of having five minutes of riding lessons when I was twelve years old. Our family owned a small farm about an hour from our house since I was in fourth grade. That was the year my teacher read us Walter Farley's book The Black Stallion in class. I was enraptured with the idea of having my own black stallion. From the first minute we got the farm, I begged my parents to buy me a horse. After all, it looked to me like all you needed to successfully own a horse was a few acres and a fence. Our farm had that. It even had some old barrels laying around. To my young mind, the only thing missing from my dream of being a champion barrel racer was a horse.

Eventually, I wore my parents down and they bought a horse. My dreams were shattered quickly. We only had him a couple of months before we sold him. Because I couldn't control him. This was one of two facts I had conveniently forgotten to tell Babs. After my parents sold the horse, I spent my lifetime blaming my parents for taking away my opportunity to be a champion. Now 40-plus years later, I was back on a horse and there were no barrels in sight. All we were going to do was walk on a trail in the woods. How hard could it be?

As with any discipline, what you see and what is under the surface are worlds apart.

Boring? It was as if I had dared the Universe to prove me wrong.

As our ride progressed, Mocha walked me right through an occupied spider web. My face took the full web, spider, and all.

> **"As with any discipline, what you see and what is under the surface are worlds apart."**

This insult was an offer into a new dimension if I chose to take it. But of course, at the time I knew nothing of a relationship where the horse would offer his legs to me, where he would give me his trust and true connection. I had no idea the magic that was really happening on this boring ride in the woods. I was too busy being offended. He continued walking as I flicked the spider away, wiped my face and shuddered. My thought, "How dare he walk me into that web."

Mocha didn't walk me through the web deliberately – he was merely taking the lead that I had unknowingly left unattended. I saw the web coming. However, in this dimension, I had not made any kind of connection or contact with him. My lessons from childhood were long forgotten, so I had few tools to move him right or left to avoid the web. What few ideas I tried didn't work. Hmm. To my way of thinking, it was almost like I was riding a faulty motorbike. If I just knew which buttons to push, he would do what I wanted. Wrong. He was simply walking down the trail, waiting for that turn toward the barn, choosing every step for himself. He knew from the first moment I got on him that he was the leader of this ride.

As we continued down the trail, a part of me began to realize what he had known from the beginning: He had all the power. I was the unfortunate passenger on the back of an animal that had survived thousands of years by running away at the first sign of danger.

My lack of awareness about the consequences of the horse being in control created a form of unbalanced thinking. What I decided, more in the back of my mind than in the forefront, was that it would be good for the horse to like me. (Even as I write this, it's embarrassing to admit.)

My sense of boredom had transformed into something more ominous. I felt the need to correct the balance of power.

I said "good boy" to him a couple of times, but not for the right reasons. Yes, it's good to praise a horse who has learned something or gotten over a fear. This was definitely not in response to him having done anything like that. Nope, it was a verbalization of my thought, "I want him to like me."

I would be on the ground, unable to breathe within seconds.

As we turned down a steep hill, the horse perked up as he had done several times before. Everything in his body language told me we had made a turn toward the barn. Even though I could not have found the way home, he knew the way and would gladly be able to take me there. He picked up his pace, clearly excited at the thought of the pile of hay waiting in his stall. Later I would learn his lateral gait on such a steep hill created a rocking motion that feels like a trot. On this day, I just wanted the motion to stop. I pulled back on the reins to slow him down. Unconsciously, I also leaned forward and gripped his sides with my legs.

I had never been on such a steep hill in Texas, where I grew up. Leaning forward was exactly the opposite of what I should have done. I was saying slow down and go fast at the same time. By now, he knew the confusing requests from the woman on his back did not necessarily mean anything. But the barn was ahead, and gravity encouraged speed. So, he obliged. With my questionable balance, I quickly went from trying to slow him down to just holding on. That strategy lasted for one more step and then I was flying.

I landed with a hard splat on my side. My friends went into action to catch the horse I had just left to his own devices. When they came back to check on me, I could barely move, and every half breath hurt like hell.

I could tell something was very wrong. My arms and legs seemed to be in one piece; however, my middle wasn't working too well. Here we were, out in the woods, where getting back on Mocha to take me home was not going to happen. Walking out wasn't happening either. In fact, I tried to sit up and failed miserably. Luckily, we were in cell phone range. Babs' husband Bob met us with a four-wheeler and a question: "Should we call an ambulance?"

After they loaded me into the ambulance, I settled back, closed my eyes, and meditated. My meditation took me back to a very different ambulance ride almost twenty years before, one caused by me being out of balance in my career perspective.

The First Ambulance Ride that Started to Wake Me Up

Everyone bustled around me, hooking up monitors and watching my funky heartbeat bounce around like a pinball. As I lay there half dazed by the fluorescent lights, my irritation grew. Where were their priorities? Did they not understand that the pressure I felt letting important work fall through the cracks far exceeded the worry that I might die?

At that time in my life, I felt like my career was just taking off. My projects mattered on a national scale; my incentive package was anyone's dream, and I knew most of the senior executives of a mega bank. (And they knew me – which seemed incredibly important to me – back then anyway.)

It never crossed my mind that if I died, someone else would be doing my work tomorrow.

Fainting on my bathroom floor that morning scared my husband enough to summon an ambulance.

An erratic heartbeat scared my high school-aged daughter enough to think she might lose her mother.

A phone call from my husband to update my parents sent their worry meter off the charts.

Me? The one lying in the bed? I was worried if I would be back at work on Monday. If I wasn't, I was sure all hell was going to break loose.

Any prospect of being in balance in my life was so far out of reach, even the potential of dying of a heart attack blinded me to the miserable state of my life.

For many years, my corporate life had been marked by questions: How does one get ahead here? How do I stay out of trouble but also get some of the limelight that seems to help get people promoted? What do they really want from me? How do I do more of that?

Getting answers to those questions had started paying off in the past few years; I had been promoted and moved to increasingly bigger roles three times in less than six years. Time after time, I had proven my worth and had been rewarded with longer workdays, more pressure, and the dangling carrot of money that grew exponentially the longer I stayed.

The prison of my own making was closing in, and I welcomed it with open arms.

All this activity allowed me to join a select club of "high potentials," meaning people who looked like they might eventually make it to the executive suite. There were hundreds, if not thousands of us, all vying for a few spots and all certain that we had the right stuff to finally get there. The pressure to reach that pinnacle was enormous.

Life was good.

At least, it was good if I ignored the fact that my soon-to-be-a-drug-addict daughter had carried a bottle of pills to school a few years before with every intention of taking her own life. It was good if I ignored my frayed relationships, starting with my marriage. It was good if you didn't ask my team what kind of leader it had. It was good if I ignored the signs all around me that my whole world was out of kilter.

Life was good if I ignored the fact that my health in my late 30s was clearly failing even as I insisted they get me out of this hospital so I could go back to work.

For me to be discharged, they just had one condition. "You have to pass a stress test." Cool! Passing tests was in my wheelhouse! For a straight-A perfectionist like me, this would be a snap.

As the cardiologist strapped me to the stress-test machine, he asked me where I worked.

When I told him, he said, "Seriously, you work there? You're the fifth person I've tested for stress-related heart problems THIS WEEK, and I haven't worked that much."

> **"Life was good. At least, it was good if I ignored the fact that my soon-to-be-a-drug-addict daughter had carried a bottle of pills to school a few years before with every intention of taking her own life."**

Suddenly, my memory flashed to the several instances of ambulances leaving any one of our corporate buildings in downtown Charlotte. In fact, we had sent two trainees from my own Credit Training program to the hospital via ambulance in the past few weeks.

His incredulity about us bankers dropping like flies got through to my numbed-out brain. Here was a guy who had endured the rigors of medical school, had to be on call at all hours and was testing me on a Saturday night calling ME out for being a workaholic. It was a clue that something might be off.

While a part of me really wanted to reject his judgment, I couldn't escape it. There was something terribly out of balance here. But it would still take more reflection, warning signals, and facing the suicide of a colleague to wake me up and allow me to see the world with new eyes.

My diagnosis turned out to be Barrett's Esophagus, a potentially cancer-causing condition brought about by stress. I had to do something, or I would likely get stomach cancer and die an early and painful death.

For the next twenty years, I entered an intense, rocky personal journey of deep self-awareness. Without a doubt, I changed my relationship with anger, stress, and all the people in my life. My husband and I stayed married. We moved to the mountains, where I became an athlete, artist, and executive coach. My spiritual life became rich and fulfilling.

My daughter entered recovery and today helps parents of adult addicts navigate the rough waters of reclaiming their lives.

As today's ambulance pulled into the emergency room, I was so much calmer than the first ride some twenty years ago. I had truly come a long way.

I couldn't possibly see it yet, but the ceiling of possibility was about to be blown off. This accident would be a gift. It would teach me that mistakes are merely calibrations, and the balance point is always moving. Uncertainty would become an opportunity to use my Tools, and pressure would be the force to build them.

But first, I would have to accept the reality of what had happened.

Lack of Knowledge — or Something Else?

After getting an X-ray in the emergency room, I looked at the clock. If all went well, I would be out of there in time to drive the boat as promised for Austin Abel, the pro water skier who runs a ski school on Mystic Waters, our 162-acre former Girl Scout camp. By now, I was breathing better and was pretty sure the doctors would tell me that I had a broken collar bone and perhaps some broken ribs as well.

My daughter Jen had followed the ambulance and was keeping me company. We were mostly bored and ready to leave.

The small emergency room was relatively busy for a Saturday afternoon, giving us plenty of opportunities to eavesdrop. In one room, someone had something going on with her foot. Maybe a broken or sprained ankle? As I strained to hear details, words like barn, horse, and gate landed on my ears. Hmm, another horse accident. No surprise, I guess. We do live in horse country and this hospital was the closest to the Tryon International Equestrian Center, where a show was going on that day.

I turned my attention to the other room behind the curtain. Soon, it became clear that yet another horse accident had brought that man into the ER. I couldn't decide if I should feel vindicated or worried. After all, these other two victims surely knew a lot more about horses than I did. "So maybe I'm not so incompetent after all," was my first thought. My second thought was "Wow, horses can be really dangerous."

I didn't have time for the third, balancing thought. Suddenly, two emergency room doctors came rushing in the room and said, "We need to get your shirt off. We see a problem on your X-ray." Given the extreme pain on my right side, it took a lot of help to get me stripped down as they shooed my now white-faced daughter out of the room.

My questions started coming a mile a minute. "What is on the X-ray?" "Am I being admitted?" "Why the hurry?" Then the unspoken question "Am I going to die?" loomed large as they asked me to turn onto my left side.

"You have a pneumothorax. We have to put in a chest tube. First, I'm going to deaden the area where we are going to stick the needle. Then I'm going to …" "Wait, what's a pneumo – whatchamacallit? I have pneumonia?" Finally, someone cleared it up by saying it's a collapsed lung. They wasted no time. Before I could ask any more questions, they rolled me to my left and started the procedure.

As soon as the tube entered the area between my lungs and ribs, I felt a release of pressure. The doctor said I should be breathing much better now. The pain in my side lessened and my breath came more easily. Ironically, my consistent oxygen levels of 98% had kept any of them from suspecting anything seriously wrong with my lungs. Plus, they noted that most people with a collapsed lung don't carry on a quiet conversation, as Jen and I had been doing right before they came running in. Evidently, meditating had made a huge difference in both my calmness and my physiology.

Over the next three days, I was a guest of the hospital as we waited for my lung to stay inflated without mechanical assistance. Between the many medical professionals and visitors, I answered the question "What happened?" the same way.

I had a knowledge gap. I did not know how to stop a horse.

That story failed to tell the truth on so many levels.

At the time, I had not yet learned about the idea of having a pressure gap.

I vaguely understood the idea of mental tools. I was intimately familiar with the impact of pressure, uncertainty, and failure. Most of my responses to pressure involved either building my skills or lowering the pressure.

One thing was sure at this moment in time. I would not be getting back on a horse anytime soon, if ever.

Maybe I Should Just Walk Away

I was on a tightrope. On one side was common sense and logic. At the time of my fall, I was 59. When the orthopedist came into my hospital room to see about my injuries, I told him to ignore the age on the chart and asked him to treat me as he would a 25-year-old athlete. Right before the trail ride, I had been cutting back and forth on my water ski and was determined to get back to it. His response reinforced my concern; he had experienced a similar injury riding. Now that horseback riding was proving to be much more dangerous than I realized, why would I risk another serious injury or worse?

On the other side was the desire to overcome my newly discovered fear. The proverbial adage to get back on the horse called out to me. Plus, I had friends who wanted me to ride with them. In their visits to me in the hospital, I started realizing that trail riding could be the MOST dangerous way for the uninitiated to get on a horse. Who knew? However, riding would also be a wonderful way to spend time with friends.

I was faced with questions and choices. Would I be able to walk the tightrope of overcoming my fear while not taking undue risk? What would I need to learn if I decided to address my fear? What would I do with this life-defining moment?

> **"That story failed to tell the truth on so many levels."**

My accident gifted me with several months to consider my options.

CHAPTER TWO

Growth in Recovery

Give and Take of Energy

The first day home from the hospital revealed just how challenging this recovery would be. While I had practiced recovery on a micro scale for many years, this injury was calling on me to practice recovery on a macro scale.

Babs brought me a book to read. It was *The Undoing Project; A Friendship That Changed Our Minds* by Michael Lewis. It's the kind of book that provokes a hard look at the way we think about things. The book planted seeds and kept me enthralled for several days.

Good thing. It was going to take a really good book to get me to sit still. Without the use of my right arm and still in pain on the whole side of my body that went splat, I was discovering just how many things I could not do. Wash my hair? Only if I found a one-handed method. Deal with the fallout of wet hair? Blow drying is a two-handed affair. I mastered left-hand brushing and air drying. Drive? I couldn't reach the gear shift.

As I moved through my first few days at home, it became abundantly clear that I live my life as a perpetual motion machine. Thanks to reading *The Making of the Corporate Athlete* by Jim Loehr and Tony Schwartz in 2001, I had learned the value of oscillation and its role in helping "mobilize energy on demand." After years of practice, I had learned to effectively use stress and recovery in short doses to be able to sustain high levels of energy throughout every day.

What I hadn't learned was how to "demobilize energy on demand."

Not to worry. My body was doing it for me.

Two weeks into my recovery, I wrote this blog:

BLOG POST

The Give and Take of Leadership

I've had recovery on my mind a lot lately. Recently, I fell off a horse, breaking my collarbone. After a couple of long days in the hospital (I also had a partially collapsed lung that required a chest tube), I spent my first full day out of the hospital running light errands. My daughter/co-worker did all the driving, so it really was much less effort than a normal full day of work. By evening though, I was disproportionately tired.

My energy expenditures to run my day exceeded the energy needed to help me heal.

Since anyone who knows me will tell you I typically have a lot of energy to spare, it was a good reminder that I don't have unlimited energy. Recovery is necessary to gather enough energy to go about my daily business. Usually, a good night's sleep, healthy eating, and meditation are enough to keep me going strong. But not when my body is injured and needs the energy to heal.

As I've been more mindful of recovery, it's reminded me of an insight I had with skiing a few years ago. One of my coaches pointed out that I was not creating enough energy behind the boat to get out to the buoy line before the boat pulled me back. Suddenly I saw the idea: I need to gather energy to deploy it.

If I don't "cultivate" enough energy, I will fall short on the result I need. What a simple concept!

Soon, I could see this idea in action everywhere I looked. The project that seemed stalled? No one was taking the reins and creating enough energy to get the team moving. My lackluster garden? Not enough soil preparation to provide the nutrients to grow wonderful plants. The friendship that seemed shaky? Neither of us was putting any energy or attention into it.

One of my clients told a story that illustrated this principle beautifully. He was the executive sponsor of a multiyear change project in his company. The pressures were tremendous and every second of his day was scheduled. At the close of a team leader meeting, one of his colleagues suggested he walk through the area where many of the people working on the project were working. At first, he declined and then thought better of it. He took an hour to walk around talking to people, thanking them for their work, asking what they needed and generally showing that he cared.

Afterward, he said he had no idea how much this visit would energize him. It reminded him of what was happening at the ground level of the project and more importantly, he said, "This single visit reenergized the whole team. And to think, I almost didn't do it."

This simple principle, whether you call it give and take, gather and deploy, cultivate and harvest, or something else, underlies all our endeavors.

We simply cannot harvest something that isn't there.

We cannot run on an empty tank without severe consequences. Leaders are truly managers of energy.

Where do you need to recover or gather energy? What are the consequences of trying to get the proverbial blood out of the turnip? What can you do to energize yourself or others?

Next time you notice something missing, look first for what you might be able to give — it might be the only resource that's needed.

What I was starting to see were layered principles that would emerge even more clearly in the months and years to come. The magic was not in my ability to amp up. Nor was it in my ability to slow down. What mattered was the adjustment. Being able to calibrate my energy to the needs of the moment became priceless attunement. So did learning to deeply listen, so that the calibration aligned with the needs of the moment.

Once I slowed down, I realized there was a real risk I would overdo it. After a few days of slowing down, I started wondering if I would ever want to get off the couch again.

This recovery was proving to be much more difficult than I expected.

To Quit or Not to Quit

For me, doing something difficult often involves going for it, getting into the swamp, hating the way it feels, thinking I can't possibly handle it, saying a bunch of cuss words, and then either somehow making it through or shutting down.

Often in the shutting down part, I also quit.

That's exactly what happened when I was co-leading a major change project at the bank where I spent so much of my corporate career.

We were integrating a major merger filled with animosity AND we were introducing a whole new process to a system that was as old as the ages. The people on the receiving end of all this change had to deal with a brash new set of bosses telling them the way they did business would have to completely change. Said or unsaid, the message was something like, "You are doing it all wrong and should have known better. We know better, so we are here to fix you."

These messages did not exactly welcome the new members to the team with open arms.

As the project leads, it was our responsibility to deliver the news and then get our new colleagues to accept the new way of doing things. Here's what I have learned in years of leading corporate change and going through my own personal change. You can't "make" anyone do anything.

What was being asked of us was extremely difficult and the pressure was enormous.

By this time, I had already started some forays into my self-awareness. It was not going well. What I really wanted was someone to give a test and then declare me "self-aware."

Steve, my co-lead on the change project, and I were off-site working with some consultants who were helping us on both the project and the self-awareness front. Everyone and everything called us up to a higher level of facilitation and leadership than I had ever experienced.

It felt impossible for me to do what they were asking. The pressure of the situation was far greater than my ability to rise to the challenges facing us. More importantly, I felt like a complete failure and loser, because it seemed I just couldn't get it. And I was getting tired of the criticism and "feedback" that my way wasn't good enough.

What it was going to take for me to change my ways felt like climbing Mount Everest. In the face of such pressure, I quit. Usually when I quit, it's an internal form of shutting down, where I pretend to be engaged and just survive long enough to get out of the situation.

In this case, the pressure was too high for that. In the middle of one of our meetings, I turned to Steve and said, "I can't do it. What you are asking of me is too much." The look of betrayal and hurt on his face hit me in the gut. He was gracious and said he was disappointed, but obviously would honor my decision. After all, what choice did he have?

In a perfect world, I would have gotten in my car and gone home. Since we were working halfway across the country and traveling together, I reluctantly stayed in the meetings. "I want to leave. Shit. I can't leave. There's no way out."

Our group had dinner together that night and all I can remember of it was that it was surreal, probably because the next morning's memories overwhelmed almost every other memory I had.

We were deep in a working session when one of our team members got a call. Kevin stepped out and, although it was rare for us to be interrupted (this was before the smart phone), we quickly went back to what we were doing. While everyone else was focused on the project, I was still wishing for my escape.

When Kevin came back into the room, he was a different man. His face was ashen, he moved with effort and his eyes said it all. He had just gotten some terrible news.

Diane, the executive sponsor of our project, had committed suicide the night before. We were all flabbergasted. Diane was the most put-together, calm, effective executive you could imagine. We all felt both honored and protected to be working on a project of this scale and scope with her generous and experienced oversight. (Note: I am using aliases for this story.)

This could not be happening.

But it was.

Our work stopped as we rode the roller coaster of emotion and sought out more information. As the day rolled on, we learned that she shot herself in the head while her husband and boss went into the house to get drinks. This may have been an act of desperation — but it was also an act of defiance. She went out inflicting pain.

And I knew just how she felt.

We spent the next several hours crying, processing, disbelieving, and theorizing. What could make her this desperate? Why did she do it this way? Had she sent any warning signals? What would make her do this?

When things didn't go my way, I would often spout off about taking my quitting to this extreme. While I would never consider myself genuinely suicidal, I could identify with the idea of saying "f*$k you" to the people putting pressure on me, especially when I couldn't see a way out of my misery.

Somehow as the day went on, I began to realize that my self-torment and helplessness would only get worse if I didn't face my demons. My way of living was eating me up from the inside out.

I was nowhere near balancing, much less dancing the tightrope.

My typical responses to pressure had been to go helpless, to hide, to pretend, or to be a child.

When that didn't work, I played the false confidence game, saying "I've got this" whether I knew what I was doing or not. When that failed, I went to the angry parent mode, full of rage, judgment, and resentment, trying to gain power over people with my condescension and strong emotions.

Over the course of that unforgettable day, Diane's death gave me a crystal ball into my future. If something didn't change, the outlook was dismal.

If I were to play at this level, this bouncing back and forth between being powerless and intimidating would have to end. It was time to grow up.

When we returned from a break, I looked at Steve and said, "I'm back in. She can't die in vain."

Steve was both shocked and relieved.

Me? I wasn't sure what I had just done.

Although I had quit quitting for the moment, I still had to wrestle with the desire to throw my hands up and walk away. The roots of this pattern were complex, and they ran deep.

Birth of Rules

In some ways, I came by my urge to quit honestly. My begging for a horse finally paid off. My parents relented and bought me a horse; just as suddenly, we quit and sold the horse without me ever understanding why. Until I restarted my journey with horses. That's when I learned we had innocently done almost everything wrong.

My memories of the practicalities of getting the horse were vague. Looking back, I wondered, "Who hauled him the 50 miles from our town to the farm?" "How did we decide which field to leave him in?" "Were we at all worried about the barbed wire fences hurting him?" "Who checked on the horse when we were gone for a week or two at a time?" "Was buying a horse named Buck a bad idea?"

"That's when I learned we had innocently done almost everything wrong."

And then this question "What made me think catching a snake and then trying to catch the horse – while holding the snake – was a good idea?"

I was on my way out with the halter and lead rope to a very large field where we had left him the last time we were there. Suddenly, a garter snake darted in front of me. Growing up outdoors and with a drainage ditch near our house, I loved playing with all kinds of wildlife, including snakes. With his vertical stripes, this one was clearly not poisonous, so I caught him. It's what I always did when encountering a snake.

Being the ignorant kid I was at the time, I guess I thought it would be fun to introduce Mr. Snake to my horse Buck. Bad idea. Horses and snakes don't want to be friends. Buck showed me that loud and clear as he ran far out of reach. I quickly dropped the snake and started trying to coax Buck back to me.

After living in the field all by himself for a while, Buck didn't want to be friends with me either.

I don't remember how long it took me to catch him. But I did learn in no uncertain terms that the only snaky-looking thing I better have in my hand when approaching a horse would be a lead rope. My parents silently marked: Strike One.

Perhaps the same day or another day – I can't remember – we had the bridle incident, where I could not for the life of me get the bridle on the horse. He kept raising his head, backing away, and showing me the whites of his eyes. I kept chasing him like a lunatic. Looking back, I just wish I could tell Buck how sorry I am for my ignorance. We never did get the bridle on him that day. My parents silently marked: Strike Two.

On the deciding day, I had managed to get the bridle and the saddle on Buck. My only goal was to get on and go. Fast. Barrel racing fast.

My mom was fishing in the tank holding in the water on the other side of the hill. ("Tank" is Texas language for a small lake or pond.) I had no idea where my dad or other siblings were. I was in my own world of delight, running on Buck around in the open field just west of the tank.

Buck and I suddenly exploded up the hill and stopped just short of where Mom was peacefully casting for bass. Mom had just swung the rod and reel back to her right, preparing to throw a cast. I was smiling from ear to ear following the exhilarating run up the short hill. She whirled around and in a way that I knew had no right answer yelled, "Did you mean to do that?"

This was no time to be strategic. I had been her daughter for twelve years. I knew that tone of voice and I had a very well-developed rule for the pattern we were suddenly living out in real time. It was damned if you do and damned if you don't.

If I said yes, I was in trouble.

If I said no, I was in trouble.

My rule told me to answer the question that was the path of least trouble. Seemed like a good idea to blame the horse, not realizing that his very existence on our farm was in question.

I can't say for sure when the rule to avoid getting in trouble was born, but I suspect it was during the windowsill incident.

When I was four years old, my parents bought a new house under construction. We would go by every day, checking on progress as the studs became drywall and the drywall became finished walls. Day by day, the construction zone slowly morphed into livable space.

It was on one of these visits that my "don't get caught" rule was born. It had probably been formed before that, but I'm getting ahead of myself.

As my parents were off in another room with my baby sister, they left me alone in the empty kitchen with the big plate glass window facing the backyard. At the bottom of that window was a big, white, freshly painted windowsill.

To my young eyes, this was the most beautiful, blank canvas I had ever seen. All that white space seemed like a good place to write my name – something I was just learning to do.

I can't remember what sharp object I used – probably a nail – but I proceeded to write my name on that lovely, somewhat soft, surface. I happily wrote the letter "L" before my mistake hit me.

If I wrote my name, my parents would know who did this. Some part of my kid brain knew that marring this brand-new windowsill might not be a great idea. Such an act would definitely get me in trouble.

So, I did what any smart kid would do. The next letter I wrote was "e." Whew – that was a close one. I finished out the rest of my sister's name Leigh, aware that I had cleverly avoided being in very bad trouble. My sister's name was now etched in both the paint and the wood. Dealing with this would be her problem.

My clever kid brain had missed one important detail. My sister was not yet two years old.

And at this moment, she was in the back bedroom with my parents.

A few minutes later, my parents came back in the kitchen. Of course, my mom saw the writing on the sill. My mom was a fiery person and we saw her flames in full glory that day. I'm pretty sure the neighbors were also getting to know the new family who would be moving in soon.

My artistic act had gotten me in trouble. That etching would stay on the windowsill for the next ten years that we lived in that house, reminding me – and my parents – just what a bad girl I was.

Eight years later, here I was on top of the world, sitting on my dream horse. Busted by the same fiery mother who had to look at that marred windowsill every day. No one to blame but the horse.

I answered, "No," feeling rather proud that I would not get punished as badly as if my gallop up the hill was an intentional act. Blame it on the horse.

Strike Three.

My parents sold Buck after that. I was heartbroken – and convinced that I answered her question the wrong way.

In the months following, I wondered. If I had chosen to say "Yes," would the outcome have been different? Would I have been scolded and told never to scare my mom like that again? Was there a path that would have let me keep Buck and become a champion barrel racer? Why did we have to quit? What would have happened if we had chosen the path to learn more about the care and upkeep of horses?

From my twelve-year-old perspective, all I knew was that we quit. For many years, I deeply struggled with losing Buck. In my child's view of the world, my dream was stolen. Many of my Rules were born and reinforced around this story.

Later, as I learned to build my Tools, my adult eyes showed me that my life was saved.

Three Buckets of Rules

As my recovery progressed, conversations started taking on a new tenor. Old patterns and Rules began rising to the surface, showing me their forms, their benefits – and their limitations.

While the bruises were fading and my bones healed, there was a consistent question explored in most of my conversations, both with friends who loved horses and friends who feared horses. "What happened?" It was a loaded question, defined by many facets. "What did you do wrong?" "Where did you make a mistake?" "Will you ever ride again?" "What would cause this to happen again?" "How do you make sure a horse never runs away with you again?"

And the question I asked myself: "If I don't get back on, does it mean I am a failure?"

These questions were deep and starting to penetrate my very identity. I didn't like it.

My various friends who had horses and knew very well the ins and outs, as well as the dangers of trail riding, provided much-needed perspective.

"There is a skill to balancing yourself on a horse moving downhill. The rider has a responsibility to coordinate with the horse so that he can carry you more easily."

"Got to keep those heels down. It keeps you locked in the saddle."

"When a horse starts running out of control, you bring them around into a circle. It's like an emergency stop."

My knowledge-hungry brain ate up the advice, starving for a technique that I could deploy should I ever choose to ride again.

Yet one conversation pointed to something deeper, something in the fog that occasionally showed itself in ever-morphing shapes and disappeared as soon as I looked at it.

"You seemed so confident. It never occurred to me that you were anything but totally proficient." So said Babs as we discussed what had happened that day. We had only ridden together twice.

Confidence. It's something I had cultivated since my first day in the corporate world – and probably even before that. I built my adult form of confidence on the foundation of so many of my childhood Rules.

"Don't get caught" developed into "I've got this." (Translation: Even though I'm faking it, I'm good at faking, so who will ever know?)

"Damned if you do, damned if you don't" developed into "I will beat myself up, so you don't have to." (Translation: I don't have to change anything because I've eaten the slimy vegetables and paid my penance.)

"Quitting is the way out" developed into "Look at this other thing I'm good at." (Translation: If it doesn't come easy, I don't want to have to take the time to develop mastery.)

This Swiss cheese confidence was destined to collapse under pressure. All the skills and knowledge in the world would not break those patterns.

In my coaching work with leaders for the several years prior, I had begun breaking lifelong patterns like these into three "buckets," with different origins and different ways out:

1. Survival Mode
2. Kid Mode
3. History Mode

Common Sources of Triggers

Survival Mode	Kid Mode	History Mode
Core Question: How do I stay alive?	*Core Question:* Where do I find my power?	*Core Question:* What worked before?
Type of Trigger: Body goes into fight, flight or freeze for survival	*Type of Trigger:* How your parents/caregivers did it based on Parent/Adult/Child	*Type of Trigger:* Personal to each person based on significant life events
Symptoms: Heart racing, butterflies Narrow focus Sweaty palms Placating	*Symptoms:* Playing one up or one down Helpless or judgmental Blaming	*Symptoms:* Assuming what someone means without asking Over-or-Under reacting Upset for no clear reason

In some ways, all three modes played out in my experience falling off the horse. When Mocha started down the pivotal hill, his big gait felt like a trot to me. The sensation of speed immediately sent a shot of adrenaline into my system. Survival Mode was triggered in milliseconds. Now I was in Fight, Flight, or Freeze. At this point, because of my lack of skills and more importantly, my Pressure Gap, I had no choice but to try to hang on when pulling back on the reins didn't work.

We all have Survival Mode, and the chemistry of it operates in essentially the same way in all of us. It's non-negotiable hardwiring granted to us at birth.

Earlier in my ride, Kid Mode had been triggered. Kid Mode is anytime we feel a power differential and we do things to get our power back. This idea started coming to me when working with Eric Berne's Transactional Analysis in a leadership program I was teaching. While I did almost no deep study on the method, what I saw was easily applicable to the corporate world.

In my Kid Mode view of the world, I pictured a tightrope, where on the tightrope itself, we walked in a Power With approach to solving problems and leading changes. With such a narrow, wobbly path to walk, we were bound to fall off on one side or the other. On one side was the Child side, where we fell into a "Power Under" approach. Every time I walked into my boss's office and said something to the effect of "I've tried everything, nothing works, it's everybody's fault but mine," I was in the "child ditch." It's tailor made for victims.

When it dawned on me that Mocha was the one in power after walking me through the spider web (albeit unintentionally), I tried making him like me – a classic Power Under strategy to even out the power differential.

On the other side is the Parent side, where we fall into a Power Over approach. Of course, more than once, I had walked into my boss's office trying to get away with the "You need to fix this" attitude. Getting all grabby with the reins and trying to be forceful instead of communicating were my feeble attempts to gain power over Mocha on the way down the hill.

Can you see how these methods cause us to over - and under react, always swinging off the tightrope?

In many ways, Kid Mode is shared by all of us, much like Survival Mode. If we were raised in any setting where there was a power differential, we have strategies for dealing with situations of Power Under, Power Over.

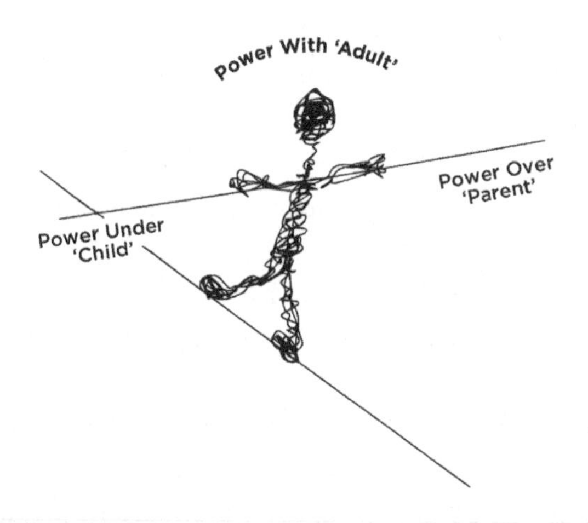

As I worked with clients – and myself – in understanding the different mindsets (Berne called them "ego states"), I needed a way to organize them. You can look at the "centered mindset" as being on the tightrope. I can fall off the tightrope by over-or under reacting to the situation, much like I did with Mocha. In that case, I bounced back and forth, from trying to get him to like me to trying to have power over him and then going back to feeling helpless. Really helpless.

Right after my accident, I started working with a leadership team whose core role in the organization was like herding cats. There were a lot of power dynamics in play. They were executives in their role, but not always in their actions. The team lamented its frustration as we worked through the give and take of its various decisions.

> **"... what they were seeking was the ability to be present when in difficult conversations, while delivering unwelcome news and in making strategic decisions."**

In many ways, we began to recognize that what they were seeking was the ability to be present when in difficult conversations, while delivering unwelcome news and in making strategic decisions. They wanted executive presence. I created the following tool for them to see where they were at any given time in their interactions.

Inferior Mindset "POWER UNDER"	**Centered Mindset** "POWER WITH"	**Superior Mindset** "POWER OVER"
Analogous to Child	Analogous to Adult	Analogous to Parent
Operates from past decisions to cope from childhood	Operates in present moment	Operates from the past observance of parents and other caretakers
Sees others as having power over them	Sees others as equals	Sees themselves as having power over others
Takes things personally "What's wrong with me?"	Takes nothing personally	Makes things personal "what's wrong with you?"
Seeks approval	Defines him/herself on his/her own terms. Distinguishes between skills and self.	Seeks to take care of
Plays innocent *"Not me"*	Owns his or her part of a situation	Looks for someone to blame *"Your fault"*
Can tend to act helpless	Allows others to live with the consequences of their actions	Can tend to be overly helpful
Gets angry and rebellious to feel more powerful	Gets the facts and stays grounded	Gets authoritative, judgmental to feel more powerful
Reflexive thoughts "I'm no good" "I should have done better" etc.	Chooses thoughts - interrupts old patterns	Reflexive thoughts "Look what you did wrong" "You are no good" etc.
Reacts to others' decisions on what is good or bad, right or wrong, black or white	Considers what thoughts and actions will lead to. Focuses on consequences and fallout	Sees the world in black and white, right and wrong, good or bad terms

Inferior Mindset "POWER UNDER"	**Centered Mindset** "POWER WITH"	**Superior Mindset** "POWER OVER"
Tends to be more emotional	Tends to be more logical and rational	Tends to be more values-driven
Looks outside of self for motivation	Internally motivated	Looks outside of self for motivation
Tends to try to prove or show that "I am enough"	Grounded and feels from the inside out "I am enough"	Tends to need others "under me" to feel like "I am enough"

How we bounce around the strategies we choose is deeply colored by our life experiences.

Our life experiences also create our History Mode – and each of us has a completely different set of life-defining moments that shapes who we are and how we make sense of the world. While we may share patterns of "trauma," our reactions to what happens in our lives, both good and bad, are unique to each of us.

Our ways of dealing with pressure start forming from the time we are born. We learn from watching our parents and other family members, teachers, peers, and other authority figures. We learn from our experiences and how we handle what happens to us. As we are growing up, we are like little scientists, studying the world and deciding who we are and how we fit in it. This becomes our "conditioning."

We document those discoveries in our bodies and our ways of being in the world. That conditioning becomes our patterns for dealing with the pressures of life. Feeling betrayed? You've got a pattern for that. Not getting what you want? You've got a pattern for that.

My own History Mode patterns played a role from the moment I accepted the invitation to ride, straight through to the accident, the recovery, and beyond. There's no getting around it.

Some of our patterns are super useful. That instinct to hit the brakes when something rolls in front of our car? Useful. That instinct to hit someone who just took something we wanted away? Not so great, especially in corporate life.

My pattern around showing confidence – my pattern of "I've got this" – was very useful in corporate life, where there is always more work to do than can possibly be done. The insatiable work monster was kept fed and mostly quiet by people like me.

Our early years as little scientists established a huge repertoire of patterns that operates like automatic programs. They run in the background without any conscious thought or help from us – and they take energy, much like an app running in the background on a smartphone.

You can think of our patterns like the buttons we push to start an app on the phone. Rather than having to open the screen and find the icon, our buttons get pushed by the pressure of the situation. Here are examples of the types of things that happen that will push our buttons and cause us to operate from conditioning (instead of from the actual situation in front of us):

- Not getting what you want
- Feeling betrayed
- Making a mistake
- Watching someone else be praised for something you did
- Getting embarrassed
- Feeling treated unfairly
- Getting "screwed" by a situation
- Wanting to please others
- Looking for approval
- Wanting to be right
- Fearing failure
- Feeling responsible for the fate of others
- Being told your work is not good

Our unconscious patterns run us, just as surely as if we were robots running on the programming code of their inventor. Learning to operate creatively and consciously requires MUCH MORE than a simple decision to change. Why? Because emotions lock the original programming into place. Until we access those emotions and then "rewrite" the program, we cannot change the pattern.

While my body was running down the hill on Mocha, the robot was running my mind. If I were ever to ride again, it seemed wise to do something about the robot. In other words, it was not a skill problem. It was a mindset problem.

But at this stage of my recovery, I preferred to think it was a riding skill problem and one that I might not ever have to address. What mattered more was getting back on my water ski.

Losing the last six weeks of my water ski season had been heartbreaking. After years of trying to shorten the rope, I had almost given up. Truth be told, I was afraid of skiing on the "22 off" line length. When the rope is that length behind the boat, the wake has a bump. Crossing the wake at high speeds in a leaning position and hitting that bump sent shock waves and adrenaline through me every time. After a few buoys, the adrenaline coursing through my system typically rendered my muscles useless.

Two days before the accident, I had finally completed a full ski pass on the 22 off rope length. It was a breakthrough a decade in the making, and a simple trail ride in the woods ended my ski season – and opportunity to cement in my new learning – in a matter of minutes.

Now I had two priorities over the fall and winter: rehab like a professional athlete and provide the corporate team opportunities to take its leadership and team to a new level.

Back on the Water Ski

Several months into my recovery, it was time to see if I could still ski. The doctor had insisted on three months off. I waited five – partly because it was the dead of winter. When I could stand it no longer, daughter Jen and I got in the car and headed to Florida. While the recovery aspect was new to me, skiing in Florida during the winter months was totally normal.

So were a lot of my old Rules that made the trip with me.

Every skier I know feels the same mix of dread and excitement at the return from an off period. Slalom skiing is an intense sport. Even the highest-level skiers acknowledge the first time back on the ski every season feels incredibly fast and unmanageable

Almost from the first moment I got up on the ski, it felt completely normal. Clearly, I had developed a lot of muscle memory over the past decade. The familiar muscle soreness the next day was a welcome reminder of how much fitness this sport offered. This time, not being able to raise my arm to brush my hair filled me with happiness. I was back!

Yet there were parts of me that were still shaken, in the way trauma can mark us forever. In walking the tightrope of confidence, my overconfidence had swung to under-confidence. Questions were rumbling under the surface. Where else in my life was my "I've got this" rule waiting to trip me up? Was I really so good at bullshitting that I was fooling myself? What kind of mark would this trauma leave on me?

The questions sparked enough discomfort to start getting through my defenses. My accident was blessing me with new insights; perhaps the trauma could be a gift.

In my blog written after the trip, I could see the forms of a new way of being starting to show their shapes.

BLOG POST

Move on or Move Deeper

I love making progress. When I was an avid tennis player, I wanted to move from being rated a 3.5 to 4.0. In my various jobs, I always wanted the next promotion or big assignment. On the potter's wheel, I've pushed to create ever taller forms. In water skiing, I've been on a multiyear quest to speed up the boat and shorten the rope.

In my mind, progress tends to involve the next measurable milestone much more than cultivating deep mastery.

While I appreciate mastery as a concept or theory, actually putting it into practice has been something I have avoided in order to achieve my beloved "progress." To me, mastery is boring. Why? Because it involves the subtleties of doing the same thing over and over, improving slowly and carefully, filling in the gaps that are easily glossed over with my need for speed.

This fall, I had an experience that has wakened me to a different need: Rather than move on, I need to move deeper. It was revealed with the one-two punch of falling off a horse (landing me in the hospital) and then having to take several months off water skiing right after I had achieved a previously unattainable milestone. Having to sit still during my recovery gave me to time to reflect.

My extreme lack of mastery contributed to the fall from the horse. While I had many important takeaways from that experience, perhaps the most profound was this:

Knowing how to stop a horse in theory does NOT translate to

embodying the energy, mindset, and physical actions to stop a horse that would rather run.

When it came time to put my theory into practice, all the knowledge in the world meant nothing. Without having practiced and learned to connect my knowledge to real skill, in the moment of truth all I could do was hold on and hope for the best. In this case, I was wearing a helmet and went down on relatively soft ground. It could have been much, much worse.

As I healed, I had a good part of the winter to reflect on the differences between knowledge, skill, and mastery. I realized that in many areas of my life, I have substituted knowledge for real skill. And nowhere have I undertaken the journey of mastery. As a result, I end up holding on and hoping for the best. When my skills fall short, the consequences are not usually as severe — so I've gotten away with it — with consequences.

When it was time to get back on the water ski, I started by slowing the boat down a little bit. Of course, this went against everything I typically do, which is to try to make progress (even though in water skiing my progress is usually baby steps).

A wonderful thing happened. First, I could still ski! This is an intense sport and anytime you come back from a long time off, there is this question: Can I still do it? Second, I moved deeper. In this case, moving deeper meant that I was able to feel things at the slower speed that I couldn't before. My coach said this: "I'm not trying to say that it was good that you got injured — but it's giving you a chance to build a better skiing foundation than you had before."

In that moment, I realized it was time to move deeper.

So, I am. Moving deeper that is.

I'm slowing down and trading progress for depth. Rather than claiming my prize of achieving the goal, I'm deliberately practicing the actions that lead to the goal. Moment by moment, I'm moving deeper.

CHAPTER THREE
Invisible Tools

When the Student is Ready

Three inner fault lines finally provoked me enough to make the pivotal phone call. One had been planted months before and lay dormant, waiting for more energy to widen the crack. In a conversation during my recovery, my friend Daryl mentioned her horse trainer Bruce Anderson and the work he did in the corporate leadership realm.

Daryl and her husband had recently moved to the area, and we became fast friends, with a shared love of the outdoors, conservation, and water. She had several well-trained dressage horses and one she mainly used to ride on the trail, named Scotty. Three months before I got on Mocha, Daryl asked me over to ride Scotty.

We were hoping I could brush up my childhood horseback riding skills so I could join Daryl out on the trails on her farm. We started in the arena. I quickly discovered I was WAY over my head on Scotty. Over my head in the same way that any typical driver might experience in a finely tuned Ferrari surging around the racetrack for the first time. (You can read the whole story in the sidebar.) Interestingly, I did not see what happened with Scotty as a red flag to my horseback riding aspirations until at least a year after my fall. Nor did I realize that this blog was a call-out to the Universe to help me deal with pressure.

BLOG POST

Where Is My Choice Here? And Yes, I Got Back on the Horse!

My theme for this week seems to be adrenaline. Let me start by saying there is a joke in our house about who is the real adrenaline junkie around here. I contend it's me. And I got a lot of adrenaline this week. It's left me pondering how to use this involuntary pulse of fight, flight, or freeze energy pulsing through my veins. What would happen if I actually channeled it instead of running away or curling up in a ball of "make it go away?" What is the best choice to make between that moment of stimulus and response? And how do I continue to build the inner fortitude to tolerate discomfort and get comfortable with being uncomfortable?

From the outside looking in, almost no one would see me as the daring one. So, if I'm the one who is such a chicken, how can I be the adrenaline junkie?

It's all a matter of perspective. I'm married to a "mountain dew" man who does everything from extreme scuba diving to sky diving to horse endurance racing to back flips off giant boathouses. By all accounts, he looks like the adrenaline junkie in our household. He has spent his whole life doing brave and daring things. Most activities don't even touch his fear system. So, while he is considered an adrenaline junkie, he has to work VERY hard to get a hit of adrenaline.

Me on the other hand? I was raised in a "don't go near the edge" household and I didn't. As a result, I was generally a careful child who turned into a fearful adult. (I hate admitting this.) My fear system gets jacked with the slightest hint of danger. Because my threshold is so low, I get hits of adrenaline all the time. That's why I say I'm the true junkie in our house. I'm the one getting regular doses of it.

So, what happened this week to fill me with adrenaline? Oh, let me count the ways. It started with the spider on the boat platform. No, I'm not scared of spiders. (I used to be but that's another story.) When I saw him as I was stepping on the platform to ski, I moved my boot so as not to step on him and the boot suddenly slipped out from under me. Imagine the feeling of hitting wet ice, add a boat with jagged edges to fall on and you will get an idea of the next move. I managed to sit back into the boat without doing the splits or crashing onto my knees.

Once I recovered my poise, I

realized that I had taken one of the biggest hits of adrenaline in my recent memory. My heart was racing, my stomach was flipping, and I generally felt incapacitated. I looked at Jen, my driver/daughter who knows my tendencies and me so well and said, "I can't ski like this." I sat on the boat and said, "Give me a minute." Of course, adrenaline takes a while to drain from your system and I said as much. She offered to ski and let me get calmed down. That was certainly an option.

And then it hit me. (The perspective — not more adrenaline.) My body had just inadvertently created tournament conditions. The feeling I was having was no different than the feeling I have before skiing in a tournament. Being able to perform with that kind of energetic surge in the body is a hugely valuable skill, and one that I have not mastered. This was my chance to practice with the inner feeling of true tournament conditions.

So I looked at Jen and said, "Let's see if I can use this. I'm gonna ski."

The first pass proved why tournament conditions are so difficult. I overshot every buoy. Even though I had anticipated being stronger than normal, it was difficult to corral all the energy surging through my body. Had I been in a tournament, my performance would have been short lived.

It was on the next few passes that I started understanding how to channel the energy in a productive way. When my mind caught up with my body's enhanced capabilities, I skied my best of the summer to that point. By far. In fact, the next day, I was missing that surge when I skied.

I came to see the adrenaline as enhancing my capabilities rather than debilitating me.

Over the past few years, I've been "rewiring" my brain to make it less sensitive to those fear hits. For example, the first time I drove a boat through a ski course, my heart was pounding, and the boat guides seemed to scream past me at Mach 4. Now I drive said course every day at faster speeds with advanced shortline skiers — deliberate practice and familiarity have made the once scary now the norm.

But of course, you know my lessons on managing fear and adrenaline were not yet over. I'm sure you have heard the old saying, "If you fall off the horse, you gotta get back on." I got to test that one as well.

A friend invited me over to ride her horse, which was one of my very favorite things to do as a young woman. Almost all of my riding had been on the very calm, nose-to-tail riding horses typical of public riding stables. Yes, I had been on "real horses" — but not that often. And all of my riding has been Western riding. The difference between Western and English are much more than a different saddle.

We started with catching and grooming my mount, which gave the horse and me a chance to know each other and build trust. Smart move. Then we mounted up in the ring and I started learning how to ride all over again. Different saddle, different reins, real horse. And unlike my ski, the horse could feel my every emotion. Just knowing that made it a little harder for me to settle in at first.

After a while, I did begin to get comfortable, and we started speeding up. Just like in snow skiing, it's important to learn the basics of how to slowdown before you get too much momentum. In this case, it's with a live animal who understands specific signals. The first couple of times were OK — I was able to get him going and stop him without too much trouble.

Then, while the horse was moving at a quick gait, I inadvertently gave a "go" signal when my deepest desire was to stop. Before I knew it, we were running. This was certainly not what I expected! You can imagine what happened inside of me. My body was now in full flight or fight mode. I was literally in flight mode — and I would have loved to be able to fly off that horse and land on my two feet.

My friend was calmly giving me instructions on what to do. I'm not sure how she could be so calm while I felt like I was on a runaway train. Damn, why won't this horse stop? Needless to say, when we got stopped, my first instinct was to get off that horse!

She knew better and I knew better. That horse would never respect me again. First, we debriefed in those few minutes while I was still astride him. We realized my Western riding style conflicted with his training. My stop signal was confusing to him, and my adrenaline sense of flight came through as the stronger signal.

So, I went back to walking for a few minutes to regain my composure and reconnect with the horse. My system was pulsing with the huge hit of adrenaline. In this case, I intentionally channeled that feeling into deep focus, connection and gratitude with the horse. He did eventually slow down, and he was simply doing his best to please me. And I had managed to stay on through the whole thing. **Whew!**

You may be wondering what all this talk about adrenaline has to do with business. At work, we rarely talk about it in these terms. We don't say, "Wow, when you called my idea stupid, I got a hit of adrenaline." Or "Dang, I get super-scared when I see you and your boss talking because half the time, it means I'm getting in trouble for something I've done." We are mature, powerful business-people — so we frame those adrenaline hits as "just business" or we don't even realize that we are in a reactive mode.

That lack of awareness can cost us.

Here's the problem with adrenaline. We don't really have a choice about when it hits us. It's based on our history, our personal fears, our experiences with parents, teachers, or bosses. When that stimulus hits us, we start operating in fight or flight mode, when the conditions actually call for us to be calm and reasonable. We are more likely to escalate a conflict, to take something personally, to get hurt or defensive, or just pick a fight.

All that energy surging through our system tells us to DO SOMETHING and we do.

It's just that we then do something that is probably an overreach for the situation.

You may be thinking, "OK, I get it. I don't want to overreact, and I don't want to damage relationships. So, I will quit having adrenaline." If it were only so simple. Our inner nervous system decides when we get adrenaline. Our conscious mind has little or nothing to do with it. Unless we do serious self-awareness training, we will get hit when we get hit.

So, we first have to learn to deal with the adrenaline hits we get. Start by being aware. Recognize that when you have that pit in your stomach or the leap in the heart, there is a chance you are surging with more energy than usual. That signal is designed to keep you alive and, when it hits us in a business environment, it drives behavior that does not match the situation. Learn when your tendency is to fight, flee or freeze.

You may also want to consider doing some inner work to rewire your system to tolerate and normalize those situations that trigger you. You can desensitize yourself if you deliberately practice doing so.

But I digress. Back to Bruce Anderson.

I had experienced equine assisted learning before and thought I had learned all I needed to know. Now that I had just been thrown off a horse, the thought of working with them was still up in the air for me. And I did NOT want to literally be up in the air like before ever again!

In the meantime, I was coaching a leadership team that was operating under extreme pressure. Every one of us needed to take our game to another level. The idea of working experientially with someone like Bruce who could potentially accelerate our learning intrigued me.

From my earlier work in a horse-focused leadership program, my big takeaway was this: Horses don't act because of the title you hold or the words you say. They engage through clarity of thought and energy – and they show you when your energy is incongruent. The challenges the team members faced were not about positional power. Rather, influence mattered. Influence was their currency and they needed more of it. Learning to influence a 1,200-pound animal would help these team members influence leaders above, below and around them in their organizational hierarchy.

Those were both logical reasons to work with Bruce, but it would take the third unspoken longing – known only looking back on it. When the pressure got high, and I went into the froth – the space outside of my comfort zone but still in the learning zone – I quit. At this point in time, I had not allowed that awareness to move into my conscious mind. It was my subconscious longing to learn to operate in the froth that spurred me to make the call.

It was October, a month after my accident, when Daryl first mentioned the leadership work with Bruce. At the time, I said I would think about it. Being the go-getter that I am, I got right on it and called him in March.

When I spoke with Bruce on the phone, he began to take me through his method. He didn't talk about himself, his clients, or how he worked. He just started doing his thing, which involved asking me lots of questions, as if we were in a coaching session.

In that phone call, I realized this was nothing like the experiential work I had done with horses before. He didn't really talk about the horses. He was mostly talking about the mental cycle that occurs when we are under pressure and make a mistake. He also said things like "We were not meant to live in man's world. We were meant to live in nature's world. As we relearn how to dance with nature in the world we were made for, we can also learn how to dance with human nature."

I didn't yet realize just how different this work would be. In fact, after we hung up from that first call, I thought I fully understood his methods – and that Bruce would see that when we worked together the following week.

My proving mindset – the very same pattern that told my friend I knew how to ride – asserted its dominance once again.

What I Thought was Micromanaging

Before we hung up from that first call, I mentioned to Bruce that my daughter Jen worked with me, and he also invited her to the "show and tell" session, which we would do at his farm in Camden, S.C. We picked a day in the next week, and he warned us to dress for anything, including mud. As Jen and I drove the 165 miles from Lake Lure to Camden, we were full of anticipation about what to expect.

Going in, I had some preconceived notions. Given that I had done one whole leadership session using horses, I expected Bruce to do the same or at least something similar. Plus, I had read a bunch of books. So, I was feeling rather confident. On our drive, I described to Jen some of the activities I had done in the one session, as well as some of the exercises I had read about in books.

She had been helping me with the leadership team, so we mapped how my preconceived notions of the exercises Bruce would share would help the team with several of its challenges. We also talked about the big stuff, like how would we feed the team and where would they sit and what if it rains and would there be a bathroom. In other words, "corporate" Lynn showed up.

The horses would see right through me.

When we got out of the car, a giant of a man greeted us. He asked if we would like to sit and visit on the porch before we got started. I was pretty sure there were no horses on the porch, so I naively suggested we get right to it. Looking back, this makes me chuckle. I would come to realize just how much my past was interfering (not informing). And even later, I would come to think of it as my past "enter-fearing." But there I go getting ahead of myself again.

Bruce handed me a rope and a halter, with these instructions: "Your picture is to choose one of the two horses, put the halter on the horse you chose and bring him or her to the round pen." A round pen is a like a corral seen in Westerns. Instead of being square, the round pen is round. Well, almost round. More on that later.

However, I hadn't gotten to the not-quite-round-round-pen yet. My mind tripped up over the word "picture." What did he mean? Did he mean goal instead of picture? What an odd thing to say. Much later, I would come to realize that horses think in pictures. His word choice was not only deliberate, it was essential. But in my rush to show off, I mentally replaced the word picture with goal and set off to crush the goal.

In my mind, this would take five minutes max. It would be less but for the two gates I would have to open and close on my way out and my way in to complete his assignment.

Here's my embarrassing little secret. I only cared about one thing at this point. I wanted Bruce to ask me where I had learned to catch and halter a horse like that. In the world according to Lynn, I was just one step shy of being a natural horsewoman. Overconfidence struck again. Secretly, there was also a part of me hoping he would absolve me from any responsibility for the horse accident. Not to mention, I wanted to see those cool activities for the leadership team.

So much for my wishful thinking and getting the horse to the round pen in five minutes. Yes, I caught the horse in short order. Then I had to figure out the halter, which was unlike any I had ever seen. "Let the halter tell you how to put it on the horse," Bruce said. Talking halters were not part of my preconceived expectations, and best I could tell, this one looked more like a rope than a halter. And last I checked, ropes don't talk.

Finally, I got the halter on and started walking with the horse. On the way into the round pen, Bruce stopped me and asked me to feel my "Negative/ Positive Pole." My what? There he goes using funny words again. Yes, I feel something. What I'm feeling is pissed. You are not letting me get this horse into the round pen, where all the fun will start.

"Your Negative/Positive Pole is like a car battery. There's a little charge of electricity inside of you. See if you can feel it." As he spoke, he moved his hands up and down in front of his midsection, with his thumbs up. "When something is off, that little charge of electricity will surge through you. Notice it and give it a number."

If I learned nothing else for the rest of my life, learning this lesson would be worth the trip to Bruce. But it would not get through my numbed-out brain for a long time.

On this day, my number on a scale of one to ten was a ten. An hour and fifty questions later, the horse and I finally walked into the round pen. Yay, I thought, now I get to do something with the horse.

Not so fast.

First, he had me take off the halter I had worked SO hard to put ON the horse. Man do I hate to do rework! In the intervening hour, my annoyance had been rising, click by click. I mostly stuffed it and tried to assume positive intent. But asking me to remove the halter was almost a click too far. However, my inner "good girl" won out and I removed the halter as ordered. I watched the horse start grazing and turned back to Bruce, still wondering when we would get to my preconceived notions of "working with the horse." I had conveniently forgotten that Bruce calls this work Natural Humanship™.

For the next hour, we talked and did an exercise with flags. Best I could tell, that was a complete waste of time. Our mission was to find the middle of the round pen and all I could think was, "If the middle is so damned important, why the hell hasn't he marked it before now? When oh when will we do the leadership lessons with the horse?" There was a lot of talk about the Negative/Positive Pole, but the noise in my head drowned it out. The noise in my head had been drowning out my God-given instincts for my whole life.

Someday I would learn the transformative power of Finding the Middle. But on this day, I just wanted to get on with it.

Mistakes

Finally, Bruce handed me a tool that looked like it might lead to doing something with the horse – a good, old fashioned cowboy lariat. The assignment was simple and clear. Take the rope from its current, unorganized state into a set of equally sized coils with no tension in the rope.

Jen and I were still standing in the middle of the round pen, talking to Bruce, who was sitting in a chair just outside the fence.

When Bruce gave me the Picture (there's that word again), I was sure it would be easy and we could quickly start working with Trini, the horse I had worked so hard to catch and bring into the round pen. She was still peacefully grazing behind us.

Lariats are stiff, making the assignment a lot more challenging than it appeared on the surface. Lariats are sort of like a garden hose that only loops when coiled just right. In just a matter of seconds, I was in deep shit. I had made several coils and they were NOT equally sized, and the loops looked like my disorganized garden hose at home. I was failing and desperate to cover it up.

As my internal tension rose, the nice, calm horse I wanted so badly to play with started walking in circles around us. With my attention on coiling the rope, I barely noticed. Bruce would say something, and I would feel the heat rise in the back of my neck. Sitting under his stare raised the pressure even more.

"Between the horse, the lariat, and the guy heckling me in the cheap seats, I felt naked and exposed."

Soon, I started to notice the horse. I couldn't help it. No longer was she peacefully grazing. She had started trotting and then running and now was kicking up her heels. Greeeaaaat. Between the horse, the lariat, and the guy heckling me in the cheap seats, I felt naked and exposed. Now I feared for my life. Horses are BIG and this one was moving faster and faster.

As I watched Trini kick and buck, it never dawned on me that Jen might be getting concerned about the chaos running around us. Nor did I understand how or why my actions might have sent the horse into such a state. It was like I was looking at the world through a rolled-up tube of paper. I did have a flashback to my accident, remembering being on the back of a horse that had kicked me off in similar fashion.

Bruce stopped me and said something about me beating myself up. I fully denied it and tried to keep convincing him (and myself) that "I've got this."

None of my bullshit games worked.

He saw me. He saw ME. Now all he had to do was coax the real me to come out from behind the conditioning of my past.

While coiling the lariat, I did not consciously feel like I was making a mistake, nor did it feel like I was beating myself up. Yet at some level, my physiology was responding to my lack of rope coiling skills as a mistake. Once the "mistake" button got pushed, the automatic cycle took me into my past. The unconscious memories and emotions stored in my body came flooding to the surface. I was no longer the grown-up version of me, but the eight-year-old being scolded for getting something wrong.

And yes, I was beating myself up. That's no way to learn anything.

When Bruce interrupted me in that moment, he gave me a different path to take. Rather than operating from the past, he took my focus into the present moment. As my tension drained out through tears, the horse calmed down and faced me.

Now we could work on the Picture. How does one learn to coil a rope without training?

The use of the word Picture began to come into focus. Bruce said, "You are trying to do everything at once. A moving picture is made of lots of smaller frames, right? What are the frames?"

Still, I stood frozen.

"Break it into the smallest steps. Try stuff. Where is the twist in the coil coming from? What move could you make to release the tension? Would you twist the rope to the right or the left?"

From my helpless Kid Mode state of being, I asked for the answer.

Which way DO I turn the rope?

He said to try it and see what happens.

But what if I make it worse?

You might make it worse. And then what?

I go the other way. But what if that doesn't work?

Try something else.

But that might not work!

You won't know until you try.

But I might die.

OK, I didn't say the last thing out loud, even though that's what my mind had been screaming from the first, horrible coil of the rope. I might die. It feels like I'm dying here.

It wasn't death.

It was a path to life.

In that moment I could not appreciate what a profound lesson this would be. As he stayed with me through the messy emotions of wanting to throw the rope on the ground and leave the problem altogether, I began to chart a new path out of my old ways.

I tried twirling the tension out by swinging the rope to the right. It made it worse, yet somehow, I was still alive.

"Let the rope tell you which way to turn it," he said.

There he was, with his talking ropes again. But this time, something inside opened, just a little bit.

As I tried working with the coils, I began to tune into the rope, which meant I made space to tune out the inner voices telling me what an awful rope coiler I was. When my attention turned to the problem in front of me, it was as if I had a whole new set of resources at my disposal.

My mind quieted and I started working the puzzle. First this way and then that way. Soon my brain and my hands made a connection and before I knew it, the lariat was beautifully coiled.

Tears began to well up as I realized that I was alive. The shame and embarrassment of not being able to do a simple task had evaporated. I had experienced a glimpse of who I was born to be, without the internal noise and drama. It was just me and the rope, patiently working out a problem, listening to it tell me where to find the relaxed path.

On this day, I was not yet clear on what I had just learned. It had nothing to do with coiling a rope. Bruce had provided a safe space for me to solve a problem. For most of my life, I had not been afforded that kind of psychological safety in most of the cultures I had experienced, whether at school or in my career. While he was providing this space for me, my intensity and fear of getting it wrong did the opposite for the horse. Trini's bucking antics showed me the cost when safety is lacking. Her response was pure, without the usual human cover-up.

More importantly, Bruce had illuminated the key to my own treasure chest of Invisible Tools. It was a magical key that would only turn when I was present.

Accidentally Showing Up

The pressure of trying to figure out the rope took me out of the moment. As I stood there struggling with the rope, it felt like I was on center court in the finals of Wimbledon. I wasn't fully in the game. A part of me was in the stands, watching myself fumble and stumble with the task, with the audience of thousands offering their critique – the imaginary critique created by my mind.

Leaving the moment happens all the time. I jump into the other person's head and start imagining what they are thinking.

When I was a kid riding my bike down the street, I used to "hear in my head" what each neighbor must be thinking about me as I passed by their house. This little mind game continued for the rest of my life, pretending I knew what was going on in someone else's head.

The same thing happened at work. Often, I reacted based on what I thought someone was thinking rather than taking the time to ask, listen, and truly hear what they were actually thinking.

One of the biggest promotions of my banking career put me in both the spotlight and the headlights. My job was to take the core training program for commercial bankers from a one-year program to ten weeks, while delivering better bankers. As things often get done in the corporate world, the decision to reorganize around this idea happened before there was any proof at all that this idea could work.

The pressure to get it right fell on me and my team. The heads of the many commercial banking divisions were anxious to see how we would solve the problem; they looked forward to the benefits of a much less costly program, while at the same time feared the possibility that they might be stuck doing remedial training for the newly minted bankers they were counting on to be very proficient, very quickly. This was a tall order – learning to assess whether or not to give a business a sizable loan is a difficult task.

It was in one of the early meetings presenting our plans to this group of executives that I had experienced an out-of-body moment of watching myself crumble from the stands and then, somehow, bringing myself back into my body.

Everyone had come to corporate headquarters for a planning session around the new organizational structure and I was one of several team leads slated to report on our plans. This was the kind of working session that would be full of probing questions, pushback, decisions, and occasionally condescension. Nothing can knock me off center like being talked down to.

The executive team would either leave the meeting confident that we were up to the task, or it would begin taking measures to make sure that someone got the job done. In other words, I had a real shot at screwing things up here.

As we were gathering for the meeting, you could cut the tension with a knife. On the surface, everything looked friendly and supportive. The undercurrent told a different story, one that carried an awareness of the stakes.

Luckily for me, I was not the first to speak – but my luck was short-lived. As I watched others stumble and fumble under the examination of the senior leaders who had much to gain and lose, my planned presentation started looking weaker and weaker. Doubt started creeping in.

Would they press me as hard on my staffing plan as they did the presenter before me?

Would they open doors for me to hire from their teams – an essential part of my strategy – or would they insist that I somehow manage with a less-experienced cohort?

What if I made a mistake?

What if I looked unprepared or even stupid?

Is this the end of my career?

The pressure started to rise as the consequences of this moment washed over me.

My mind started chattering ideas to help me out. To get an idea of the self-talk, picture a parent watching their kid play a sport. Instead of yelling for me to choke up on the bat, it said things like, *"Come on, you know these people. They like you. Be sweet and cute so you can get your way!"* OK, maybe if they liked me enough, they would overlook the potential holes in the plan. But wait, they like the guy talking right now. He is choking. What about him? Then my competitive side started saying things like "*You can do better than him. He's being too cautious. Show 'em what you got!"* Even though we were all really on the same team, I found myself thinking I could do better than the other presenters. I NEEDED to do better than the other presenters. Now I wanted to win.

None of my mind-chatter nonsense helped. It came my turn to speak. My body tensed. A flood of sensations coursed through my torso; I was feeling like I had just been gut-punched. I looked down to open my presentation. When I looked up, I had that sort of tunnel vision that was like seeing the room through one of the peepholes in the door. The expectant faces of these executives entered my brain looking like distorted figures in a funhouse mirror. The words coming out of my mouth felt equally contorted. About two sentences in, I had enough presence of mind to be aware that I was speaking gibberish with a trembling voice that I didn't recognize. With a sinking feeling, my mind chatter told me I was going to get exactly what I had feared.

Here I was, a grown-ass woman with a big job and yet a skill I learned as a toddler was suddenly out of my reach. I could not talk.

The pressure had gotten to me. I was sinking.

A huge part of me wanted to run out of the room. In some ways, it already had, leaving a shell of me behind to face the music. I needed to find my voice and find it now; if I couldn't handle the pressure of talking about my plans, what would make them think I could bring those plans to life?

> **"Here I was, a grown-ass woman with a big job and yet a skill I learned as a toddler was suddenly out of my reach. I could not talk."**

Then I stumbled on an analogy that somehow got me out of my head and back into my body. I said, "These young bankers are coming in believing they are ready to run the ship, even though they can't yet read financial statements. What we have found is that we must balance helping them see the reality of their lack of skills with giving them a sense of progress. It's like a roller coaster. If they can feel the click, click, click as the car heads to the top, they will have the patience to see the training program through."

In what seemed like a magical moment at the time, I could feel the room change. As my physical demeanor shifted, my voice came back. I was fully present in the room. I quit pitching and started talking through our plans. Their eyes changed – from hard and skeptical to interested and excited. We had an engaged discussion where we jointly solved problems, developed strategies, and made decisions. By the end of my part of the meeting, the executives expressed their full support of our direction. I left the meeting with confidence and clarity.

Looking back on this event, I've wondered what shifted that day. Did I suddenly rise to the pressure? Did I find a level of inner strength? How did I get myself back to the present moment? Or did the people in the room lower the pressure? When their eyes changed, was it a way to encourage and support the clearly faltering me? Were they taking the role of audience member who showers the performer with positive vibes? What would have happened if they had gone harsh instead of friendly?

Without a time machine, I will never know for sure. However, with an increasing knowledge of the Pressure Gap, I believe their friendly faces and positive vibes helped lower the pressure.

The Pressure Gap

Pressure has a way of interfering with our most basic skills. We know how to talk – until we are faced with a huge audience or a make-or-break sales presentation. We know how to write and yet can't seem to hit send on an email that makes a bold offer. Pressure can even make walking next to impossible, especially for someone with a fear of heights, like me.

Here's an illustration you can test right now. Find a 20-foot span where you can walk comfortably on flat ground. Walk for 20 feet in a straight line. Now, reverse direction and walk the same span as if this were a 12-inch-wide beam. You might have to put one foot in front of the other.

Did you fall? Did you even feel wobbly? Probably not. The pressure created by the first task was really low – you handle that level of pressure all day long. The pressure created by the second task was also low, although slightly higher. Keeping your balance along a 12-inch beam is slightly more difficult than regular walking.

Now for the next task, it's best to use your imagination, unless you have a balance beam handy. Imagine that you are going to walk across said balance beam, like the one gymnasts use at the Olympics. Chances are the pressure created by the height of the beam will test your mental Tools if you really do it. Personally, just imagining it can create the sensation of falling in my body. While I can easily walk a four-inch-wide span across the floor, I cannot do the same four feet off the floor. I have a Pressure Gap.

For the final task, again, use your imagination. In this case, imagine that you are going to walk across a 12-inch-wide inch beam (three times wider than a balance beam) that is several hundred feet off the ground. We have already established that you have the skills to walk a 12-inch beam without falling over – so this is well within your skills.

Envision yourself walking across that beam several hundred feet above the Earth. Everything on the ground is really tiny. You wouldn't be able to recognize your own mother from this distance. You might be tempted to stare at your feet, even though that's not how you normally walk. But remember, the beam is 12 inches wide! You have the skills to do this all day long. I'm going to take a wild guess here and say you would love to have something to hang on to while up there. Or better yet, that you would like to be roped in. Or if you are like me, you might say to hell with it – never going there.

The "Pressure Gap" is the difference between the combination of your skills and mental Tools to handle a situation and the pressure created by that situation. You can close the gap by either reducing the pressure or reducing the pressure or building your mental tools, which will raise your pressure threshold.

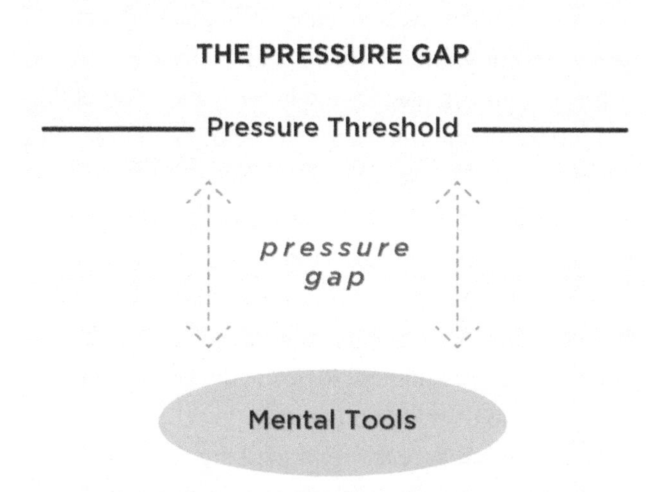

Once I understood this concept, all of Bruce's micromanaging started making sense. He was creating micro-moments for me to choose a new way. With my usual "hurryupitis," my goal was to get what he was doing by noon of the first day.

Ha, in my dreams. It would take a lot longer. A whole lot longer. If I were to have the courage to return.

We Can Never Go Back There Again

Jen's turn with the horses happened after lunch. After coiling the lariat – which felt like a lifetime – the three of us went to a local restaurant. In a different setting, this big, imposing man was nothing like the guy who had micromanaged my every move that morning. I was still trying to put my finger on his methods, and I peppered him with questions during lunch. What I was starting to learn was unexpected. He was not "certified" in some course or method of working with horses. He had learned what he was teaching the hard way. The really, really hard way of trial and error. No wonder the exercises I was looking for were nowhere to be found.

He spoke sentences like, "I'm here to help the horse to help himself survive in the world we have created," and "I'm teaching you to live in the world you were made for instead of the world we have made," and "It's not the horse; it's the pressure created by the horse," and "Forget the goal. Break it down frame by frame," and my least favorite of all "I don't WANT the horse to do the picture."

He had other confusing terminology, like AlphA and TyranT. These did not mean what the dictionary said, and he spelled them with the capital letters at the beginning and end. He used these words to describe a mindset. Instead, AlphA meant that you were letting the horse – or situation – tell you what to do, when to do, and how to do. TyranT meant the past was interfering, causing us to over - or underreact.

The idea of over - or underreacting piqued my attention because it resonated with the "change tightrope," a mental construct I had been using for years. The visual of a tightrope started for me in the context of leading change and dealing with the balancing acts of leadership. For example, in dealing with resistance to change, the typical leadership strategies fell into two buckets. The first was to be too easy on people, which forced the leader to personally take on too much as deadlines slipped. The second was to be too hard on people, which drove resistance underground, letting the leader have the illusion all was OK, but causing conflict and chaos in the people who were upset and didn't want to change. Both sides of this equation slowed change down. Walking the tightrope meant allowing people to have their normal reactions to change while at the same time, requiring them to do good work.

As our lunch wrapped up and we headed back to his farm, my head was spinning. I had both loved and hated my experience from the morning. Bruce's methods for leadership training seemed to have some promise – but I wasn't sure what it was yet. It did feel like I had released something in my round pen session that had nothing to do with horses.

It went without saying, at least as far as I was concerned, that Jen would get a chance to play with the horses after we finished eating. In my mind, she was excitedly looking forward to it. Even though I had been her mother for thirty-six years, you would have never known it. Boy did I misread the situation.

When Bruce handed Jen the halter and lead rope, the scene played out very differently. He gave her the same instructions he had given me. But everything was different. Jen had no experience with horses, halters, or lead ropes. And the halter wasn't talking to her any more than it had talked to me.

She slowly walked out into the field and greeted one horse and then the other. Animals love her and the horses were happy to have her hang out with them. When it was time to put the halter on, all she saw was a tangled mess. After one attempt with putting the halter on, her solution to deal with the pressure was to throw the rope down and walk away. At that moment, we saw a very different Bruce. All this while, I was still thinking she was having fun.

Instead of the micromanaging questioner, she got support. Instead of telling her to listen to the rope, he showed her how it fit the horse's head. Instead of asking her why she tied it this way and not that way, he helped her make the special knot. Step by step, frame by frame, he showed deep support and kindness with both Jen and the horse. Slowly but surely, she and Bruce solved problems together, eventually bringing the horse to the round pen.

Later I would come to learn that Bruce could see that Jen was well over her pressure threshold. He was letting her tell him what to do, when to do, how to do — i.e., being AlphA. Rather than adding pressure by asking her tons of questions, he reduced the pressure by offering support. In other words, he avoided pushing her buttons, where he had pushed every button I had to get a reaction out of me. Even later, I would come to learn the benefit of having someone push my buttons.

On this day, I was thrilled and sure that Jen was loving the experience. One of these days, I will remember that she can hide what she's feeling better than anyone I've ever known.

While they worked, I planned. My experience with the lariat had made me realize the potential depth of this work; now I had to figure out how to make it work for the leadership team. Clearly, it would be different than what I had anticipated.

"Even later, I would come to learn the benefit of having someone push my buttons."

Eventually, Jen's session was over, and it was time for us to go. We had a three-hour drive home in which to debrief, and I was picturing a rich conversation about possibilities as we rolled on down the highway. As we left, Bruce had one request. He wanted to speak with me the next morning to review the session. It seemed really important to him. I promised to be available and got in the car.

Before I could get the seatbelt on, Jen looked at me and said, "We can never come here again. And there's no way you should bring the leadership team."

It was going to be a long drive home.

CHAPTER FOUR

Failure is not Failure at All

A Pony Opens the Door

A month later, Jen was skipping along with a new pony in the round pen saying, "It makes me so happy!"

Jen had come to the farm still carrying the skepticism from our first session. In the ensuing month, we had many conversations about our experience and Jen had thawed enough to come for the next session. What had bothered her most in the first session was watching Bruce micromanage and pepper me with questions. When she learned that I was not nearly as bothered, but more curious, she let go of some – but not all – of her resistance.

This time, I had asked a close friend, Gail, from the corporate world to come be a "guinea pig" for a session with Bruce. Gail was like a second mom to Jen; we both agreed it would be good for Jen and me for her to be there.

In some ways, Jen and I represented two opposite ends of the spectrum. I was keen to learn more, and Jen was in the "no way, no how" camp. Having a third person might help calibrate whether there was anything to this work or not, and we could approach anything that came up from different perspectives.

As soon as we pulled into Bruce's farm, Jen spotted the new pony. He was truly a small horse – more like the size of a Great Dane. Jen is good at hiding negative feelings; when something as cute as this pony is around, her delight practically drips off her skin.

The session with Gail went for a few hours and I noticed that Bruce was repeating himself from the last couple of conversations. He was saying the same phrases over and over again, like "It's not the horse, it's the pressure created by the horse," and "When your mental tools are not equal or greater than the pressure of the situation, then you over – or underreact;" "It's not the thing you are doing, it's the mindset *while* you are doing the thing that matters;" "It's not a mistake, it's an opportunity;" "It's not the work with the horse that matters; it's *in* doing the work with the horse, you are recalibrating your mental tools and becoming more of *the* You;" "The round pen is a metaphor for your life," and the dreaded, "I don't want the horse to do the picture!"

> **"It's not the work with the horse that matters; it's IN doing the work with the horse, you are recalibrating your mental tools and becoming more of the You."**

Every time he said that I remembered myself lying on the ground unable to breathe, wondering what had caused the horse to throw me into the dirt. At moments like this, I thought, *"Bruce, I most certainly DO want the horse to do the picture! And my picture is to stay ON the horse. What kind of horse trainer/people trainer/leadership trainer doesn't want to get the job done?"*

My first inkling of an answer to that question came the day after our first session. Bruce and I spoke as promised. I didn't share Jen's reservations, which she had listed in exhaustive detail over the drive home. I did mention one small moment, when we pulled off the highway and found ourselves behind a line of cars at the exit.

I made some comment like, "Wish I had my James Bond car with a weapon that would move all these cars aside." Something made me tell Bruce about this exchange with Jen and he said very matter-of-factly, "Good opportunity to work on patience." This seemingly small moment in an otherwise eventful day was like a little miracle – one that I would understand much, much later.

Hmm. One of the things I had often experienced after leaving countless meditation retreats was that my good feelings seemed to evaporate on the drive home. A truck would cut me off, a wreck would back up traffic or any number of other everyday occurrences would take me from cool-headed meditator to road rage madwoman in the blink of an eye. It had never occurred to me to use these things to make myself better. Instead, I would just beat myself up for being bad at staying grounded. Perhaps the horse NOT doing the picture offered a good opportunity to work on myself.

Nothing changed in that moment – but a seed was planted.

Resistance Melts

During the day, as Bruce worked with Gail, Jen had her eye on that pony. When Gail and Bruce finished, Gail left, and we decided the three of us would debrief in what I would later come to call a "porch session." The porch overlooked the round pen and the pasture where the horses grazed. It was a gorgeous spring day, and everything was just starting to turn green. Chickens were running around, the peacock occasionally spread his magnificent tail and hummingbirds darted in and out of the feeder. I made note of a lariat (or was it a noose?) hanging in the nearby tree but didn't have the courage to ask about it until many porch sessions later.

We took our seats and began discussing the events of the day. Before I knew it, Bruce had asked Jen if she wanted to give it another try. *Wait – give what another try? Jen is not heading for the car? She is carrying a halter? She's heading for the round pen? Ooooohhh, of course. Not the round pen. She's heading for the pony!*

Even though our intention in the debrief was to focus on the session we had just completed, the conversation had somehow come around to the prior month. In what seemed like a flash, Bruce said something, and Jen was ready to try again.

Looking back on it, that pony catalyzed another miracle moment. He was only going to be there for a short time while Bruce "babysat" him for a friend. His cuteness factor was just high enough to override Jen's wall of resistance. Had we come another time, the pony wouldn't have been there – and I might never had gone back.

As Jen skipped around in the round pen, the pony opened her heart. She was having fun – and was putting herself in danger in ways she did not recognize. Quickly Bruce saw that Jen was not respecting the pony the same way she would have a full-sized horse. He would give her a task (Picture) and she would try to use force to move him around. Though small, this pony still weighed well over 200 pounds.

At one point, he said, "What makes you think this pony can't hurt you? He's got teeth and he's got hooves." He pointed out that she was underreacting to the pressure of the pony – a sure sign that she was in TyranT mindset.

Bruce's TyranT mindset was still somewhat of a mystery to me. He mentioned the past interfering. As had happened before, I recognized that he and I were often talking about the same or similar ideas, with different language. In my language, what I was seeing was both Kid Mode and History Mode in action. On the Kid Mode tightrope, Jen was falling off on both sides – child and parent. From the Child Power Under side, I saw:

- Jen wanted the pony to like her;
- She was naive to the danger in front of her.

From the Parent Power Over side, I saw:

- Jen letting the pony get away with doing whatever it wanted;
- She was overly helpful when she decided it was time for the pony to do the picture;
- Attempting to use force when being helpful didn't work.

Rather than the give and take of Adult Power With, she was following a common pattern: feel powerless, then try to grab power, overshoot the mark, try to make up for the pushy moves and then continually porpoise back and forth without ever really finding the balance on the tightrope again.

I was reminded that this very pattern played out the day of my accident. First, I wanted the horse to like me. Then I started to recognize the danger, so I tried to find a way to get power. When he started to run, I completely overreacted and the consequence was a big splat.

Seeing my own pattern play out in my daughter, right in front of my eyes, evoked a strong recognition of History Mode. Where else would she have learned such a pattern, other than to watch her mother do it hundreds of times over her lifetime?

In all my years of working on myself, through the journaling, reflections, meditations, grounding, and every other method I had tried to break my longstanding patterns, I had never found a way out that stood the test of pressure. Something told me I was about to learn something big, so I grabbed my phone and started the video.

The Round Pen as a Metaphor for Life

The fifteen minutes that followed were pure magic. I was no longer an outsider, trying to see if this fellow Bruce had something that would work for clients. Suddenly, I was a mom, filming as Jen reached point after point of trying and failing and learning, repeatedly. Instead of resistance and covering up, as I had shown the month before, she was open-hearted and smiling. Even when she was making "mistakes."

Perhaps the most powerful exchange occurred when Bruce asked her, "Were you doing TyranT mindset?"

Jen: *"Yeah, I think so."*

Bruce: "Definitely – because you weren't applying the pressure the pony was telling you to, because you were so engrossed in the excitement of working with the pony."

Jen: *"Yes!" Smiling from ear to ear.*

Bruce: "And you were like Bruce, f__ you, I don't care what your picture is because I'm just having too much fun!"

Jen: *"Because I just love the pony!" Giddiness exuding from her pores.*

Bruce: "But where else in the job place are you doing that? Can you do that? You understand? You can't be doing that shit in the job place. You can't let the past interfere."

Jen: *"Oh – yeah!" Lightbulb moment.*

Just that exchange busted so many assumptions. TyranT mindset does not necessarily FEEL bad; it can be exciting. Laughing doesn't make everything OK. The sensation of excitement can be misinterpreted, just as the sensation of anxiety can be misinterpreted.

Back to the exchange on the video:

Bruce: "So what I'm showing you here – the nice thing about the pony was – did you ever feel in danger?"

Jen: *"No."*

Bruce: "But, by him being so small, were you having a hard time getting your picture done?"

Jen: *Laughing – "Yeah!"*

Bruce: "And at the same time, you think he's small ..."

Jen: *"I wasn't being as cautious and as demanding ..."*

Bruce: "Because you assumed because he was small ..."

Jen: *"I thought I had more control than I really did."*

Bruce: "Yeah. But who was the one that was lacking control? You or the pony?"

Silence.

Jen had not really thought of herself as lacking control. Neither had I. She had been dancing around laughing, having fun trying to move the pony. Even though the pony was not going where she was directing, it all seemed like fun and games.

Bruce pointed out that her desire to help was actually putting her in danger, and she was not aware of exactly how painful a kick or bite could be. He pointed out that having the pony run wild was "not beneficial to him."

There he was, using that terminology again. His words echoed back to me, "I'm here to help the horse to help himself to live in the world we have created." The modern world is the world we have created. Horses are of the natural world. But a horse who is allowed to succumb fully to his wild nature would be way too dangerous for humans to work with day in and day out.

Bruce was saying out loud what Jen was learning. Believing that she could control the pony was a faulty assumption.

Without me knowing it at the time, Bruce had just revealed a core point – perhaps THE core point in his method. Jen had lost her power by believing she had power where she didn't. It would take me many years and even more horses to begin to grasp the depth of this lesson.

She could choose to work with the horse by using domination and force or form a relationship of trust and connection. In the dominance game, it's all about Power Over and Power Under. This was the game I had played my whole corporate life. Kid Mode reigned supreme.

Bruce was showing another way to dance the tightrope. Instead of using force, fear, and intimidation, the hallmarks of dominance, he was showing Jen how to dance between applying too much and too little pressure, with the intention to push the horse's Negative Pole up. Doing so allows the horse to choose how to balance his Negative/Positive Pole. Using dominance can get things done – but with a cost. It creates compliance. Out of fear, a horse might freeze, or run away. (People do the same thing.) But the horse could also fight. As Bruce pointed out, the horse has teeth, and it has hooves. A kick or a bite can be devastating and even fatal.

However, Bruce's main focus was not on what Jen was doing. Instead, it was on where it came from.

Bruce: "Yes. But notice your emotion, how the past was interfering. And you were trying to fill a void. You understand? And therefore, by doing that, you're actually saying to the pony it's OK to do what it's doing, when it's not OK. You understand what I'm saying?"

Bam. There it was.

Jen was caught in a pattern. She was feeling emotion. Lots of emotion. In order to address the feeling, Jen was filling a void. She was allowing the cuteness of the pony to override her own insecurities. We all have insecurities, and we have strategies for filling the void they create. Jen was operating on invisible Rules. She might as well have been a robot – albeit a happy one. Bruce was here to show her a way out of the Rules. That much I could see. This very type of "rule breaking" had been at the root of my coaching work for years.

But something was different here. Now I had seen Bruce debrief different situations in the round pen, and in every case, there was a parallel with life. When he said, "The round pen is a metaphor for your life," he was able to back it up with lessons like this one.

Let the Situation Tell You How Much Pressure to Apply

After Bruce revealed what was really going on, Jen got very clear on her Picture. With some coaching on reaching for her Tools – listening, hearing, patience, problem-solving – Jen helped the pony to help himself move with ease around the perimeter of the round pen.

Several times, Bruce pointed out that Jen had found her AlphA mindset, meaning she was letting the pony tell her what to do and how much pressure to apply.

The pony didn't talk any more than the rope had.

However, the pony did show her what worked and what didn't.

Bruce's approach interrupted some of my big assumptions and looked very different than what I expected. *Where were the instructions for how to move a pony or a horse around? How does one apply pressure if you can't touch the animal? Why does Bruce keep handing us a lariat without telling us how to use it? Surely, we missed a training session in "horse school" about ... everything one needs to know?*

Instead, Bruce kept saying things like, "Pay attention to what the horse is telling you! Use your mental Tools – listening, hearing, patience, timing, feel, problem-solving, discipline." Outside of maintaining safety, he was giving us no Rules. Just Tools. It was an empowering message – both for Jen and for the pony.

"Remember," he said, "the pony will tell you how much pressure to apply. Let him tell you what to do, when to do, how to do."

Eventually, those words would come to mean freedom in contexts far beyond the horses. In this moment, they were still creating cognitive dissonance.

- In my head I'm looking for Bruce to give some answers, share his rulebook and educate us on the ways of horses.
- I'm also sensing that if I could just get out of my own way and the incessant desire to be perfect, there is something to this idea of allowing the situation to tell me what to do.
- The two thoughts felt like a major contradiction, yet they also seemed to go together, like two rhyming words in a poem.

Seeking a way to resolve the dissonance, I remembered using that principle outside of the training with the horses.

Just the week before, I had a conversation with Scott, a client who had been trying to avoid firing one of his most trusted team members, Bob. His company was growing at an astronomical rate and Bob had been struggling to keep pace. Instead, he had been missing deadlines and showing up late for work. Scott had been very clear on his expectations, yet Bob was only making matters worse. Finally, Scott realized he had to fire him, and called me in hopes that I would offer another alternative. I asked Scott what was making him so concerned. He simply said, "He's been great until the last few months; I just don't want to fire him." I said, "What makes you think you are the one firing him? Doesn't he know what you expect? You've been very clear. He's firing himself." Bob had told Scott how much pressure to apply; if Scott had not listened, Bob would have caused even more damage than he already had.

Rather than creating dissonance for Scott, the idea that Bob was firing himself gave Scott some peace of mind. Letting him go was exactly the right move for both the company and for Bob. Later, Scott rehired him – because Bob needed that level of pressure as a wake-up call and was able to get back to where he needed to be.

I was starting to see that what Bruce was teaching went far beyond the round pen. My perceptions were coming from standing outside the fence. For the whole day, being outside was my safe vantage point. But not for long.

Bruce invited me to join Jen in the round pen. Our task was to contain the pony in a six-foot square with nothing but our energy. I really would have loved to have that halter and rope back. I wanted more control. More than once, Bruce had to remind us we couldn't touch him. Otherwise, he gave no other specific steps to take. Rather, he kept talking about letting the pony tell us what to do, when to do, how to do.

This was incredibly frustrating to say the least. The pony was doing whatever he pleased while we ran around trying to contain him. Not only did we look like Keystone Cops, but it also felt like mistake piled on mistake piled on more mistakes.

Try one thing and it's too much. Try another thing and it's too little. Back and forth, never quite getting the hang of it, we were feeling the frustration build.

The thoughts behind my thoughts started making me feel like a failure. My direct thoughts were things such as, "*Why isn't Bruce helping us? Where is that pony going now? What should I do next?*"

My indirect thoughts didn't have words. They had energy. And the energy weighed me down. It was that energy that the pony was responding to. If they DID have words, it would be things such as, "*I'm going to get in trouble. Why can't I get this? What's wrong with me? How bad do I look?*"

I wanted to get the Picture right; my very identity was resting on this.

Bruce wanted us to use the pressure created by the pony to build our mental Tools.

I wanted perfection.

Bruce was showing a path to progress. It went something like this:

- The pressure wasn't there to crush me; I could choose to allow it to elevate me.
- The uncertainty and not knowing what to do are an essential part of creativity.
- Failure is not failure at all.

In this path, I was learning – no, relearning – a principle that would serve me deeply. Let the situation tell me the best response. My past can inform – but be mindful when it interferes. Or EnterFears.

When we stopped feeling like we were making mistakes and started listening to the pony, it became easy to contain him in the six-foot square. The answers were not in the seen thing – they were in the invisible part of the equation.

I didn't know it yet, but this work would eventually teach me that most of my assumptions about balance, pressure, uncertainty, and failure were upside down or backward. My assumptions about trail riding were just as inverted.

CHAPTER FIVE

Assessing Risk

Horses and Survival Mode

After my first two sessions with Bruce, I began taking a variety of individual clients – not the leadership team – to work with him over the next several months. I wasn't even remotely ready to consider getting back on a horse again, but I was still hanging out with my friends who had horses. Also, Tammy Tappan, owner of Equestrian Artists at Tryon International Equestrian Center, had asked me to include my pottery in her gallery. Her horse paintings had stopped me in my tracks the first time I saw them. Every time I walked into her gallery, I could feel the familiar tug of wanting to be with horses. Trips to the gallery offered me more excuses for going to the Center. More than once, Tammy offered to take me on a trail ride with her horses. And more than once, I told her I was not ready.

The more I was exposed to the horse world, the more I heard from lifetime horse men and women about the life with horses. Perhaps the most common phrase I heard in this phase of my recovery was this, "I've been injured more times than I can count." While feeling somewhat vindicated about my own accident, this dawning awareness did little to build my confidence about ever riding again. Instead, I started learning more about horses, trail rides, and the risk I inadvertently took to take the lead on a trail ride.

My inverted assumptions about trail riding – albeit innocent – started with ignorance around the mind of a horse and ended with naïveté about the complications of taking a fight/flight/freeze animal out for a stroll through the woods.

It's never just a stroll for the horse.

Riding horses has been done by humans for thousands of years. Yet when you stop to think about it, riding horses should not be possible. We are getting on the back of a huge animal and asking it to give its body over to our direction. In the pecking order of life, horses are prey, humans are predators. So, the prey animal is allowing a predator to get on his back, usually after throwing a saddle up there. Which is made of a dead animal. An animal we have already killed.

Yet somehow, mankind has learned to work with these magnificent animals over the centuries. Seeing the world through the eyes of a horse has helped me understand the survival instincts of life. While humans are predators in the big picture pecking order, we are both prey and predator in our own lives. Anyone who has ever felt the hair on their neck prickle while walking in a big city or felt the glare of an angry boss knows the feeling of being prey. Learning to develop trust with a horse has helped me understand myself so much better and it's transformed my understanding of the human survival brain.

Because of who they are, horses are profound teachers, if we are willing to give ourselves over to them.

As Dr. Allan J. Hamilton, M.D., says in *Zen Mind, Zen Horse: The Science and Spirituality of Working with Horses:*

> *The reason the horse can become such a gifted teacher for us is because he does not need an inner voice. He doesn't think in words at all. He feels. He experiences the simple energy of his emotional state of being. More than thirty million years of evolutionary pressure have turned the horse into the quintessential prey animal. Rather than using words or vocalization to communicate sounds that help a predator pinpoint its prey – horses learned instead how not to talk, to make sounds, and how to make sense of being, not thinking.*
>
> *Horses infuse emotional meaning into body movement. They pour this vital emotional energy – chi – into every gesture and glance, lending them the nuances of tone, accent, and value. By sensitizing themselves to chi, horses can not only convey the*

meaning of what they want to share with other members of the herd but can also feel the palpably sharp energy emitting from a stalking predator's eyes locked intently on its prey. Evolution has driven equids to the farthest limits of nonverbal, right-sided brain function.

Out on the trail, these sensitivities are amplified. Now you have a prey animal carrying a predator into the wilderness. The lead horse has the most responsibility. Its large eyes and huge nostrils are always on guard for danger out in front and from the sides. The horse in back tunes in for threats from the rear. The horses in the middle just focus on what the lead and trailing horses communicate.

The pressure is high, especially for the flight animal. Should an event happen – and events often happen – it's entirely possible for both human and horse to be scared. Unexpected gunfire, a snake slithering, or a pack of dogs challenging the path might or might not send chills down a human's spine. However, the horse will always have his survival instincts on high alert. The horse might take off running. He might rear up. He might decide to suddenly roll back the other way. He might buck. He might just jump to the side. He might stand still.

It's best if he stands still.

Even when he's standing still, a fearful horse radiates with energy. A rider can feel that. Moreover, any sudden dancing or prancing of the nervous horse can elevate the unprepared rider's fear to extreme levels. Now the horse has to contend with whatever is happening OUT there and what is happening UP there, on its back – the place where a cougar might drop in an ambush.

Here's the one thing a horse will never conclude: that he's the cause of the fear in the predator on his back. It's our job as his rider and leader to be the responsible one and manage, not hide, or not pretend away our fear.

Horses are masters at reading incongruity. Hiding feelings of any sort telegraphs nothing but trouble for an animal who stays alive by reading intent. Remember my story of coiling the lariat? The horse began running and then kicking and then bucking because I was trying to look calm, cool, and collected while my inner turmoil escalated. The horse felt the mismatch. She stopped her antics when I quit pretending. When I started working through the problem step by step, moment by moment, my inner turmoil melted away and the horse turned and calmly watched me coil the rope.

When I decided to go out on the trail, in the lead, on a horse I had ridden only once, my starting assumption was that trail riding was nothing compared to getting a horse to perform something far more advanced. (My other assumption was that getting on the horse mattered more than anything else. More on that later.) Growing up going to the rodeo, I watched horses do all kinds of specialized activities, such as exploding out of the gate to catch a calf or running around the barrels. The 2018 World Equestrian Games were held near where I live and I watched people with their horses do all kinds of advanced skills, such as jumping over six-foot fences, dressage (which looks like horse dancing to me) and racing with carts. It all looked dangerous and thrilling at the same time.

I was both impressed and keenly aware that I knew nothing about how to get a horse to do any of those things. However, trail riding – that I could do. Or so I thought. On the surface, it looks like anyone can do it. However, any true horse person will tell you nothing could be further from the truth.

Unlike working in an arena where there is a defined space and a clear job for the horse to do, the trail offers pressure and uncertainty. Whether the unexpected will be unmanageable or not is yet to be seen. In fact, in many ways, trail riding is the most dangerous of horse activities, especially if the horse and human are not prepared. Remember, anything can happen out there. Deer crashing through the trees, pigs rolling in the mud, snakes crossing the path, bicycles and motorcycles sharing the trail, crossing streams, uncertain footing, loggers cutting down trees.

Going out on the trail can either be a house of horrors or a series of opportunities to learn and grow. Later, I would come to realize what Bruce was saying. At this point, I just wanted to avoid the house of horrors.

Many people who own horses share the same belief I did about the difference between performance riding and trail riding. They say, "It's just trail riding." Followed by the deadly thought: *"How hard can it be?"*

"Going out on the trail can either be a house of horrors or a series of opportunities to learn and grow."

Warwick Schiller, professional horse trainer, compared trail riding to having the right tools to fix a blown tire on the horse trailer on this Facebook post:

It's (fixing the blown tire) quite a simple process, providing that before you left home, you had the right sized socket, breaker bar, a jiffy jack, and a fully inflated spare.

I often get asked, "What would you do when

out riding on a narrow trail and your horse gets upset, and there's no place to circle him to get him under control?"

My answer is usually, "Just put a little bend in his body, and if all of the training I have done at home is solid, he will come back down and relax." Most times the reply I get after that is, "That wouldn't work with my horse, he won't even relax when I do that at home."

About this time, I usually suggest they talk to the guy with the gun.

"The guy with the gun?" they ask.

"Yes, the guy with the gun pointed at you who forced you to take an unprepared horse out on a narrow trail."

Usually about this time they start to figure out that maybe that wasn't the best situation to put their horse in.

I have sometimes felt bad for pointing out that maybe their horse isn't ready for trail riding ... there's a Buck Brannaman quote that gets around social media that goes something along the lines of, "some trail riders say they don't need that fancy arena stuff, they just want to trail ride. They just want to die out among the trees."

Trail riding is like going out on the freeway with your car. It may be ok to drive around the pasture or paddock at home in a car that's not safe, maybe the brakes are iffy or the steering not so good, but when you get out where you may have to take some evasive action to circumvent situations that are out of control, it's a really good idea to be prepared.

Clearly, trail riding is no walk in the park. Both humans and horses must prepare themselves for the pressure and uncertainty they will face. Yet with all this survival instinct in play, horses do learn to be safe on the trail. The folks who offer public trail rides prepare their horses with the mental tools to handle the unexpected. While the unexpected can happen – and it does – they have developed the tools to handle the pressures, uncertainty, and fear. They don't put just any rider on any horse in the lead.

We Have Survival Mode Too

So, it was here in the lead where I discovered that I was the one lacking mental Tools. Survival mode took over. Fear flooded my system. I was now the predator on the back of a horse. It never dawned on the horse that he was the source of my fear.

As with any endeavor, horseback riding has two tracks: the skills of the activity and the ability to bring those skills to bear under pressure. I was completely unaware of the gap between my skills and the situation into which I had gotten myself. I was also unconsciously operating on two false sets of beliefs, one about the safety of trail riding and the other about the nature of horses.

The modern world with all its progress has divested us from nature, and the nature of horses. It's taken us away from our own nature. For most of human history, horses were our primary mode of transportation. Knowing how to care for them, communicate with them, and work with them was an essential part of life. With the advent of the car, horses haven't gone away. However, for most people today, it's possible to live a full life without ever encountering a horse.

"The modern world with all its progress has divested us from nature, and the nature of horses. It's taken us away from our own nature."

Today we interact more with machines than we do nature. Machines are logical, they have rules and procedures that ensure they work as we want them. We push a button and get an immediate response. Not so with nature and not so with horses. When I pulled back on the reins that day, I expected it to be like hitting the brake on my car or my bicycle. He should stop.

He went faster. When he did the opposite of what my Rules said he should do, I had no other way to meet the moment.

I lost my balance, both literally and internally.

As I shared my story with many people, my basic premise for the accident was I didn't know how to stop a horse. Most riders agreed and they all had a method to stop a horse. Do this, that, or the other thing with the reins and with your legs and the horse will stop. There is a skill to stopping a horse, especially one that is running faster than the rider wants.

Bruce's diagnosis was different. In his way of thinking, the pressure of the situation was greater than my mental tools. The question was not whether I had the skill to stop the horse; the question was whether I could use the skill under pressure.

Of course, as he shared this theory, I kept thinking: *"But seriously, how do you stop a horse?"*

My controlling mindset was sure the answer was in the reins. What I did not know yet was that you can stop a horse with nothing more than a clear mental Picture and energy.

Finding the Heat

Growing up, we cooked hotdogs and s'mores over the campfire almost every weekend. Getting too close to the fire taught me about getting burned. There was a just-right place to stand, where I could cook a hotdog or marshmallow without cooking myself. Get too far away and nothing got cooked. Get too close and it was me that got cooked. Depending on the wind, that just-right place could change and move. Finding the safe zone was a constant balancing act that required my attention.

Getting burned can be a metaphor for more than touching a hot stove or getting too close to a real fire. We humans have well-developed systems to keep us away from things that hurt.

In my year of recovery after my horse fall, I tried to find that just-right place to stand. My mind provided both the fire and the solace. Sometimes, it fed me sensible thoughts. More often, it fired noisy thoughts like bullets from a gun. *"You were overconfident." "You will never get it." "It was a freak accident that will never happen again." "You just need better skills." "You would be crazy to ride again."* Notice how the thoughts careened between both extremes. They either pulled me into the fire or kept me outside the fire. Productive learning and growth could not happen when there was no heat or too much heat.

None of these thoughts chose the path of productive discomfort. Nowhere did I ask, "How can I use the heat to gain traction?" Instead, my thoughts kept me spinning my wheels, rushing to land on an answer that would stop the heat and take away my discomfort.

What was most unsettling was the gap between what I believed I could do and what my accident revealed. Like a dog with a bone, my mind gnawed at the gap, wondering what moves I should have made with my hands, my seat, my legs.

To completely mix my metaphors, I was barking up the wrong tree. The problem was not in my skills – although my skills needed improvement. The problem was in my relationship with pressure. What I've been uncovering is the Pressure Gap, much richer – and scarier – territory.

The tangible territory of the skill gap is so alluring. Sports offer excellent illustrations of the skill gap. In basketball, a player might hit a certain percentage of shots in scrimmage games and not even come close to the same rate in a big game. A swimmer might get a certain time every day in practice and fall short under the pressure of the meet. A tennis player might be able to ace every serve in practice and yet end up double-faulting in the tournament. In every case, they have the skills to perform in low-level situations.

Increase the pressure, and they can't perform at the same level. In other words, they are not bringing their level of skills to bear when it counts. For me, it's as if my skills go offline when I need them most. In the heat of the fire, there is no time to read the rule book. The only thing that matters is the mental Tools I bring to the situation. Those Tools are the gateway to effectively managing my skills and embracing the discomfort of the pressure. If my Tools are not up to the task, my skills lie behind a wall of fear.

Considering My Choices

The groundwork with the horses introduced a novel perspective on what was needed to get back on the horse.

With this new vantage point, it wasn't just a matter of getting back on or not. There were three options.

1. I could choose to never ride again — a logical choice as I was now 60 and didn't want to risk another serious injury.

2. I could take riding lessons — the mainstream choice, which would educate me on the rules and skills of equitation.

3. I could work on my mental Tools — the messy choice guaranteed to be full of pressure, uncertainty, and failure.

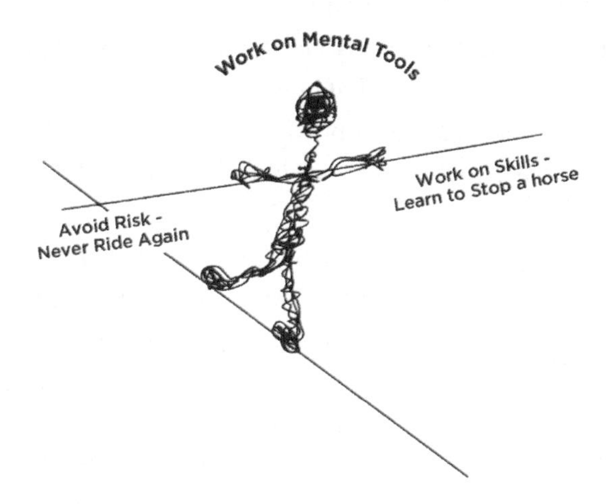

Choices 1 and 2 offered two sides of the risk tightrope. When assessing risk, one side is risk avoidant. The other side is risk dismissive. In my credit training program, we had to teach aspiring bankers to see the full picture of risk. Those with a risk avoidant tendency had a difficult time making lending decisions. They felt much safer leaving the bank's money in the bank. (And they may very well have had some of their own money stuffed in mattresses like their grandparents had.) Those with a risk dismissive tendency minimized the genuine risks in the deal. Every deal looked good to them, because they only saw the money-making potential while being blind to many ways the loan could go sour. (And these same trainees seemed to consistently have the story of the one that got away.)

We wanted our bankers to walk the tightrope, which meant training them to see and mitigate risk while recognizing when that risk was too much for the bank to take.

To walk away would put me in the risk avoidant camp, for which there were plenty of good reasons. However, I knew myself well enough to know it would feel like I let my fears win.

Choosing to take riding lessons that focused strictly on riding skills seemed to minimize the genuine danger I was beginning to see in horseback riding. While I would become a more skilled rider, what good would my skills have been if I could not access them under the pressure of a horse that was choosing to act like a horse, rather than a machine?

I couldn't decide. While working with horses on the ground was slightly intriguing, I still carried the belief that getting ON was the only interesting part. The day of my accident, I remember going through the motions of brushing the horse, putting on the saddle and putting on the bridle, focusing almost strictly on the goal of RIDING the horse. In fact, I was so excited about being ON a horse again, I stopped and took a picture looking down on his head. That was about 15 minutes before my fateful thought, *"This is sort of boring."*

"A part of me knew it would be like shaking up my internal snow globe. There was no telling where things would land."

In my two sessions with Bruce, I was shown the messy alternative. To truly change, I would have to feel the pressure and go deep – to my core. A part of me knew it would be like shaking up my internal snow globe. There was no telling where things would land. What I wanted instead was a set of Rules and steps. Bruce kept talking about my Tools – listening, hearing, patience, timing, feel, problem-solving, and other actions in the unseen territory.

My beliefs were acting like a heat shield, keeping his methods at bay. I was speaking one set of beliefs while showing a contradictory set of beliefs when under pressure. While I espoused giving up perfection, I was totally seeking perfection. While I coached people (and myself) that beating ourselves up avoids change, under the pressure of getting it right with the horses, I beat myself up. While I wrote eloquent articles about the value of mistakes, I still cringed when I made a mistake.

These old beliefs were not living in my head, they were living in my bones. They were like computer code, the Rules running my every action. Extricating myself from them was not merely a matter of changing my mind. Only the heat of pressure would burn them out of my cells. I had little to no ability to apply my knowledge under pressure. While my head was attempting to apply its knowledge, the beliefs in my bones were directing my actions.

Yet in that first year, I kept coming back to Bruce with clients – me on the outside, them in the fire. Looking back on it, I believe it was to help them learn what I thought I already knew.

Yes, I had knowledge of the concepts Bruce was sharing. I had been teaching many of them for years. Plus, I was thrilled with the experiential aspect of working with live animals in a somewhat unpredictable environment.

But my old beliefs still held me in their prison. I was still thinking of the work as a finite set of lessons rather than infinite possibilities.

Remember the example with the Pressure Gap? Just because we can walk on a twelve-inch beam on the ground doesn't mean we can walk the same path when the beam is elevated even four or five feet off the ground. Just because we can talk doesn't mean we can be coherent when we are in front of people whose opinions matter to us and the stakes are high. The consequences are higher.

I had been walking on a twelve-inch beam on the ground; it was a safe distance. My pressure threshold was about twelve inches high.

At this distance, I could throw logs on the fire of knowledge without ever truly feeling the heat. I spent a little more than a year skipping along my safe twelve-inch beam, away from danger but no closer to deciding whether to get back on another horse.

CHAPTER SIX

The Decision — Sort of

Barely a Baby Step

As I learned more and more about horses, safety, and trail riding, it became clear to me that I would not be getting back on THE horse Mocha anytime soon. The truth was, I had been traumatized. The accident had shaken my confidence on two levels. First, it showed my lack of riding skills and the true danger of the sport.

More importantly, I lost confidence in my confidence.

I had encountered a domain in which I could not bullshit my way through. I was now learning that horses are expert BS detectors. It was tempting to regain my confidence by leaving it untested by the experts.

But my inner cowgirl, the one who begged her parents for a horse, kept whispering in my ear, with sounds that could only be heard by my heart.

Something bigger was moving me toward a life-affirming choice. Suddenly, horses were everywhere – even in places they had never been before. Like down the road from me.

The World Equestrian Games came to town twenty minutes from my house. It was like the Olympics for the horse world. In the months leading up to the big event – ironically a year to the day after my accident – the nearby venue held qualifying events to see who would make the cut. The only

Western discipline that showed was an event called Reining. Even though I had grown up with rodeo and barrel racing dreams and cow horse cutting connections, I had never heard of Reining.

Curious as to what it was all about, I made a point to be at one of the preliminaries. The minute the horse and rider came out to perform, I was smitten. The riders and horses seemed to move as one. This was the kind of riding I had dreamed about doing when I was growing up.

As a child, I had drawn thousands of pictures of cowboys and horses galloping. In Reining, not only do the horses run full speed, but they also do a dramatic sliding stop where the horse pushes his back legs underneath him in an extraordinary feat of athleticism.

Imagine a horse sliding into second base and you will get the picture. It's jaw dropping.

Plus, these were American Quarter Horses, and they were gorgeous. Many were palominos, with long, flowing, blond manes. They were unlike any horses I had seen in the other disciplines.

This Texas girl had found her dream horses.

Within a month, I would learn that longtime friend Janice had gotten involved in Reining. In all the time I knew her, she had never even mentioned horses. Now I discover that the Oklahoma barn where she trained her horses was very close to where my family in Texas lived. It had to be more than a coincidence. When she suggested I come visit her there, I jumped at the chance.

She told me to bring my boots.

I laughed.

I had seen those horses in action. Not only were they extreme athletes, but they were highly sensitive to their rider. One of the interesting things I had noticed about reining horses was how many stallions were being ridden. In every other discipline at the Games, the male horses were predominantly geldings. (Which in dog terms means neutered. Removing his man parts makes the horse much calmer and safer.) Not so in reining; stallions were the norm. All three of Janice's horses were stallions.

When I walked into the barn (with my boots), the same warm feeling I experienced as a child walking into the rodeo returned. The feeling was home. I almost choked up as I walked through the barn, greeting each horse.

Next to the barn was a huge practice arena. The arena was full of horses and professional trainers, teaching the horses to make their moves. Janice went out to ride a stallion and I was so impressed as she did spins and ran at high speed around the arena.

She got off and handed the reins to Trevor Dare, who was training one of her horses. He looked my way and gestured for me to come over. My heart started pounding. Facing the prospect of getting back in the saddle for the first time since my accident sent crazy sensations through my body. I started stretching, going through the routine I do before a big ski tournament to help calm my nerves.

After getting myself as calm as I was going to get, I walked out into the arena. I looked at Trevor and said, "Just because I look like I know what I'm doing, don't believe it. Hold the reins please." He walked me around the arena as I tried to find my seat in the saddle. He kept checking in, asking if I were ready to take the reins. No way was I going to let him give me the reins. I had just seen this horse – a stallion no less – running full speed. I wanted the safe ride, the easy ride. Inside I was a kid on a pony ride.

In truth, I was overreacting to my fear. I didn't yet have the mental Tools to properly calibrate what I could and couldn't handle.

As I got off the horse that day, I realized that I had broken through a barrier. It was barely a baby step, but it was enough to take the next step.

Back in a Saddle

Cedar Creek Stables is about 20 minutes from my house. I had seen their signs for years, and a month after my accident, my daughter Jen had taken her cousin to ride there. Upon returning, she said it was a good thing I couldn't go. Not only was the entire ride going either up or down steep hills, but they also walked the horses through the creek. She couldn't imagine me being OK with that after my accident, especially since going down a hill had played a part in my fall.

After returning from my trip to Oklahoma, I simmered for a few more days. In the afterglow of spending so much time with the reining horses, I wanted something more than a pony ride. The next frame in my picture would be to simply get back in the saddle again. I called my friend Marla and asked if she would join me on a trail ride at Cedar Creek. Notwithstanding the hills and creeks, I assumed this would be the safest way for me to practice getting back on a horse.

When the owner Howard handed out horse assignments, he had a twinkle in his eye as he told me I would be riding Ben. Marla would be on Hidalgo.

The barn was a short bus ride away. On the ride, I did my best to calm my nerves. It was difficult to believe that something I had loved so much as a child now filled me with this level of fear. As the bus bumped along the road, I called up my childhood excitement, remembering how it felt whenever we talked Mom into taking us out to the local stables. By the time the bus pulled in, I was ready to go.

As we walked into the barn, they pointed me to Ben. Now I understood the twinkle in Howard's eye. There was just one problem. No way in hell was I getting on Ben. Ben's a draft horse. He was a foot taller than the next tallest horse. I'm tall, so Howard probably thought a tall horse would be fine with me.

Nope. Nope. Nope. Just No.

Marla quickly volunteered to ride Ben before I walked the half mile back to the car. I would ride Hidalgo, a normal sized horse. Problem solved. At least for the moment.

The ride took us over the creek and up a hill. Up, up, up we went. I tried to remember the instructions. *Was I supposed to lean forward or back on the way up? And which way on the way down?* Damn. For every up, there would be a down. Based on how far up we were going, this was going to be a long way down.

When we got to the top of the hill, they stopped on flat ground to do a saddle check. Our job was to simply stand still and wait. My horse was antsy, his feet moving right and left. Looking back, I realized he was reflecting the state of the nervous woman on his back. While they had given us a set of four simple moves to get the horse to go, stop, turn right, and turn left, it was abundantly clear to me that once again, I had no control over this horse. My safety was in the herd, in being on a horse that did this every day with people of all skills and with a guide in the lead to handle the unexpected.

"My horse was antsy, his feet moving right and left. Looking back, I realized he was reflecting the state of the nervous woman on his back."

For my entire life, when someone asked me, "Do you ride?" the answer had always been "Yes." Now, I was beginning to understand the difference between being able to get on a horse and being able to ride. Like being able to clean a fish compared to doing brain surgery. Or launch a paper airplane compared to flying a fighter jet.

Sitting on an antsy horse during saddle check, being told to relax, loosen the reins, to sink into my seat was like asking me to go from the miniature golf course to winning the Masters. I was still a passenger, but now the fog was clearing. I was truly becoming aware of how much I had to learn. That was just in the horsemanship domain. Since I started working with him ten months before, Bruce had shared a whole different world in the "humanship" domain.

Maybe this ride could check a box. In the simplest of terms, I had fallen off the horse. Now, I had gotten back on and even put on my big girl britches by holding the reins on my very own. Maybe I could call it good? But first, we had to make it back to the barn.

I tried not to think about what was coming. The hill where I had my fall was tiny compared to this one. We were at the top of a mountain and the barn was at the bottom. A potentially traumatizing downhill walk was in front of me.

Sure enough, as we started down, the guide told us to lean slightly back as the horse made his way down the hill. At this point, I truly began to understand what genuine anxiety feels like. Adrenaline started shooting through my body and with every slight bump or misstep, I felt like I was going down. My mind catapulted a thousand thoughts a minute – most having the word "shit" in them. I tried to breathe deeply, but that seemed to just tell my brain that things were really bad.

Somehow, someway, we finally made it to flat ground. I was so relieved. Then I remembered that we had to cross the creek again. This time, we wouldn't just cross it. We would walk in the creek for quite a ways. My mind sent out more shitty thoughts. *"Really, let's just check the box and tell everybody you got back on the horse." "Anybody can ride these horses; why are you making it so hard?"*

As we splashed through the creek, my body hurled sensations of impending death and my mind believed every one of them. I marveled at how calm and normal everyone else seemed to be. I wondered how the horses knew where to step when they couldn't see the bottom of the creek. I waited for it to end. By death or by walking in the barn. I really didn't care. It just needed to end.

Finally, the ride was over. When I got off, my knees hurt, and I could barely walk. I had done it. I rode a horse, by myself, and went home in a car instead of to a hospital in an ambulance. I could now officially check the box and say I got back on a horse. It was done. Or was it?

By the time I got home, my knees were fine, but my mind wouldn't let it go. While standing outside the fire over the past 10 months watching others work with Bruce, I realized my passive engagement had shown me that horses had something to teach me. My internal conversation went something like this:

I checked the box and my knees hurt, so that was a good excuse to never go back.

I'm pretty sure I already know what Bruce is teaching. Just do that.

But if you know it so well, why were you so freaked out on a trail ride designed for beginners?

Learning to reach for my Tools instead of my Rules sounds like an interesting possibility.

But all the other people riding horses aren't doing this messy, internal work. Why me?

How will you feel if you walk away?

The next week, I called Marla. "Wanna go ride?"

Marinating

Big decisions – those moments in time, put-a-stake-in-the-ground, out-of-the-blue declarations – usually marinate with me for a long time. What looks like inactivity, or tentativeness, or even fear is often just the process of letting a pending change seep in.

This awareness is in contrast with my machine-thinking, where I want to push a button and everything old is suddenly new, like laundry that goes in soiled and comes out fresh and clean.

I crave the machine response, but change doesn't work that way. At least, not deep, change-how-you-live-everyday change.

While I can't exactly pinpoint the moment that I became a slalom water skiing addict (the good kind of addict), I can point to moments that created tiny sparks that eventually led to a raging fire.

During the time when I was traveling every week to Washington, D.C., and New York City, I got a message from my husband. We had been living on Lake Lure for a couple of years and the ski boat was going largely unused. We were both too busy with work to really enjoy our home. He asked what size life jacket might fit me. Having never had my own ski jacket, I guessed medium and forgot about it.

When I came home late Friday from that trip, I walked into my dining room where a beautiful vase of hydrangeas, a new wetsuit, and life jacket awaited me. He had also left a note that read, "Can't wait to ski with you in the morning." I melted. This hesitant skier would most certainly ski with him in the morning.

Soon thereafter, I saw friend and neighbor Ina out skiing behind her deck boat with another local acquaintance, Lori. At that point, I knew enough about slalom skiing to know that the right boat is everything. The wake produced by a ski boat is designed to be small so you can zip through it at high speeds. A deck boat is not a ski boat. So, I invited them out on my ski boat. Watching Lori zip back and forth across the wake blew me away. She was positively glowing as she got back in the boat, and I knew I wanted a rush like that. But I had also taken some bad falls in the past.

After marinating in Lori's joy, I made an offhand comment to Bob Washburn, a longtime local resort owner, that I would love to learn to cut across the wake like Lori. I just didn't want to fall. His response was quick, "I can teach you how to cut without falling." So, we booked some ski lessons.

The next year, Russ and I found a random ski course on a lake where we took our boat on vacation. I drove the boat with him zipping back and forth, terrified that I would run over the buoys strung together to guide the boat's path.

The next year, we bought our own portable ski course and put it in the lake we were visiting. I couldn't get around a single buoy. But at the end of that trip, I told him I was going to find a ski school to teach me how to go around those elusive buoys.

Many more ski mornings with Ina and Lori and ski school experiences transpired before the day I realized I was a true water skier.

None of these moments were THE moment. I honestly can't point to the exact moment, and that's the point. I guess I knew it was serious when I went along with my husband's crazy idea that we should build our own ski lake.

Talk about big change. A Saturday morning diversion turned into us owning a ski lake, along with a leadership retreat center, farm, and much more. All because of a series of tiny sparks, cultivated over time.

The fall from the horse was a Saturday morning diversion, between ski sets. On the morning of the accident, I skied and as I left to go ride horses for a couple of hours, I said I will be back to drive Austin Abel, who runs the ski school on our lake. Instead, I spent the afternoon in the emergency room and the next three days in the hospital.

Still Seeking the Skill to Stop a Horse

Now that I was back on a horse a year and a half after the accident, I was done marinating. Some part of me wanted to push a button and declare, "I'm back on a horse. Now it's time to get back on THE horse."

Every time I pictured returning to the farm where I had the accident, the screen went blank. There were too many steps not yet taken between here and there. Rather than judge my paralysis, I listened. I stayed in touch with Babs, who took such good care of me after the fall, and kept her apprised as I kept taking baby steps.

My opportunities to ride covered two ends of a very large spectrum. On one end was Cedar Creek, which offered guest rides and a confidence-building experience. On the other end was my friend Janice's reining horses in Oklahoma, which showed me a world of possibility that both set my heart on fire and seemed very far out of reach. The difference was like driving a typical car on the road versus getting a chance to hang with the pit crew at a NASCAR race.

The next four months went by like a blur. I started going to Cedar Creek regularly. Marla joined me one more time, and then decided to start taking English riding lessons closer to her house. I didn't feel ready for lessons, and certainly not on a tiny English saddle. My flavor was definitely Western riding. My only goal over the four months was to make it down the hill without the adrenaline-rushing, heart-pounding sensations.

Yet some part of me wanted the thrill of the ride. After my first trip to Oklahoma, I knew I would be back. I wasn't dreaming of being a Reiner yet. But being on a farm with hundreds of horses and a chance to ride a "real horse" was alluring. Plus, my family was right down the road. My dad had been having some health challenges and coming to Oklahoma was a way to check on him without seeming overly worried.

The next time I went to Oklahoma, they put me on a beautiful, blue-eyed

Cremello stallion, one of Janice's horses. This time, I took the reins. Already, the trainers in the barn were asking me if I was ready to trot or canter or spin. It was a good kind of pressure. Over a couple of visits to that arena, I managed to walk, trot, and canter. Plus, I was able to do a few slow spins on the back of a very well-trained horse in controlled conditions.

In both the trail rides and in the arena, I was still having adrenaline-rushing, heart-pounding sensations, even though these were relatively controlled settings. In Bruce's language, my Negative Pole was at a ten on a scale of one to ten. That's a lot of energy, and there was no doubt the horses could feel that. I thought something was wrong with me and longed for someone to tell me I was good – that I could go back to ride THE horse. But it would have been a lie. I wasn't good and the answers were not coming from someone else. But I didn't know that yet. I still just wanted to learn to stop a horse, because every time I got on one, it felt like it was nanoseconds away from galloping off, with me holding on for dear life.

By this time, I had been bringing clients to Bruce for a year. We had a session soon after my experiences in Oklahoma. I mentioned my excitement and continuing trepidation to him.

We were finishing a porch session where Bruce and I were debriefing the work. Now that the client had left, I turned the subject to me. All this adrenaline was starting to take its toll, and he gave me the same spiel I had been hearing him give my clients for the past year. "*Yeah Bruce, but I don't want messy Option 3 – I want easy Option 2,*" I thought. So partly out of desperation to move away from the personal stuff and into the skill stuff, I asked him a question, "Do you give riding lessons?"

The answer was yes.

I wasn't really thinking through the ramifications of taking riding lessons almost three hours from my house. I just knew Bruce could help me work out what was happening when I was on the back of the horse. I booked a session for a couple of weeks out, excited to get on a horse under Bruce's tutelage.

It turned out Bruce and I had very different definitions for "riding lessons."

CHAPTER SEVEN

Imbalance is a Good Thing

The Balancing Act of a Lifetime

When I signed up for riding lessons, I sought balance. My conscious self wanted balance on the horse. Losing my balance had cost me dearly. My deeper self sought more.

The only tightrope I've ever walked was a slackline a foot off the ground. Yet the metaphor of walking a tightrope resonates with me. When I was leading major change initiatives in my banking career, it was always a balancing act, of regulating the heat, by acknowledging the emotional turmoil we were creating, while at the same time keeping the focus on deadlines and clients. When leading process improvement, I deeply learned the benefits of balancing speed and quality – going slow to go fast almost always netted a better result. As a business leader, I find the balancing acts are constant, such as focusing on the short term versus the long term, on cost management as well as customer service. As a lover of food, the balance is in the exchange of calories consumed with calories burned. (One of the benefits of slalom water skiing is the intense calorie burn!) As a coach, I'm always balancing challenge and support. Every balancing act feels like walking a tightrope to me.

In my own self-awareness work and in assisting others in theirs, I've come to realize that the biggest balancing act is the one between our two basic human needs: Attachment and Self-Expression.

Dr. Gabor Maté is an addiction researcher who frames addiction as an ill-fated solution for an Attachment problem. Our human needs are non-negotiable. We need others AND we also need to be who we are. It's the balancing act of a lifetime.

Unlike many tradeoffs, Attachment and Self-Expression do not offer an equal opportunity of choosing one over the other. Because our basic survival needs favor the Attachment side of the balancing act, we tend to choose getting those needs met above everything else. We need to meet our basic survival needs of food, water, shelter, and safety. We need warm hugs. We need to know we are cared for. We need to know we belong. We need to believe we are enough. We know those needs are met by how we feel. No amount of talking to our brains is going to give it to us. A warm hug on paper and a real warm hug are very, very different.

When we don't get what we need, we do other things to make the empty feelings go away. We have a lot of strategies for satisfying our need for love, approval and caring. Shopping, eating, working, exercising, gambling, sex ... and drugs.

When Attachment needs are not addressed, it's almost impossible to be true to ourselves. Authenticity and Self-Expression go out the window. We lose touch with our inner guidance and awareness of who we truly are. We lose access to the healthy Tools needed to take care of ourselves.

As Maté says in his book In the Realm of Hungry Ghosts:

> *"I believe there is one addiction process, whether it is manifested in the lethal substance dependencies of my Downtown Eastside patients; the frantic self-soothing of overeaters or shopaholics; the obsessions of gamblers, sexaholics and compulsive Internet users; or the socially acceptable and even admired behaviors of the workaholic. Drug addicts are often dismissed and discounted as unworthy of empathy and respect. In telling their stories my intent is twofold: to help their voices to be heard and to shed light on the origins and nature of their ill-fated struggle to overcome suffering through substance abuse. They have much in common with the society that ostracizes them. If they seem to have chosen a path to nowhere, they still have much to teach the rest of us. In the dark mirror of their lives, we can trace outlines of our own."*

My addictions fell in the socially acceptable realm of the workaholic. It has been a try-harder-beat-myself-up-prove-I-can-do-it sort of strategy that worked very well in the corporate world, until I began to see it for the losing game it was. The pattern made me susceptible to the siren song of more money, more status, more responsibility in exchange for the warm hugs of belonging and the elusive feeling of being enough. Everything was fine when the pressure was low. When the consequences raised the pressure, work became everything, and life faded into the sunset. It was this realization that motivated me to leave the banking world and start my own firm.

First Riding Lesson

After leaving Corporate America, I thought I had beat the pattern. My work/life balance was exceptional, and I rarely caught myself looking for approval or beating myself up. But Bruce did. Over and over again, he caught me beating myself up in cagey ways in those early sessions.

He could see what I still didn't know that I didn't know. In my mind, I was moving away from fixing me and instead learning the skills to ride a horse.

When I pulled into Bruce's farm for my first riding lesson, I opened the back of my car and pulled on my boots. My heart fluttered a bit as I anticipated getting to ride either Marley or Mac, a new gelding that had arrived recently. We started with a porch session, as we had with all the leadership sessions we had done. Since this session was labeled "riding lesson," I was looking forward to hearing some new ideas from Bruce. When we began, things started feeling suspiciously like every other session we had done. Later – much later – I would understand that his repetition was intentional, to balance out the repetition of my old patterns. On this day, I just wanted him to tell me how to ride a horse, so I could learn to stop the horse.

Then he asked me a riding question. "What are you trying to accomplish with these lessons?" I replied, "I want to learn to ride safely. I've come to recognize the danger I put myself in on the trail. I could walk away, BUT, I have several friends who would love for me to ride with them."

I didn't mention the tearing sensation ripping me down the middle. Back and forth my thoughts were bouncing. *"Who would I be if I didn't get back on the horse? Why would I ever risk such an injury again? How can I walk away from this? How can I ever do this?"*

Then he asked, "Are you ever going to get back on THE horse?" I gulped and said, "Yes, I would like to. If possible." Once I said it out loud, I saw it as a stretch goal and set about proving to him that I would be ready sooner rather than later. In fact, I thought he might give me a checklist of skills, like stopping from a trot or making good circles. I should have known better.

"Good," he said, "Now put that Picture aside. The work we are going to do is not about that Picture. It's about breaking the work down to the tiny Frames that make up that Picture."

Dang it. His guidance was still sounding like the work we had done in the leadership realm. I hoped he understood I was here to ride. However, by now, I knew better than to argue. Besides, he confirmed that I had my riding helmet as we walked down to the horse pasture. Surely, I would be riding today. Please.

Not so fast. He handed me the halter and lead rope and asked me to pick a horse to "ride." My instructions were like the ones from the year before. Bring the horse into the round pen, close the gate, take off the halter and wait for further instructions. At least I could see that Bruce had brought a bridle and saddle down to the area. I wondered what the first step in a real riding lesson would be.

He asked me if I remembered how to find the middle of the round pen. "*Are you kidding me?!?!? Not this again!*"

It would be several more lessons before I realized how Finding the Middle unlocked an essential part of me and turned everything I understood about balance on its head.

The Balance Point is Always Moving

My awareness of dynamic alignment slowly opened from the back of a boat. In my quest to run the slalom course, I kept running into the dilemma of having far less time to practice than my brain and body needed to coordinate the intense and fast movements over a mere twenty seconds. Not only does it happen fast, but slalom skiing is also physically intense.

Slalom skiing involves a boat going straight down the course, while the skier swings from side to side. In the ski course, the skier goes through the first gate, around six buoys and out the end gate.

The swing of the skier is like that on a swing set, except with far greater speeds and done while moving down the lake. While the rope is fixed to the pylon in the center of the boat, it swings big, wide arcs as the skier banks the ski on edge to slingshot through the boat wake and then banks the ski on the other edge to cast the ski out and around the buoy.

It's a constant game of beating the boat from one buoy to the next.

With each ski pass for someone in my classification lasting twenty seconds, there is not a lot of time to practice. A practice session behind the boat is typically six passes through the course. While some try to do more, typically, the practice quits being productive because the skier is exhausted. This is even more true at the elite level, where a pass is sixteen seconds for pro men and seventeen seconds for pro women.

Whether it's seventeen seconds or twenty seconds, learning the intense moves while on the water is no easy task.

I needed a way to practice off the water.

Like many skiers, I tied a rope to a post and practiced leaning against it in a simulation of the body position at the apex of the turn on the water. The angle of that lean determines the speed of the skier from buoy to buoy; the deeper the lean, the faster the ski moves.

Practicing this lean seemed like the answer to my dilemma. At every opportunity, I went to the post and did my best imitation of my body position on the water. I wanted to build the muscle memory so that I could do this elusive move while behind the boat.

It turned out to create more problems than it solved.

My brilliant idea did not consider the much bigger problem in slalom skiing and in most endeavors, whether business or sport: The balance point is always moving.

When I leaned against a fixed post that was not moving down the lake like a boat does at 30 miles an hour, I created a form of static muscle memory. With my hands on the handle, I would have my coach review my form. *Were my arms relaxed and in the proper position? Were my hips in alignment with my shoulders to create a good, stacked position? Were my shoulders where they needed to be relative to my feet and hips?*

It felt like such a productive exercise – and it was – to a point. Unfortunately, it was a single point in a game with countless variables. In a way, it was like the analog clock with no battery. Even a dead clock shows the correct time twice a day.

Doing this practice gave me such confidence. It was like being able to hit a bucket of tennis balls or practicing five hundred times for my TEDx talk.

Every time I took my practice to the ski course, I felt ready to apply that lean as I crossed the wake – and every time, I ended up way out of balance on my way to the buoy. Sometimes I could recover; more often than not, I could not get back into good ski position to continue the pass.

Puzzling through what was going on took numerous conversations with my trainer and ski school professional, Austin Abel. He has a dual quest. First, he's always taking his game to the next level. Second, he's constantly working on how to coach others to ski at their next level.

One day, he was in the boat and I was in the water resting between ski passes at the end of the lake. I both celebrated and complained about my lean through the wake. Yes, I had achieved the position I had worked so hard to learn on land while leaning against the pole. But the pole on land is a fixed balance point. Skiing 37 feet on either side of the boat has almost infinite balance points. Just like an analog clock, my lean against the boat was in the correct position one time on the arc. Keeping that position for more than a split second threw me out of balance.

As we were talking through this, he said, "Your lean was great. You just stayed in it too long."

The boat is dynamic and the pole on land is static.

What I needed more than the ability to balance from a static point was the ability to move incrementally as the conditions changed. Reorienting was more important than chasing something that was in the past.

"Reorienting was more important than chasing something that was in the past."

Never once in the ski course am I at the same angle relative to the pylon where the rope attaches. I'm always moving either right or left. In addition, my body is never at the same angle relative to the vertical and horizontal axis. I'm either standing tall toward the sky or leaning ever more or less toward the water at varying degrees from start to finish.

In other words, my body moves in dynamic alignment to the boat in thousands of variations over those twenty seconds. The permutations of the two axises are incalculable.

My lean drill only showed me the perfect alignment relative to the boat for a single point in time that lasts less than a second in the ski course.

Fixing my mind on that single point of success set the conditions for multiple points of failure. With that insight, we started working on dynamic alignment.

I would come to learn that not only did I need to reorient my body. My mind played an even bigger role.

All too often, my mind and body were not in the same place. When things were going well, my mind tended to jump ahead. The thought, *"I'm about to run this pass"* guaranteed that I would NOT run the pass.

When I had a bobble on the ski, my mind would take me to "oops-land" where I wished for a do-over and punished myself for screwing up with whatever wrong move I had just made.

If I had enough bobbles or falls, my mind would transport me all the way to childhood while it reminded me of whatever rule I had made up for how to still look good while screwing up or deal with the mistake when it was time to explain myself.

My mind would even jump into the boat and wonder what the driver was thinking. If people were watching, the pressure was even greater.

With my mind all over the place, it was a wonder I could ever calibrate my body to stay in dynamic alignment.

The balance point is always moving.

Imbalance is a Good Thing

It turns out imbalance is more important than balance. Pay attention to the subtle moves of anyone doing any sort of balancing act. The tightrope is never completely still. The bicycle always moves from side to side. The rowing boat tips and corrects constantly.

I once watched a trick golfer hit a golf ball three hundred yards while standing on one of those big balance balls you see in the gym. His legs never quit moving as they adjusted and corrected and reoriented to keep him stable as he stood on the wobbling ball.

When we treat balance as the sole objective, we miss the point. Balance comes and goes and comes again so quickly. George Leonard, author of *The Way of Aikido and Mastery*, said, "The student asks the master how he stays in balance. The master replies 'I'm out of balance much more than you are.

I've simply learned to regain my balance more quickly.' "

The skill of returning to balance matters.

Balance is an act of constant calibration and recalibration more than a goal to be achieved.

Not only is the balance point always moving, but we also only have movement by getting imbalanced.

When we are moving, it's a constant act of getting out of balance and then back into balance. Rather than being like the top of the hill to be conquered, balance is simply a reference point.

Watch a young baby learn to walk. Recently, I watched a mom teaching her son. First, Mom helped him stand up and he teetered, tottered, and swayed. When he swayed far enough forward, he took a step. Two steps later, his bottom half could not keep up with his top half and he fell forward to his hands. Next try, his top half could not keep up with his bottom half and he was suddenly sitting on the ground. Next try, he was able to take a few more steps. Slowly he was learning to make the corrections to string the actions together into a walk.

Walking is an act of losing and then regaining balance. We just do the losing and regaining in such small increments that we no longer realize that we are out of balance.

To move things, we must get out of balance and then regain that balance, preferably in a way that keeps us aligned and safe.

One of my artistic endeavors is throwing clay pottery on a wheel. Learning to center a lump of clay is a critical building block to creating a cup, a plate, a bowl, or a tall vase. The initial lump starts out of balance and then through the act of centering, we bring the clay into balance.

That centered lump is just that – a centered lump. To make something on the pottery wheel, you then must take the clay out of balance. Lifting a wall of clay is an act of disequilibrium, stacking one layer on top of another. In and out, over, and over, the clay goes out of balance and then back into balance.

The art is in the give and take. Push too much and the wall collapses. Push too little and nothing happens. Some of my early mugs are super thick on the bottom. As a rookie potter, I just couldn't get the bottom level of clay out of balance enough to move up the cylinder. The thick bottom makes those mugs too heavy to drink from, but they are great pencil holders.

There's a subtle problem with disequilibrium. It feels wrong. The physical sensations of being out of balance are uncomfortable. That's the point. However, we interpret that discomfort incorrectly. We tell the story (usually subconsciously) that we are making a mistake. At some level, I wanted Bruce to show me how to ride a horse without feeling any disequilibrium.

What he was here to teach me would turn disequilibrium into a gift.

Finding my Center

On this day, all I knew was that once again, we were doing Bruce's maddening exercise called Finding the Middle. To me, it seemed like an unnecessary impediment, keeping me away from the work I came to do. *How was this silly exercise going to help me with anything involving the horse?*

Nonetheless, I went along, because apparently the only way I would be able to do what I wanted was to humor him by Finding the Middle of the damn round pen.

His first step was to ask me to just go to the middle and find the closest approximation to the very center of the round pen. Once I did that, I just needed to make a mark in the dirt with my heel. I thought *"OK, this won't be so bad. Surely I can get close enough for him to let me move on."*

I walked into the middle, looked around a bit, made a tiny adjustment in my placement, and made the mark with my heel. As I was looking around, I had noticed one weird thing. The round pen didn't exactly seem round. Oh well, this was close enough. I recalled that we did this the prior year and the whole process was rather elaborate. However, I had succeeded last year, so in my mind, that box was checked. I expected this time we would move through the Finding the Middle step very quickly.

Bruce asked me if my heel mark was on the middle. Thinking this would hurry things along, I gave him a smart-ass answer along the lines of, "It's as close as I can get without a measuring tape."

When working with a horse in a round pen or round corral, the human typically stands in the center and does different things to encourage the horse to move in circles around him or her. From the center and staying in a 6-to-8-foot diameter, the human can get the horse to walk, trot, or canter and, with the right moves, can get the horse to change direction.

Knowing this, I was pretty sure a close approximation of the center was good enough to move to the next step. I was wrong.

"Well," he said, "let's go through a process that will get you closer." Dang it.

He handed me four blue flags and said, "Let's start at the beginning." Step by step, he guided me to first divide the round pen in half, and then half again. The clock in my head kept ticking, wondering if there was going to be any time left in our session to do what I came to do.

After going through the agonizing process of planting the four blue flags, we knew that if the division was accurate, we would be able to pull two strings from each point and the intersection would be the middle of the round pen. At this point, I still thought we were trying to find the actual middle of the round pen.

It would be many, many more sessions before I realized we were recalibrating me to find MY center.

So, after we found what we called the middle of the round pen – and after I was more than satisfied that we had the precise middle pinpointed enough for me to be able to move on, he gave me the orange flags.

Now this was starting to seem like an even bigger waste of time. I thought we were Finding the Middle and we had found the middle. My patience wearing thin, I took the flags, because I was pretty sure not taking them would make working with the horse take even longer than it already had.

He had me go stand next to one of the blue flags and look at the blue flag across from it to see if there was equal area on both sides of the imaginary line. I'm not big on rework — and this exercise felt like we were just redoing perfectly good work we had already done. Still, I humored him.

Then he asked me to do the unthinkable. He said take three steps to the right and evaluate the division of the round pen from my new vantage point. *Why in the world would I do that?*, I thought. He reminded me of my Negative/Positive Pole. He said I could also call it a "spirit level," like the ones carpenters use. "That feeling of being off does not mean you have made a mistake! That feeling is your Negative/Positive Pole sending you signals that there is something for you to pay attention to or that is not beneficial to you!" *But I don't want to feel disequilibrium!*

The feeling was exactly his point. He had to yell to raise the pressure enough to get me moving. He wanted me to move back and forth, forcing the internal bubble in my spirit level to move way out of center and then back again. "Now move back to center and then three steps to the left," he said.

As I was standing three full steps from the blue flag, he asked me to feel my Negative/Positive Pole relative to whether there was half of the round pen on each side of me.

"Hell no!" I thought. Watching my reluctance to move even an inch, you would have thought there was a pit of alligators sitting there. Now he wanted me to feel it when every bone in my body was screaming to move me back to the comfort zone. Clearly, I wasn't going to die if I pushed my bubble that far off center. But tell that to my body, where the sensations were screaming "Danger, danger!"

My Survival Mode and reality could not have been further apart. His tone of voice, intended to push my Negative Pole up, was doing its job. Every bone in my body remembered getting in trouble with my parents, my teachers, my bosses. The past came flooding in, warning me that when I feel this way, I better get in line, because I'm making a big mistake here unless I do what "they" say to do.

Bruce was pushing my "mistake button," not to drive me crazy, but to heal me. He was intentionally setting the conditions for me to go into my old stories and the uncomfortable emotions, so that I could choose different actions than the ones I had programmed myself (or been programmed) to do.

He said, "Give it a number on a scale of one to ten. How far off is it?"

With that distinction, the fog began to clear a little. I gave him a number – something like an eight or nine.

"Now go back to the right. Give me a number." This time it was clearer that the blue flag across from me and my position did not represent a fifty/fifty split of the round pen. Now my number was more like a five.

> **"Now my feelings were not telegraphing that I had made a mistake; instead, they were providing the warm voice of guidance."**

The noise faded into the background and the inner electric charge became my primary focus. It was like a tuning fork, telling me which way to move.

"Move back and forth, paying no attention to the blue flag under your feet. Just keep moving back and forth until your poles are balanced. When your number is zero and the imaginary bubble within feels centered, plant the orange flag."

As I followed his instructions, the external world dropped away. The only thing that mattered – for a brief, exquisite moment – was how I felt. Disequilibrium became my friend. Now my feelings were not telegraphing that I had made a mistake; instead, they were providing the warm voice of guidance.

Back and forth I walked, tuning in to the little electrical charge called my Pole, giving it a number as I made smaller and smaller swings. Finally, my Negative Pole balanced – the number was zero – and I planted the orange flag.

I mentally returned to the real world and noticed that my orange flag was a few inches from the blue flag.

It would be yet another year before I truly understood the depths of what had just happened, even though Bruce gave me the full lesson that day.

"The orange flag represents The You," he explained, "not A you, the conditioning done by domestication. Domestication made you believe that's who you are. It's not. It's so ingrained in you that every inch of your being believes it's you. This exercise helps lift that veil. It allows you to consciously see the difference between A you and The You. When you are tempted to beat yourself up over making the mistake of planting one of the flags in the wrong place, remember, your inner guidance found the second place. *Did you notice the voice in your head wondering what I was going to do with your mistake? Did you feel the urge to hit yourself with the 2x4 for getting it wrong? Do you really want to give your power over to those voices from your past?* Are you really going to look outside yourself for approval and acceptance when you have this power within you? When you learn to use your Poles to guide you, it doesn't really matter what 'they' say. When the chatter in your mind starts, all you have to do is listen to your Poles. The chatter won't matter, because you will be tuning in to one of the Tools God gave you to guide you."

My ears heard his words, but it would take a lot more for me to grasp the wisdom and freedom in what he was teaching me.

The next five or six times we started a session in the round pen, we started with this exercise. Every time, I had the same response. "Why the hell am I doing this?"

It became clearer the day Bruce threw me yet another curve ball.

CHAPTER EIGHT

My No-Riding Riding Lessons

The Horse is Your Responsibility

As I was nearing Camden for one of the sessions, my phone rang, it was Bruce. "Do you trust yourself to trust me?" he asked. I quickly answered yes and then wondered what was about to happen. He gave me directions to a new location.

When I pulled into the new farm, Bruce had a lesson going on. Rather than working in the round pen, he and another person, a professional horse trainer, were working on trailering a large horse.

Putting a horse in a trailer is no small task. Well-trained horses walk on calmly. However, just as with the dangers of a trail ride, asking a flight animal to subject itself to a tiny, rolling prison is a very big ask. Things go wrong. People get injured or die. Horses get injured or die. Yet moving horses from one location to another is necessary, so we humans train them to do it.

The professional trainer in this case had been involved in a traumatic trailering situation. She had reached out to Bruce to help, because she was caught between a rock and a hard place. She would rather never have to trailer another horse; she also could not continue to be a professional horse trainer without being able to do this essential task.

I got out of the car and leaned against the hood to watch the lesson unfold. She would walk the horse to the trailer. Bruce, who was sitting out of her sight in the front of the trailer, would ask "What's your number?" as she brought the horse near the trailer.

Step by step, he would ask her, "What's your number?" And then "What do you need to do to balance your poles?"

I watched this session with great interest, because in my mind, he was working with an experienced horse trainer who clearly did not need lessons the way I did. I was aware of how dangerous it can be to trailer horses. Observing her reactions, it was clear that this woman had been injured and had seen horses injured in the process. She was working with Bruce to recover her confidence.

After their session ended and she left, we sat down near the trailer to debrief what I had observed. They had been working with a rescued Thoroughbred who had been mostly living on his own in a pasture for many years. He had only recently been gelded, so he still had a lot of his stallion tendencies. In other words, he was a lot of horse to handle.

While we were standing near the trailer, Bruce gave me his halter rope and said, "The horse is your responsibility. You don't have to hold the rope the whole time. It's fine if you drop the rope and let him graze around us. But remember, he's your responsibility."

We were not in a fenced area. It was wide open.

At first, I held the rope. I didn't dare let it go. After all, my catastrophe-fortune-teller-mind had already pictured the newly gelded Thoroughbred running to the highway a mile away.

After a few minutes, Bruce asked me to trust him again. "Drop the rope and let's talk. The horse isn't going anywhere. But remember, he is your responsibility."

My Rules were screaming in my ear *"Don't let go! You know better than to take that chance! What if something happens?"* Bruce's point was to build my Tools, and it felt like we were back with the flags in the round pen. I had worked with him long enough to know he wasn't going to let it go. So, I dropped the rope, more to humor him than to trust myself.

As we were talking, the horse did indeed keep grazing. As he nibbled the yummy clover farther and farther away from me, I felt a familiar tick — tick – tick, like an inner time bomb waiting to explode. It was a feeling I had discovered many years ago with my daughter Jen.

At the time, I was still in the numbest of my numb years. She disappeared and my Negative Pole (a feeling for which I had no name in those years) pierced through the armor to get my attention.

Jen and I were at the library in Charlotte one evening. She was in second grade, and we had just moved across country from Texas to North Carolina. I was in a constant state of feeling overwhelmed, trying to orient in a new job, in a new town, in a new state as a single mother while at the same time, she was doing the same with a new school, in a new apartment, and lots of new expectations.

I found us a table and familiarized her with the layout of the large library so she could find what she needed for her assignment. My plan was for the two of us to work at the table once she found the materials she needed.

I had brought my own work to do as well, so I sent her off to explore and was quickly buried in some work long since forgotten. Having a few minutes to myself was heavenly.

At some point, I felt the inner tickle that something was off. My attention started dividing between whatever I was doing and glancing up, expecting Jen to come around the corner any minute. The sensation sort of felt like a ticking time bomb where the beat was getting ever faster and ever louder. With every peek, the inner tickle got stronger and more annoying.

So did the inner struggle. A part of me did not want to be the helicopter mom who hovered and worried over every little assignment. Another part of me was anxious and impatient for her to be finished so we could go home. Still another part of me felt she needed some space to learn how to navigate. Feeling this thing, whatever it was, was the price I had to pay to be a better mom than the control freak I really was. Nonetheless, the super anxious part of me worried she had been kidnapped.

Finally, I couldn't stand it anymore and I got up to take a spin through the library and see where she was and how she was doing.

I found her working just as she should have been and immediately the sensation of something being off diminished.

At the time, it did not occur to me that the feeling I was experiencing was a good and useful thing. I treated it as an indicator of what a bad mom I was. The feeling was the feeling. It's as natural as the air we breathe. The problem was the story I was telling myself about the feeling, both that night and every time I felt it.

Bruce was helping me rewrite that story.

When the horse moved out of my arbitrary range, it felt like the inner ticking had become a bomb that was about to go off. I went to pick up the rope and bring him closer to where we were talking.

Bruce asked, "What made you go bring him back?" I would start answering with things like, "He was getting too far away. I worried he would make a break for it. I thought someone might come up and spook him." In other words, I explained myself, something I had been trained to do my whole life.

Secretly I was thinking *"If I lose this horse, you are going to kill me. I do not want to be the one who caused this horse to get hurt. I don't want to get in trouble."*

All the visible justifications felt so rational and right to me – and no way was I going to tell him my secret fear of failure. But he kept pressing and I kept fishing for the explanation that would get him to leave me alone.

We repeated this pattern several times. I would drop the rope; the horse would follow his nose to yummy grass farther and farther away and my little inner time bomb would go off. I would bring the horse back, drop the rope and Bruce would ask me what made me choose that moment to bring him back.

I would fish for a better answer and only one answer satisfied him. No amount of logic, rationale, or pleasing him stopped the pressure he was applying. Most of the time, he had to come up with the answer for me: "You went to get the horse to balance your Negative/Positive Pole."

"My conditioning was interfering and my need for approval was fighting with my inner rebel."

He asked, "What was your number when you went to get him that time?" Now I had to admit that I had been trying to be tough. The last time, I had allowed the horse to drift a pretty good distance. Perhaps to avoid the interrogation? Maybe to get Bruce to think I could tolerate the pressure? Possibly to test myself. Maybe to see when he would jump in? Probably a mix of all those reasons. My conditioning was interfering and my need for approval was fighting with my inner rebel.

"Oh, I don't know. I guess it was about an eight," I said.

"What made you wait that long? Why would you let your pole go as high as an eight before addressing it?"

My Kid Mode brain went into "damned if you do, damned if you don't" territory. Still caught in the belief that my job was to please Bruce and show him I could handle the pressure, I underreacted to the signal my Negative

Pole was sending. At some level, I was aware I was underreacting. Damned if you don't.

But my inner kid voice screamed, *"The only way to be safe is to hold the rope!"* Of course, this method did not consider that I would never have been able to hold the rope if the horse truly felt like he needed to run away from danger. Bruce was not satisfied when I held the rope. Damned if you do.

Bruce watched my inner turmoil with amusement. My choices of micromanaging and not intervening went to war with each other. My kid voice continued to nudge, scream, beg and plead with me to find a way to please Bruce, to get his approval or get him off my back.

I was missing the point altogether.

Finally, after several repetitions and some additional coaching from Bruce, I started tuning in to the ticking time bomb as a signal rather than a threat. This was not anxiety, and it was not a test of me to see if I could please Bruce.

This was a recalibration of my instincts. This was body, mind, and spirit training. We were developing my Invisible Tools.

We continued to talk, the horse continued to graze and when the signal reached a certain level, I brought the horse back into the range that balanced my Poles.

Bruce's training with me that day had nothing to do with pleasing him, and nothing to do with me making mistakes. Pushing my Pole up over and over again had everything to do with helping me recalibrate my system. He didn't care if I did things his way; what he wanted was for me to respond deeply to the situation in front of me, not from my Rules of my past, but by impeccably using my Tools to address the situation in front of me.

Responding Under Pressure

Bruce's methods were showing me new possibilities for something I had been practicing for years: I could react or respond. Reacting came from my past. In Bruce's language, that mindset was TyranT. Responding happened in the present moment. That mindset was AlphA.

It wasn't the labeling that made the difference. It was his absolute commitment to offering situations to respond rather than react under pressure. No matter how many times I told him it was the horse that "made me do it," he came back with the answer, "It's not the horse. It's the pressure created by the horse."

His methods went to the very core of my being.

In the twenty years prior to this chapter of my life, I had been on a journey to learn how to respond rather than react. My early corporate persona was a take-no-prisoners hard ass who felt almost nothing. That personality worked great for the type of roles I had. Internal auditor. Credit review officer. Loan underwriter. Guard at the gate for the safety of the bank's money. There were rules and I followed them to a T. I expected everyone else to follow them too.

Then the bank decided to re-engineer the way it approved commercial loans. Somehow, I was tapped to lead that project. Now my job was to rewrite the rules of Commercial Lending. I was called on to be a leader. In the year of the re-engineering project, I began to see glimpses of another way of being, another way of interacting with others. However, my personal operating Rules were strong, and my style was both compliant and authoritarian at the same time. I did what I was told and expected others to do the same when I was the one doing the telling. Looking back on it, I can see the mechanistic nature of my thinking. Being the one rewriting the rules meant I had to at least consider looking at creativity and spontaneity. A tiny spark was lit.

When I was asked to lead Credit Training for the entire bank, I realized that my job was now to facilitate true learning, especially since I had been charged with taking a one-year program down to ten short weeks. I had been subjected to some of the traditional credit training, where we sat for hours listening to someone drone on about how to analyze financial statements, fill out a credit approval report or call on a bank customer. The learning yield with this method was low and we were never going to shrink the program from fifty weeks to ten by selling and telling. We needed a better way.

My team decided to move to a more experiential learning model, where we facilitated opportunities for the trainees to learn and grow by trial and error. In one brilliant move, the design team recommended that we quit treating the new trainees like royalty when they arrived for their ten weeks of training. Instead, we built a treasure hunt. The only instructions the new bankers got when they arrived in corporate housing was how to get to their desk the next morning. There, they would find the first assignment, which was to find the fax machine. (This was a few years ago!) At the fax machine, they would receive further instructions. By the end of the first day, they would have familiarized themselves with their new work environment, gotten signed on to the computer and gotten busy completing their first assignment. Where our prior methods had yielded trainees who expected the answers be given to them, this new approach created hungry explorers who relished the hunt for their own answers.

Taking this approach forced those of us in charge of the program to change our leadership style. No more command and control. Lectures, where we ran the show, were traded for a facilitative teaching style that encouraged the trainees to ask questions, push back, and struggle with their learning process.

Not only were we training our participants, but we also had to retrain ourselves. I almost washed out of my own facilitator training program. My old Rules of command and control were so comfortably ingrained in my mind, and seemed effective, at least to me. Learning to facilitate versus deliver a lecture was excruciating. The process added more sparks to my self-awareness journey. Eventually, I got pretty good at facilitating and so did many of my team members. Others opted out because they did not want to examine their own beliefs and assumptions. They most certainly did not want the uncertainty of facilitating a session where they would be called on to respond in the moment rather than react in a predictable fashion.

We truly changed the culture of learning. During this time, we were willing to do the hard work of working on ourselves and to set the conditions for deep learning.

Through this and many more experiences, I had come to believe I was a master at responding rather than reacting.

Another Level of Mastery

Working with Bruce was starting to show me another level of mastery.

After every session of Finding the Middle, I would finally get to work with the horse – on the ground. Bruce breaks everything a horse does into four parts: Movement, Direction, Rhythm, and Track. The actions happen in that order. A typical assignment started with his Picture. It looked like this: "Get the horse moving, he picks direction. Once he's moving at a walk, keep him going in that direction for one full rotation in the round pen. Let the horse tell you how much pressure to apply. When he reaches the start line, turn your back in the opposite direction from where the horse is moving, relax and drop the Picture from your mind."

It sounds so simple. It is – IF you can stay in AlphA mindset. However, TyranT mindset is always there, promising a better way to handle all the ways things can go off plan. The horse doesn't move. The horse moves at a faster rhythm. The horse starts to move and then turns around. The horse stops to graze. I had watched many videos and live demonstrations of this type of work; it looked so easy. I had NO idea how much unseen energy work was happening to get a horse to move in such ways.

I needed to come to a whole new level of listening and observing to stay in a responsive energetic space. In one of my early round pen experiences, I was in the middle and the horse got to be wherever he wanted to be. My Picture was to achieve "movement" with the horse. At the first sign of movement, I was to immediately turn my back and let the horse be.

I won't bore you with all the ways I had at my disposal to achieve that goal. It doesn't matter anyway – because I WAY overshot the goal. The horse's ear twitched and then he raised his head and I kept adding pressure.

Pretty soon I had him walking along the rail. After a couple of minutes, Bruce stopped me and asked how I did. I was so proud of myself. After all, I had that horse MOVING, Thank You Very Much.

Then he asked me to review what had happened and the signals I had missed. "Did you see the ear twitch?" "Did you notice his head come up?" "Did you notice him shifting his feet before he started walking?" Weeeellllll ... Maybe?

"Did you not count the ear twitch as movement? Or did you not think you caused the twitch?" Truth be told, I was waiting for the kind of human signals that conk me over the head.

What I thought was good, Bruce called out as TyranT mindset. But here was the confusing part; he was OK with it. "I don't want the horse to do the Picture. I want you to have the opportunity to build your Tools. What you just saw was how focused you get on the goal, so much so that you forgot the Frames that make up the Picture. You need to break it down frame by frame. This time, you overreacted. Where was your listening and hearing? Where was your patience? How do I know when you are in TyranT? Because you are either over- or underreacting. You are beating yourself with a 2x4 for making a mistake. You are not letting the horse tell you what to do, when to do, how to do. Be the conduit! Just as with the flags in Finding the Middle, you don't have to listen to the voices from your past. The answers are right in front of you, in the here and now. The horse will tell you how much pressure to apply. You will constantly be adjusting. A mistake is not a mistake – it's an opportunity. When you feel your Negative Pole go up, listen to it, and listen to the horse. Then adjust as needed. When he completes the Picture, let him know by releasing the pressure. Let's try it again."

Bruce shined a light on something I thought I was long past. I wanted to be perfect. Better than perfect if possible. When it wasn't perfect – and it can never be perfect – I beat myself up in ways that offered complete deniability. It wasn't beating myself up if I was just getting frustrated for not being able to do something, was it? It wasn't perfectionism if I just wanted to be good, right?

Even though I had been working on these very tendencies for many, many years, I had mostly been successful when the waters were calm. In the space of the meditation retreat or working off grid in the mountains, I could maintain my composure and respond in the present moment. With any form of pressure came my old ways, in a new package. Just because I wasn't raging or being bitchy did not mean I wasn't operating on old Rules. The spiral into feeling not good enough was so automatic it was invisible. The neural pathways were like well-worn deer tracks in the woods. The energy followed the path of least resistance. I left the moment and operated from my Rules of the past.

For several more lessons, we had many, many repetitions in the round pen. Sometimes I would slip into AlphA, but TyranT would be waiting to pounce as soon as Bruce raised the pressure.

On one memorable day, I had been making progress. More and more often, I was able to reach for my Tools. I was also getting more skilled in working with the horse from the ground, especially in creating Movement, Direction, Rhythm, and Track. While my ego wanted to give me credit for getting good at this, the truth was that the pattern was getting somewhat predictable. Then on a calm day, nature offered some chaos to test my ability to reach for my Tools.

On a clear, sunny day, I was at the far end of the round pen standing a good distance from Bruce, who was outside the fence. Mac the horse was standing between us when a huge tree branch from at least fifty feet up suddenly cracked and fell to the ground about a hundred feet from where we were standing. BOOM! As flight animals, when horses hear sounds like that, they run first and ask questions later. The two horses still in the pasture took off away from the sound at full gallop before the branch even reached the ground. So did Mac. Toward me. He was seeking the safety of the herd – and as far as he was concerned, I was the herd.

Except I wasn't the herd. I was a much smaller, squishy human.

In his flight mode, he would have run me over before I could have taken two steps. While I was still processing the branch as it fell, Mac took off in my direction. Quickly, I realized the danger wasn't the tree branch – it was the thousand pounds of hooves, muscle, and panic running straight at me.

I had two choices. I could react in a self-protective mode – which would have been to either turn and run away or drop and curl into the fetal position. Both would have done what self-protective actions often do: give me a false sense of security that only makes things worse.

The choice to respond felt riskier. I could reach for my Tools and respond by raising his Negative Pole enough to turn him away.

Suddenly Bruce's coaching of "Let the horse tell you what to do, when to do, how to do," was a matter of life and death. The pressure that created the danger was extremely high. Mac's oncoming energy was showing me the tunnel vision of Survival Mode.

In a split second, I made the second choice. I raised my arms and started waving him off. Then I started jumping. In Mac's eyes, the jumping, waving woman in front of him was even MORE of a danger than the tree branch behind him. He stopped in his tracks. I dropped my arms and stood quietly. He stood quietly. The other horses in the pasture had stopped and were now standing quietly. The danger was past.

I looked over at Bruce and he said, "Well done."

AlphA under pressure. No second guessing. No beating myself up. No quest for perfection. Allowing the moment to be and then pass. Allowing the next moment to come in, be, and then pass. Flow. Feel. Listen. Hear. Patience. Timing. Observe. Feeling from within the sweet succession of the frames. Allowing that to be my reward.

This was the essence of Bruce's Natural Humanship Method ™. Just as the Dog Whisperer Cesar Milan found that most of his dog training was actually people training, this horse whisperer was retraining the human, under pressure with no predictable outcomes.

Slowly, I started realizing what was different in this work. No more road rage on my way home. When traffic built up, I used it to practice patience rather than get myself worked up. When I was driving home in a blistering thunderstorm, I drove it Frame by Frame rather than wondering through the panic how I would ever make it through. When I got home, I welcomed discomfort as an opportunity to try out the new Tools that the work was unleashing. When I made a mistake, I was more likely to recalibrate rather than beat myself up.

Yet, even as I felt myself changing, I still wanted more information about the horse. I still wanted to get ON a horse – and be able to stop the horse.

Then by chance, I met a woman twenty minutes from my house named Lynn Brown. Lynn practiced Natural Horsemanship. She even ran guided trail rides. Surely with her I would get on a horse.

CHAPTER NINE

Filling in the Holes

Swiss Cheese

When I walked into the barn at Transitions, Lynn Brown greeted me and introduced me to Phoenix, the horse that would be one of my greatest teachers. His first greeting was a toothy nip on the back of my hand. We were going to be such good friends! While I came hoping to ride, he was not saddled.

It was a hint of things to come.

Even though I was well into my lessons with Bruce, my proving mindset popped up repeatedly. I still found myself wanting to prove to Lynn that I was ready to ride. Given that she regularly ran guest trail rides, I was sure she would put me on a horse today.

She started by asking me what experience I had with horses and what I was trying to achieve. After I described both, she asked, "Would it be fair to say that you want to build a solid foundation of horsemanship?" She didn't ask me if I was ready to ride today. She didn't ask me if I knew how to saddle a horse. (Which obviously needed to be done if we were going to get on with my desire to ride today.) She didn't ask me if I knew how to do groundwork.

She didn't have to ask me anything more. Phoenix was telling her everything she needed to know.

Lynn's way of working with horses focuses on developing trust and connection with a relaxed horse, rather than using force, fear, and intimidation to get the horse to do our human bidding. Horses communicate with subtle clues, and she was reading Phoenix to get a sense of how relaxed he was in my presence. What I saw was a still, compliant horse just waiting to be saddled.

What she saw was a frozen, shut down horse just waiting to be killed.

Rather than begin the lesson with all the ways my body language and energy were sending scary messages to the horse, she started with Swiss cheese. "You have been around horses and learned some things. What I have found with a lot of my students is that their horsemanship knowledge is like Swiss cheese. They know some beginner things and intermediate things and even advanced things. But they also don't know some beginner things and so forth. There are holes in their knowledge. Most of the time, those holes don't matter. But sometimes, an event happens and all the holes line up. That's when we have disasters."

As she was speaking, scenes from my accident flashed through my mind. Thinking I knew how to stop the horse by pulling back on the reins. Thinking I could stay balanced in the saddle only to be quickly bounced out of my seat. Thinking I knew how to fall in a safe way only to land with a bone-shattering splat. Not even realizing that a horse could be operating in a fearful state of mind. All the holes in the Swiss cheese lining up perfectly so that I could be chauffeured by the ambulance crew for a three-day, two-night stay at the local hospital. Those innocent holes now appeared more ominous. If I were to ever get back on THE horse, I needed to close those gaps.

So yes, it was fair to say that I wanted to build a solid foundation of horsemanship. It would have to start on the ground.

Lynn approached the work with horses very differently from Bruce – and yet her lessons were very complementary.

We did a herd-watching experience on my second lesson. She drove me up to an enclosed arena where her six horses were standing around. In my eyes, they looked like every other herd of horses I had ever seen. Horses standing there looking around, not really concerned or noticing anything.

Before we left the barn, she asked me to not speak as we went up the hill. When she did finally utter a word, she simply asked me what I observed. My ill-informed eyes had seen very little. "Well, one of the horses is swishing his tail. That's about all I see," I said.

She then took me through the basics of horse body language. It was a direct lesson in understanding the 50,000 years of DNA in a prey animal who communicates in subtlety and energy.

First, she shared horses have four basic needs: safety, comfort, food, and play. *"Hmm,"* I thought. *"Sounds a little like human needs as described by Maslow."*

Second, she explained that horses communicate with energy and gesture. They read each other and every nuance of our human body language; there was a whole language going on here that was invisible to me.

In watching the herd of horses, she pointed to the pecking order. Yes, horses have a pecking order, just like chickens – and just like humans. Did I notice the shift they made when we came near and then again when we started talking? Could I tell which horse was the leader? Which one was keeping watch? Who was the low horse in the hierarchy? Which ones were connected or disconnected from the other horses?

After we looked at herd dynamics, we moved to individual horse body language. She had me looking at their eyes, postures, legs, and mouths. Were their eyes soft and blinking or hard and fixed? Did their body appear soft and supple or more like a stiff board? Was a back leg cocked or were all four legs squared off? Were their lips compressed or were they licking and chewing?

In a short time, a whole new world opened up to me. A horse can either be in a comfortable place or a paralyzed place. To the untrained eye, they look almost the same. Horses are masters at stuffing their worry into a compact package. Quickly, I began drawing parallels to my experiences in a variety of corporate settings.

Listening, Patience, Timing

On one memorable day, back when I was a banker in Texas, I was returning from a client meeting with a long list of promises to fulfill. Several of us on the floor shared an assistant, who was normally a very sunny, helpful person.

On this day, she did not look up when I approached her desk. She was frequently busy and focused, so I thought nothing of interrupting her. When I started talking, she did not look up. I missed the first subtle signal. Even though a little whisper in the back of my mind was saying *"Something's not right,"* I started to dump my list of to-dos on her. Rather than listen to what she was telling me – albeit with energy and gesture rather than words – I added more pressure. I justified it to myself. After all, helping me was her job. A part of me was beginning to see that she might be in anything but a relaxed, comfortable state. The go-getter in me dove in anyway.

Bad idea. Really, bad idea. After a few more sentences, she turned on me with a fury that would have knocked back an F5 tornado. Pouring pressure onto an already pressure-filled situation was not the right move.

As I sulked back to my office, head down, our manager took me aside. He had witnessed the takedown and was smiling in a conspiratorial way.

"You picked a bad time, didn't you?" We talked for a moment about my poor timing and lack of patience. He shared a little of the backstory on what had been going down at the office while I was out with clients that day. Had I been reading the situation, I would have seen dozens of signals that would have told me to be patient. It was a painful lesson on timing, worth its weight in gold.

Now back at Lynn's farm, I realized there were more lessons from this story. Adding pressure to a horse who looks calm and relaxed but is in Survival Mode while hiding his worry, can lead to unexpected explosions. Spend any time around people who take their horses out of their usual environment, be it on the trail or in a trailer, and you will hear things like, "He was fine and then suddenly he ran the other way," or "He's always been so easy to get on the trailer; I have no idea what got into him."

Go Slow to Go Fast

During my early lessons, Lynn took me into the world behind the horses' eyes. When I was a kid watching Westerns or going to the rodeo, it looked to me like all you had to do was hop on the horse, give it a kick, yank the reins and off you went. I honestly thought the most difficult part was swinging the leg over. How naive.

Working with Lynn and Bruce, I learned that horses are always, always, always assessing their safety. Their body language constantly telegraphs how safe – or unsafe – they are feeling. My first assumption went out the window. Just because a horse is standing still does not mean he feels safe. (I now realize how incredibly well-trained movie horses are.)

By learning to read the signals, communicated by their eyes, ears, tail, feet, and more, I was now much more highly attuned to how my gestures, energy, and even breathing and heart rate affected their sense of safety and trust.

The more I learned, the more I wanted to know. After many lessons with Lynn – still on the ground – I was sold on the process of developing trust and connection with the horse. I had also started connecting many more dots between what I was learning in the barn and how it impacted the ways I developed trust and connection in my human relationships. Every session with Lynn started with a debrief of how I had applied the principles she was teaching me in different situations, most involving no horses at all.

One day I came into the barn and Lynn said, "Today, you are getting on."

After months of groundwork, it was finally time for me to start riding Phoenix. By this time, many more of my early assumptions had been blasted to oblivion. I was enjoying working with the horse on the ground, whether leading him up and down the road or moving in the round pen. Now, it was finally time to saddle up. Well, sort of saddle up.

"You have developed good trust with Phoenix. Today we are going to start by having you develop connection through your seat," Lynn said as she showed me the bareback pad we would be using. The pad connected to the horse much like a saddle but had none of the support of the Western saddle in the form of stirrups, saddle horn, and wooden tree that holds the rider in place. The only thing that would be holding me in place as he moved would be my balance and connection to him.

She talked me through the process of saddling, focusing especially on being gentle and connected when it was time to tighten the cinch that held the pseudo-saddle in place.

I was about to realize that just because I had changed my mind did not mean I had changed my ways.

I started out very present. My Invisible Tools of listening, hearing, patience, and timing were all in play as I began saddling Phoenix. Lynn had reminded me that he was a rescue horse, once destined for Olympic greatness. He had been training in a high-performance show barn where the horses were treated like machines rather than sentient beings.

In his performance life, his daily routine involved being brought out from his stall – which might feel like prison to an animal whose DNA is programmed to run free over wide-open spaces – tied up on each side of his face to be brushed, have his hooves picked, and then saddled.

Phoenix's fear had boiled over years ago in the show barn. One day, he said enough is enough and flipped himself upside down while tied up to be saddled. At that point, his rider decided he was more trouble than he was worth and moved on to another horse. Lynn eventually rescued him, and he had become her star lesson horse.

Now he was standing patiently, waiting to be my teacher. Step by step, Lynn continued talking me through the process of saddling, which I had learned to do in middle school, back when my assumption was: Once a horse is "broke," he is safe to ride. I didn't know it yet, but my proving mindset was just waiting to pounce.

When it came time to pull the cinch tight, I had gone through all the steps she explained, all the while staying present as I worked with Phoenix. Just putting the pad up there was a process of letting him sniff it and waiting. Move in and move out. Give and take. Try again and assess. Each moment was designed to give him space to realize that it wasn't going to kill him. Finally, he took a deep breath and relaxed. The pad was on his back.

In my mind, we had just reached the pinnacle. It felt like I had summited Mount Everest. As my inner self did the happy dance, Lynn explained how the straps went through the different loops.

My inner celebration completely drowned out the guidance Lynn was providing. In that moment, I totally went back to my past. It was TyranT mindset in an instant. What happened inside reminded me of what happens when I'm in a deep meditation, or in flow while water skiing. As soon as I think to myself, *"I'm doing it,"* I'm not doing it anymore.

When it came to the cinch, I had one goal: it should be tight. This was a Rule I had learned as a pre-teen. A loose saddle can come off to the side and lead to a bad accident. I failed to hear Lynn as she described the Frame-by-Frame, moment-by-moment method which would help me reach the goal while at the same time, keep Phoenix's mind feeling safe and connected to me. I gave it a good yank, just like I had been taught as a kid – and just like the cowboys do in the movies. Phoenix stomped his hoof, swished his tail, and brought his head around, as if to say, "What the hell!"

All were signals that the horse was feeling very unsafe. Phoenix just showed me how far I had to go.

Some horsemen would ignore that kind of behavior because the horse didn't run or bite. Others would force the issue, insisting through fear and intimidation that the horse comply. Some would take that as a signal to abandon the ride and hope for a better day tomorrow.

Lynn's standard is to do none of those things. Early in my lessons, she said, "You need to realize that every time you ask something of a horse, you take a little bit of his confidence away. It pays to let him know when he's giving you what you are asking for. They want to please us."

She showed me how to tighten a cinch without the yank. It was a much more humane process, and the result was just as effective. However, just because I had succeeded in getting the cinch tight, there was no way she was letting me get on the back of this horse while he was in a fearful state of mind. His pot wasn't boiling yet – but it would get much hotter if we didn't turn down the temperature before making such a big ask.

We slowed way down. We walked the tightrope. We were not harsh, and we were not soft.

Instead of force and fear or quitting and placating, we stayed with him. The horse's stomping didn't stop me from saddling or riding him. It just meant that I had to restore safety and regain trust and connection before I could make that kind of request of him.

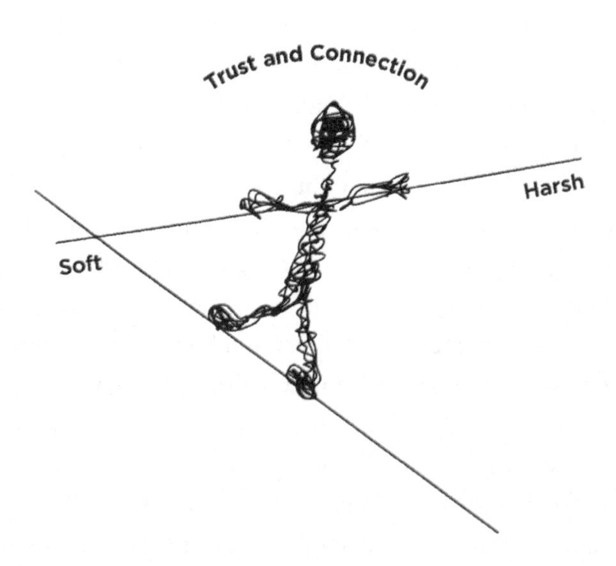

Once he let us know he was relaxed, I had the first of many terrific rides. In each moment, she showed me how to continually bring the horse along and pay attention to the signals that he was with me (AlphA) and not in survival mode (TyranT). It was a constant series of making requests and reassuring the horse. We had to go slow to go fast. When I skipped steps, it took much longer because I had to dig myself out of the hole I had created.

The Gift of Stressors

Dancing among several activities revealed the holes I had been digging my whole life – but also the positive side of the stressors that create pressure, uncertainty, and fear. When riding at Cedar Creek, just walking up and down the steep hills flooded my body with adrenaline. So did a bobble on my water ski. Walking near the edge of anything high off the ground was enough to make my knees turn to Jell-O®. Just about anything physically scary sent a flock of butterflies through my entire torso. It's a wonder I didn't take flight at every possible trigger.

It wasn't until I started applying the lessons from Bruce and Lynn – as I was riding Phoenix – that things really started to change.

Once I began to see pressure as a gift – albeit only occasionally – a whole new world opened.

First, I had to own what I was starting to call my Mistake Cycle, which I did more often than I did the What's Next Cycle. Thinking of it as the "What's Next Cycle" turned my mind to focusing on the next frame rather than allowing my past to interfere.

My words and beliefs simply did not fully align with my feelings and actions. This was not because I'm some huge hypocrite who means one thing and says another. It's a battle between my intentions and my conditioning. Old habits die hard. Decades of the survival training called life had established their ways with me. While my brain and my mouth espoused the value of mistakes in the learning process, my body braced for the consequences. With the slightest hint of a mistake, every cell in my physical system vibrated with warning signals that bad things were coming, just like what happened in Finding the Middle.

It took the pressure of getting back on the horse – with the gift of teachers who could show me the incongruity – to begin unwinding the twisted chords that held me in a stiff, pseudo-safe place. I had chosen teachers who went way beyond riding technique and equitation. Both Bruce and Lynn had seen the cost of the human-created Mistake Cycle on the horse and the human. Their approach worked at the root cause of many of the problems with horses, which is the way humans dealt with things not going perfectly.

My own perfectionistic tendencies would cause me to either beat myself up – or beat up others around me when mistakes were made. More than once,

Bruce called me out for beating up the horse when I couldn't get him to do what I was asking him to do. I didn't think of it as beating anyone up at all. In my mind, it was just the normal frustration of learning. In truth, it was the Mistake Cycle in action. It was as if Bruce could read my inner dialogue – and not even the parts that I could hear. He was reading the dialogue behind the dialogue – the energy that was running my actions.

In his book *Open*, Andre Agassi describes in agonizing detail just how the Mistake Cycle works on our inner dialogue:

"After years of hearing my father rant at my flaws, one loss has caused me to take up his rant. I've internalized my father – his impatience, his perfectionism, his rage – until his violence doesn't feel like my own, it is my own. I no longer need my father to torture me. From this day on, I can do it all by myself."

It wasn't necessarily a raging father or mother that had caused me to take up a rant. It was the whole gamut of teachers, and parents, and siblings, and bosses and so much more. It wasn't necessarily a rant in the traditional sense of the word, which I envision like a temper tantrum. It was more like a low level of frustration, just as Bruce had described dozens of times with my clients and me in the round pen with the horse, "You feel a mistake and start hitting yourself over the head with a 2x4. You start second-guessing yourself. You get up in your head rather than letting the horse tell you what to do, when to do, how to do. You leave the moment. That's the past interfering."

In my mind, I started to spell interfering this way:
The past is EnterFearing.

My fear of mistakes was causing the very thing I was trying to avoid. It was not intentional; it was automatic. And I had repeated it millions of times in my life.

In the face of a variety of behaviors, Bruce could repeat the Mistake Cycle to his clients with confidence, because everyone he had ever worked with found themselves in the cycle. Not every time nor all the time. It happened when the pressure got high enough. He also frequently described the other side of the fear; rather than making myself feel better by buying another car or working myself to death or eating another bar of chocolate, he suggested that our own human endorphins offered a genuine reward. One that couldn't be taken away.

If I were to get out of the proverbial hole I kept digging, my actions and feelings would be the thing to lead me out of it, not my brain and my mouth.

Pressure would get me into a feeling space where true change was possible.

Phoenix offered me a golden opportunity to feel differently.

Learning or Locked

From across the arena, Lynn yelled, "Your back is locked again!" Every time I asked something of Phoenix, my flow went out the window. My body went from moving with the horse in harmony and balance to rigid and stiff as a board. I sat up straight as if saying, "Now I mean business." With my body, I talked *at* Phoenix, rather than *with* him.

All I wanted to show my teacher was that I "knew" what to do. In my own mind this felt like the way to ride, me telling the horse what to do and the horse instantly responding.

Except what I was doing gave me the exact opposite of what I was trying to achieve. My stiffness communicated danger to the horse. Sitting up took me out of my balanced seat and made me more likely to fall off. All I was showing Lynn was that I still had a lot to learn.

I was unintentionally creating the very thing I was trying to avoid.

Without Lynn watching me and calling out what was really happening, I would have blindly felt great. As soon as she pointed out my locked-up back, I could feel it. I just couldn't imagine doing anything differently. My automatic response was to brace for danger. *What if he ran away? What if he bucked? What if he stopped suddenly and I went flying over his head?* My mind threw a thousand potential catastrophes at me.

She pointed out that my own nervous state was causing the horse concern. When I didn't breathe, he moved with more stiffness, trying to figure out my instructions and make sure I wasn't about to kill him.

By this time, we had been working together for several months. Knowing how to do this versus actually doing it under pressure were clearly two different things. I was in the Froth, that place of discomfort where the old way doesn't work, and the new way doesn't work either.

The Froth is my term for the productive learning zone. Like the froth at the edge of the ocean, where the bubbles are water and air mixed, the Froth is a state of mind and body sensation where the old and the new mix together. In the Froth, I feel agitation. I am toggling back and forth between the comfort of the deficient old way and the tentativeness of the new way.

Would I ever get past my fall? We were about to find out. "Relax! Breathe! Now slight pressure with your right leg while you look left. And stay relaxed!"

> **"The Froth is my term for the productive learning zone. Like the froth at the edge of the ocean, where the bubbles are water and air mixed, the Froth is a state of mind and body sensation where the old and the new mix together."**

In one of the most vulnerable moments I've ever experienced, I somehow finally let go. I took a deep breath, relaxed, and gave the slightest pressure with my leg. The horse smoothly turned, and we moved together in a flow that could only be called magical. Just writing about it almost makes me want to cry with joy.

In that moment, the sensation that coursed through my body felt like I was opening to a flow I had been seeking my whole life. I felt it down to my toes, which suddenly felt light and fluffy, rather than tight and gripping. I was dancing the tightrope on the back of a horse.

For the rest of the day, I felt the sensation of doing things from a relaxed and focused state of being. My feet felt both lighter and more grounded at the same time. My body moved with ease. Later, I came to realize it was the stream of endorphins, those feel-good hormones that Bruce had promised as a payoff. I had caught my first true glimpse of what was possible.

In the afterglow of the experience, I reflected on how I had been approaching every aspect of my life, from daily routine to the dangerous. Bracing with fear was second nature. After the experience with Phoenix, I played with ways to bring the "flowy" feeling into everyday life. My awareness on my feet was particularly keen. The more I tuned in, the more I noticed how often my feet often clenched in a death grip. Yet with some attention and intention, I could let go and my toes and feet would relax. My fluffy toes would return … for a moment. When I faced the next thing, whether a phone call, a personal encounter, the next ski set, or the next horse, my feet would brace for danger and death. My movements lost their flow. My awareness would tune in and I would rock back into fluffy toes. My awareness would shut down and I was back to grippy toes. Rocking, back and forth, I've been tuned in to my feet ever since, constantly increasing the time I spend in fluffy toes, becoming ever more aware of the dance between bracing and embracing.

Bracing for danger and falling into my Rules lock me up, both in mind and body. Embracing pressure, uncertainty, and fear as an opportunity to use my Tools opens me up to handle anything.

Now I could see – in a way that I could bring into practice – that it was the very act of facing pressure and uncertainty that would become the medicine to heal me.

CHAPTER TEN

The Mistake Cycle

Getting Myself out of a Pickle on the Water

Soon after my magical moment with Phoenix, a test came in my personal life that involved a rowing shell, blowing winds, some friends, and my husband Russ.

After he bought me a rowing shell the previous year for my birthday, my husband was excited that I would finally get to go row with our friends John and Christa from across the lake. The three of them had been going out together for years. Now I would make the fourth.

There was a reason it had taken the better part of a year for this day to arrive. We had been down similar roads before, and it had not gone well. My fear almost always got the better of me, and my husband's teaching methods – whether in scuba diving, rock climbing, or boating – only magnified the pressure. He came from a family that literally threw him in the water to learn how to swim. Over the past 25 years, I was still helping him understand that throwing me in the deep end was not the way I learned. In fact, it was a good way for him to get his eyes scratched out. I needed baby steps.

Walking down to the boathouse that morning, I mentioned that I would need his patience as I figured out how to get in the boat without tipping over, and then manage the very long, clumsy oars. I had only been in it once before and appreciated just how difficult a sculling boat is to maneuver. I never got more than 50 feet from the safety of the shoreline. He promised to be very supportive and helped me get the boat all set up. Then he said, "Go ahead and start rowing across the lake" to our friend's house.

He might as well have asked me to start flapping my wings to fly there.

As I pushed off the launch, I discovered just how many tiny corrections it took to stabilize a boat only as wide as my hips. Tipping and rocking, I found the simple act of reaching for the oars sent me into awkward maneuvers and the distinct awareness that I could fall into the very cold lake any second.

Then, as if I didn't already have enough pressure, the wind started blowing.

By now, I had managed to move away from the safety of the launch platform at the boathouse. But I was still near the huge structure with ten feet of oars sticking out from either side of the boat.

Sculling boats are designed to move in reverse. A normal stroke of the oars will catapult the boat several feet through the water. Leaving the area to reach open water required me to do the opposite of the natural stroke. I had to somehow push the oars rather than pull them to get clearance from the structure. Given that I had been in this boat only once and did not come close to effectively moving the oars either direction, the pressure was rising.

Did I mention that the wind had started blowing? By now, it was howling.

As I wrestled with asking my hands to do the opposite of what felt natural, the wind pushed me toward our pontoon boat hanging on a boat lift. The sharp propellor and I were about to have an unfortunate meeting.

In what I can only call a split-screen moment, I saw two Lynns.

One was the Lynn I had always been. In moments like this for much of my life, I had gone into panic. It happened during a dive trip in the Cayman Islands where I freaked out during one of my first attempts to scuba dive off a boat. It happened rock climbing where I got about ten feet off the ground and then screamed like a banshee to get down. It happened when I was thrown from THE horse that landed me in the hospital. Panic had been my go-to for most of my life. I knew this Lynn well.

On the second screen was the Lynn who had grown from the pressure of the round pen and had learned to reach for my Invisible Tools. This Lynn had options. I could scream and flail and end up swimming in the 50-degree water to avoid the propellor.

Or I could solve the problem.

I decided to stay with it and solve the problem. I would have to redecide many more times before I reached safety.

I took a deep breath and calmly looked around for a way to avoid being pushed into the hanging boat. The oars that had been so awkward before suddenly became my friends. I shortened one and used it to push myself off the side of the boat slip just a split second before I would have made contact.

Now I was free of the structure. At that moment, my husband saw the weird oar set-up and yelled over the wind, "You never shorten your oars!" The Lynn of the first split screen would have been defensive and pissed that he was trying to help me without really helping me. Moments like these have been the beginning of many epic fights. This time I just said, "You do when it keeps you from getting sliced up by a propellor!"

I was not out of the woods yet. With the wind starting to look like it might whitecap, the tiny boat and I continued to be blown down the lake. By now, John and Christa had arrived at our side of the lake. John was a veteran of the rowing shell, and he quickly assessed the situation.

The pressure was much higher than any rowing skills I had amassed in my one time trying the new boat. While the others in our group would be able to go out for a fun and exciting morning challenging themselves in the wind, the best thing for me was to wait for another day. We needed to somehow get me back to the boathouse.

By now the wind had carried me several hundred feet down the lake. I would have to row against the wind to return to the launch platform on our boathouse.

Lynn on Screen 1 wanted to be rescued. Perhaps someone could get a motorboat out and come drag me home.

Lynn on Screen 2 realized that getting home was on me.

The only way it would happen was if I were able to listen WHILE feeling the intense pressure. This was no time to beat myself up over my lack of skills or to wish I were at home having a hot cup of tea. Nope. The situation was my opportunity to rewrite my past. I simply needed to use my Invisible Tools. Doing so was simple – but certainly not easy.

John started coaching me on how to hold the oars, how to lean forward as I drew the oars back, turn them in slightly to make contact with the water and lean back to create the stroke. All of this had to happen while keeping the boat balanced. All of this going against a stiff wind. Every move was filled with tiny corrections toward balance.

As I listened to his coaching, I began to get a feel for the stroke. Once he saw that I had a rhythm, he quit talking and allowed me to focus. Stroke by stroke, frame by frame, I stayed present with the boat, the oars, the wind, and the water.

Before I knew it, I was at the boathouse. Now I just had to back my boat into its platform without a rear-view mirror or eyes in the back of my head. By breaking it down step by step, moment by moment, I was able to park the boat on the first try – even though the wind was still howling.

The feeling of success was one of the most satisfying things I've ever experienced. Rather than berate myself over not being able to "hang on the water with the big kids," I acknowledged that I had overcome incredible fear and panic to get myself out of quite a pickle. Much like the moment when I finally relaxed with Phoenix, I allowed the endorphins to be my true reward. The sensation was like my inner energy had gone from jumpy and miserable to silky and smooth. It's almost impossible to put into words.

It was at this moment that I knew something truly had changed in me. It would be one of many moments when my husband noted that his formerly fearful wife was able to show up even when the pressure was high.

Pressure can act as a barrier to being good at the skills we can do with ease when there's no pressure. That's the essence of the Pressure Gap. Pressure can come from anywhere. It could be from having an audience, hoping to impress or at least not embarrass, or from being alone wishing for support and feeling at loose ends. Pressure can come from danger and pressure can come from fear. The gap occurs when we feel pressure – from any source – to the extent that our skills suffer. Here's how Bruce described the gap to me many times: "The pressure was greater than your mental tools to deal with the pressure."

What I discovered on the lake that day was that I could actually LEARN a skill while under extreme pressure. Bruce's methods of applying pressure when the stakes were high with horses translated from one domain to another. In this case, I was able to access my Tools to stay dry on my journey back to the boathouse.

This method worked in "real life." I still wasn't sure how or why. And I didn't know just how critical the next opportunity would be. But first, I reflected on my dual-screen experience with the sculling boat.

Reflecting on the Mistake Cycle

When I reflected on my sculling boat adventure, it was becoming clear that the Rules of my internal operating system were being rewritten. Had the scene played out with Lynn on Screen 1, the day would have ended with Russ and me in a huge fight. It's almost impossible for someone who lives to face danger to understand how deeply fear can run in another, even in moderately challenging conditions. The Rules of Russ's operating system came from succeeding after being thrown in the pool. The Rules of Lynn on Screen 1 were written by hearing a mother scream, "don't go near the edge" for most of my life. My Rules had built giant fences around anything remotely dangerous. This gulf between our approaches to life had been a source of conflict from Day One.

Early in our marriage, I got certified to scuba dive. The first dive Russ and I attempted to do without the oversight of an instructor was a two on a scale of one to ten for him and a ten of ten for me. Russ was an advanced diver and simply could not see why I found diving off a boat in the middle of the ocean with big waves a challenge. He knew the conditions would be better once we got below the water. I was sure I would die once I got below the water.

Our wildly divergent operating systems were invisible to us, yet were running the show.

To stay married, we had reached détente. I quit scuba diving, rock climbing, mountain bike riding, and more. I found water skiing through girlfriends who allowed for my baby-step approach to learning.

When Russ bought the rowing shell for my birthday, it had been parked for a year and a half awaiting a day when I could learn to row. In a perfect world, I would not have started the way we did; however, I had no one else to teach me. It was a risk I was willing to take.

Through my work with Bruce and Lynn, I had been slowly raising my pressure threshold. As a result, I had been more welcoming of pressure and the opportunity to relax in the face of making mistakes. Going out on the sculling boat offered exactly what I needed. The unexpected wind was just a bonus.

What was missing that day was just as important as what was present. Rather than the self-judgment that stuck to my mistakes like a tick on a dog, I coached myself through each mistake. The idea was to allow whatever did not work to roll off me like water off a duck's back. When the wind blew me toward the hanging pontoon boat, I focused on solving the problem, not agonizing over my predicament. When I found myself blown way out of my comfort zone relative to the boathouse, I asked for help to get home rather than second-guessing the decision to be there. What was missing was running on my Rules; instead, when the Rules offered the quick answer, I mostly reached for my Tools. By the way, the Rules almost always offer the first answer. The change happens by shortening the time span between running on Rules or choosing to reach for the Tools.

My Rules involved getting after myself, like I had a sports mom living in my head constantly telling me to choke up on the bat. While she presented herself as a "helper," her interference amid pressure only reinforced my Mistake Cycle rather than help me shed mistakes and have access to my skills.

Bruce's methods of repetition in our leadership work with the horses showed me that my perfectionist tendencies were part of the Mistake Cycle. Once I experienced his way of "listening to the feeling," the screaming sports mom was no longer screaming in my head. The repetitions showed me that I can operate under pressure if I break it down frame by frame and allow the situation to tell me what to do. The sports mom is not providing help. Her screams instead EnterFear and move the focus to my mistake instead of my abilities to solve the problem at hand. Rather than something to be lauded, perfectionism was interfering with my ability to do anything under pressure.

The same basic cycle showed up for the many clients I took to work with Bruce. Yes, we each had our own specific nuances; however, the basic pattern was the same. At the onset of something feeling off, the cycle gets activated.

My personal version of the Mistake Cycle involved a set of steps that looked like this:

1. Physical Sensation: Something feels off
2. Conscious Story: I've made a mistake
3. Unconscious Story: Something is wrong with me; I'm a mistake
4. Emotion: Anger, frustration, shame, fear
5. Wish: I must stop the sensation so that I feel OK about myself
6. Action: Erase the mistake, cover up the mistake, panic when it doesn't work, have a fight

The whole cycle happens in a nano-second, outside of my conscious. Without the frame-by-frame breakdown, it looks like this:

1. Mistake
2. A moment of "aarrrghh"
3. More mistakes while trying to fix the first mistake

This Screen 1 method had its benefits. There was something cleansing about the pain of self-criticism. Once I had taken the punishment, it felt like I had a fresh start. Interestingly, true learning almost always involves discomfort, even pain. My theory about why we beat ourselves up is that it covers the pain of the learning process. It's a pain we know well, and since we are the ones doing it to ourselves, it feels controllable. And to some degree, it works. Occasionally, I would get better at a given skill. The self-judgment gave me the comfort that I was trying.

However, the cycle was also self-limiting. I would leave the cycle committed to never again having to feel that yucky "something-is-off" sensation. So, I would take less risk, and when the sensation showed up, I just repeated the cycle. Then I wondered why fear was running my life.

Treating mistakes as a signal that something is wrong with me perpetuates what doctor and author Brené Brown calls the "shame spiral." The little electrical charge that tells me something is off triggers a cascade of emotions, stories, and actions that take me away from solving the problem at hand. Suddenly, I become the problem, hacking away at the outside noise in a fear-based attempt to feel OK about myself.

On the other side of fear are my Tools. After the Finding the Middle exercise had been repeated ad nauseam, I was finally seeing the benefits. The physical sensation is just a sensation; what I do with it determines my outcome. Instead of thinking of it as a problem, something I don't like to feel, I thought of it as a signal. The sensation became my friend. I could either use the sensation to help me solve the problem (Screen 2) or I could try to make it go away (Screen 1). By choosing to solve the problem, to listen to John in the scull, to stay with it, not only did I survive, I raised my pressure threshold.

Good thing, because I would need my Tools the following week in a situation that made my accident look like a walk in the park.

Controlled Chaos

After many successful rides on Phoenix, riding instructor Lynn graduated me to Shahlik, a grey Arabian. She said, "Only people who ride like me can ride him. He has a dominant mind, and it takes a really confident rider for him to trust the rider as a leader."

I knew enough about horses by this point to recognize that Arabians are known to be a more spirited breed. Between Lynn's caution and what I knew about him, I had never expected to ride Shahlik, or Shah as he was known around the barn. He was certainly a much more spirited horse than Mocha, THE horse from my accident. Yet here I was, under Lynn's tutelage, learning to ride Shah.

After a few lessons in the arena, Lynn and I headed out for the second of our "controlled chaos" rides. Lynn was on her horse Martini, and I followed on Shah.

By this stage of my training, I had spent a lot of time in different settings with horses. I had spent time in a variety of barns, involving every discipline from dressage to fox hunting to herding cattle to trail riding specialists. In all my visits, I came to learn that there were two basic schools of thought around working with and around horses. One involved controlling the conditions to keep the horses calm and the riders safe. The other involved preparing the horse and rider to handle anything that came up. They were an almost perfect parallel to the shorthand I was developing. In the first, controlling the setting involved a lot of Rules. In the second, preparing the horse and rider involved developing Tools.

Lynn's teaching fell into the Tools way of thinking.

Week by week, Lynn had worked with me on building my confidence through building my Tools. We did not avoid danger. Instead, we embraced the situations that were difficult, and she trained me how to help the horse to help himself in each scary situation.

Given my accident just two and a half years before, simply grooming a horse was a scary situation for me. Getting on was a scary situation. Trotting was a scary situation. Yet, with patience, she continued to add pressure and I continued to build my Tools.

Eventually, she had to manufacture scary stuff for me and the horse to handle. The "controlled chaos" rides raised the pressure even higher. She would set the conditions for the horse and me to face a situation. She would be nearby to offer support. She set up a circumstance where the horse might be resistant, refuse to move a

"We did not avoid danger. Instead, we embraced the situations that were difficult, and she trained me how to help the horse to help himself in each scary situation."

certain way, or have to deal with the unexpected. Our intention was for me to keep a strong connection as the horse's leader, even when things didn't go according to plan.

We did this type of practice first in the arena, where the fence offered a stopping place in case things got out of hand. Lynn brought in all kinds of distractions, like flapping tarps, swim noodles, buckets of water, and scary things we had to step over. Shah and I learned to face danger together.

I did not accept controlled chaos as a great idea at first. In fact, it seemed positively insane that Lynn insisted on creating fearful scenarios. After all, did she not remember that I got to spend three days in the hospital thanks to fearful things?

Her reasoning challenged one of my beliefs. I believed that you could never show fear to a horse, because they would pick up on it. Not to worry. I had earned my stripes working in Corporate America. I was an expert in how not to show fear.

My well-worn strategy was to put on my "I've got this" face and make everyone believe that my confidence was real. Remember my experience with the bucking Trini in the round pen? The more I doubled down on proving I had things under control, the more upset she became. Over time, my lessons with Lynn, Bruce, and the horses taught me that seeing things for what they are mattered far more than the cover-up. Truth be told, the horse sensed my fear and no amount of covering it up would cover it up. In fact, incongruity telegraphed the message that I could not be trusted.

If I were to get back on THE horse, I would have to learn to face this level of pressure by reaching for my Tools rather than reaching for my habits of stuffing, covering up, or panicking.

Moving outside the arena was a huge step. The stakes were higher when there were no fences to somewhat control the environment.

When we headed out that day, it was clear from the beginning that things had changed since my lesson the week before. With a new driveway being built on the adjacent farm, dump trucks were now going up and down the usually quiet road. Both horses vibrated with alertness.

Lynn reminded me to relax.

As predictable as the sunrise, here came my first thought: *"You've got to be kidding me, I'm sitting on a thousand pounds of speed and agility, and you want me to RELAX?"*

Followed by my second thought. Here was an opportunity to

welcome pressure.

"Remember my Tools. Take deep breaths. Get deep in my seat." We were both profoundly aware that should we mentally project bad stuff, the horses would pick up on that. We had the potential to make matters worse.

A part of me remembered that, somehow, I had managed to live without horses most of my life. Why in the world would I risk another injury or lose another ski season? It was April and summer was just around the corner.

Yet here I was, riding in a much higher pressure-packed situation two and a half years after the accident. My pressure threshold had been raised significantly, and here was my chance to raise it even higher. Needless to say, I was in the Froth.

I had learned to reinterpret the sensations that led to panic and instead, to balance my Negative/Positive Pole. The question was how much pressure would take me out of the Froth and into the paralysis zone.

Once we hit the paralysis zone, learning is almost impossible. We are over our Pressure Threshold. At this stage, we are so flooded with emotion we cannot learn. We can only survive. I've heard trainers refer to horses who are above threshold to refer to this in the horse's mind. Paralysis doesn't mean we can't move. Its means we are in the full-fledged fight, flight or freeze stage of Survival Mode. We react with tunnel vision and without choice.

Ideally, on this ride, I would stay in the Froth. Slightly uncomfortable, but still able to make choices.

We walked along the driveway and Lynn reminded me to relax my ankles. "Oh yeah," I said, "heels down." One of the cardinal rules in horseback riding is Heels Down. The attending nurse in the ER after my accident asked me what had brought me there. "Fell off a horse," I said. "Got to keep those heels down," he replied. News to me. That's how ignorant I was about riding at the time. I made a mental note to always remember Heels Down.

Yet when I said heels down to Lynn, she said, "Imagine you have an egg on the ball of your foot. Feel your seat and let your legs drape like loose towels." When I followed her guidance, I suddenly relaxed, became more anchored to the horse, and as if by magic, my heels went down. By forcing my heels down, I was adding tension to the situation. It turns out Heels Down is the result of a relaxed rider; forcing it doesn't set the conditions we want to create.

As we were making our way along the open space that ran between the busy road and the creek, I mentioned to Lynn that I had been learning to row a sculling boat. I started to describe the success I had reaching for my Tools in the big wind incident just a few days before. My point was going to be how my training with the horses, especially the mental training, had helped me deal with the pressure.

As we talked, one of the huge construction trucks appeared around a bend and started coming down the hill toward us. Lynn asked how rowing could have anything to do with horseback riding. "When something happens out there," I began, "I reach for my Tools instead of ..."

Before I could finish the sentence, a big turkey exploded from the tall grass underneath us. This was right under Shah's nose and behind Lynn's horse Martini. Shah's head came up, turned left, and I saw the whites of his eyes. The energy underneath me felt like a rocket ship.

Shah launched into a run to the left as Lynn's horse Martini took off the other way.

Well Lynn. You wanted to learn to stop a horse. Here's your chance.

I felt the panic rising in me. For a split second, all my training went out the window. Again, the unhelpful first thought arose. My immediate reaction was to do exactly what I had done on the horse that threw me two and a half years before. I wanted to pull back on the reins, as hard as possible. After all, we were now heading straight for the oncoming dump truck and sure disaster.

In the whirlwind, a part of me waited for Lynn to yell out instructions, as she had so often before in our training. Just the week before, we had been near this exact location, practicing emergency stops. I heard nothing but the truck and immediately sensed she was dealing with her own spooked horse.

Whatever happened next was on me.

I could either reach for my Tools or react from my panic. Immediately I turned my mind from panic to focusing on What's Next. I had a problem to solve; freaking out would only add fuel to the fire. Beating myself up, second-guessing our decision to be there, or feeling like a victim of the circumstances would use precious time and energy that I needed to face the pressure. Plus, focusing on any of that would take me outside of myself.

Coalescing my mind around solving the problem kept me within myself.

Things happened fast. I shortened the reins against his mane, took the right rein and brought his head around while bending his right hip around. In the blink of an eye, we were stopped, facing the creek. The truck was gone. Lynn was standing there with her horse, and we were alive. We had only gone about two horse lengths away from the spot the bird launched.

Shah was calm and quiet. I was calm and quiet. Lynn said, "Well done."

> "Coalescing my mind around solving the problem kept me within myself."

In moments like these, it's tempting to stop, go back to the barn and wait to ride another day. Any horse trainer worth his/her salt will tell you that succumbing to that temptation will lead to unintended (and unfortunate) consequences. Horses make connections between what happened before what happens next. If running off at such a provocation sends us back to the barn, then perhaps he could test it next on a dove or maybe a cricket. In other words, getting out of work by spooking can be "trained" into a horse by a well-meaning rider.

So, we continued our ride. However, it was not only for Shah's training. Going back to the barn would have also told me that I could not handle it, even though I had just handled it. If I were to use this event to raise my pressure threshold, I had to stay with the pressure rather than do what I had done for the past 61 years of my life: Tuck my tail between my legs and go home.

Given how spooked I had been by my accident – now two and a half years behind me – I was curious as to whether the fear would come flooding back as we continued riding in the field alongside the road. Would I be able to bring myself back down?

In the past, the adrenaline hits my brain delivered would render my muscles useless and activate my monkey mind to run a mile a minute. No amount of deep breathing or calming practices would bring me back. Only time would help, as I silently committed to never let it happen again. Without really realizing it, such events had incrementally shrunk my world for many, many years.

This time, I carried on, able to keep my wits about me as the adrenaline drained from my system. I allowed myself to relish in my newfound skills as we encouraged the horses to explore the very area that had created the chaos. As their confidence and curiosity rose, so did my own.

Later, as we were walking back to the barn, Lynn and I talked about the strategy we had used to build our confidence. She said, "You would not believe how many experienced horse owners would have gone back to the barn. Eventually, they quit riding out when there's any chance of something happening, including on windy days. I would rather give my horse the tools to handle the scary stuff, and to do that, they need a confident leader."

I had been around enough barns by this point to see exactly what she described. By the time we put the horses away that day, I realized that I was feeling very much like I had the day when I finally relaxed with Phoenix, and the day I got the sculling boat home in the windstorm.

Bruce had often referred to this feeling as natural endorphins. However, Bruce is a horse trainer, not a scientist. Plus, Bruce had not read the myriad books I had on developing calm under pressure and on dealing with uncertainty. In fact, he had developed his methods completely based on trial and error. Based on what was happening with me, it was clear he was on to something. My shorthand language of reaching for my Tools versus reaching for my Rules was working as a method for keeping me within myself in times of pressure and uncertainty, but I didn't know why. Nothing in all my prior reading and years and years of meditation and other practices had moved the dial as much as it had been in the past two and a half years. There had to be something to the biology of it.

Endorphins Or a New Car

It turns out that endorphins play a specific role in our biology. They help us cope with stress and pain. Sounds about right – every time I went into the round pen, I felt the stress. But there was something good about this type of stress, just like the intensity of water skiing, which also gives me an endorphin kick.

The first time I felt relaxed on Phoenix – after I thought I would die – the sensations lasted all day. The good feelings streaming through my body acted as a natural reward for a job well done.

In fact, dopamine also played a role. Dopamine is known as the reward hormone because it gets released after we reach a goal and it creates that afterglow.

> *"The process of learning and remembering things often feels hard and indeed can evoke agitation. Most people don't realize it, but that agitation is the entry point to learning. Literally, the adrenaline that causes agitation signals the nervous system that it*

should be ready to change. Without it the nervous system is not as primed for change – the process we call neuroplasticity.

Once you understand this, you will more likely embrace (as opposed to avoid) agitation. Also, after a period of challenging focus and learning there is an associated increase in feel-good molecules such as dopamine (and to a lesser extent, serotonin).

The takeaway: Learning is a process that starts with focus, alertness, and agitation, ... and the process is consolidated during sleep and non-sleep deep rest (NSDR).

We all have the capacity for neuroplasticity. Don't hesitate to lean into it as a process. Recognize the agitation as part of that process. The feel-good part arrives at the end, or days later when, as if suddenly, you have acquired new abilities.

Much of our feel-good neurochemistry is wired for release only after a mental struggle to arrive at some answer or insight. Learning (and applying knowledge) is the ultimate drug."

Andrew Huberman, Instagram May 17, 2022

Learning is the ultimate drug – IF we embrace it. Early on, I wondered why Bruce thought beating myself up was so bad. After all, I'm trying to be better. But wait, am I? Does it work or not? I've come to believe that it does not work. In fact, not only does it NOT work, it's like giving back the treasure right after we have found it. In a way, pressure unearths the brilliance we have buried underneath our Rules. However, it may not look like treasure when we've just been through so much discomfort. It's not yet as shiny and beautiful as we pictured. Beating ourselves up is like walking away from that exquisite, rare piece instead of carefully brushing off the dust and dirt to reveal the beauty underneath.

When I was about eight years old, my sister and I went to see our grandparents in Oklahoma. They loved having us come visit and offered many fun things for us to do. My grandad mentioned going to the zoo about an hour away. I asked, "Do they have elephants?" Don't ask me why, but at the time, I was obsessed with elephants. It might have been because I had seen a TV show with elephants. But all I wanted was to see the huge, gray beasts in real life. He said he was pretty sure they did and soon we were in the car, heading for the zoo.

The whole time we were in the car, while we paid our entrance fee and as we made our way into the zoo, I asked, "When will we see the elephants?" My vision of gray elephants danced in my head. My grandparents kept telling me to be patient and we would eventually get to the part of the zoo where they were kept. I don't remember being interested in anything else, until the moment when I became the worst spoiled brat ever.

Finally, we got to the elephant enclosure. My heart sank. These were not the elephants I had imagined. These elephants were reddish brown. Looking back on it, my heart sinks again, as I remember how horribly I behaved. "These are not real elephants," I cried. I turned and tried to walk away as my grandparents, thoroughly horrified at my public display, tried to explain to me that the elephants were really gray. They were just covered in mud. Not good enough for me. I wailed that the whole trip was wasted. I'm pretty sure I ruined the day for everyone over my childish refusal to see the real elephants standing right in front of me.

As an adult looking back on it, I can't imagine how heartbroken my grandparents were with my behavior. They had given me exactly what I asked for, and I rejected it. I beat them up over the elephants being covered in dust!

The learning process by definition is covered in dust. We are unearthing our true abilities, and the process can be messy and make us wonder if there is anything worth having for all our effort. We have to take the time to see the treasure for what it is. Beating ourselves up clouds our vision and makes us walk away from the treasure.

Bruce was keenly aware that our consumer-based society takes advantage of this process. He often said, "We can either take something that is less and use it to enrich ourselves – here, I will sell you my hat – or we can lift it up. We can use the pressure to help us grow."

With all the inputs coming at us, agitation is everywhere. And if we don't realize that much of the agitation is an artifact of the modern world, we seek respite in other ways. We buy a new car, get some new clothes, go buy something we don't need on Amazon. We may get a little hit of endorphins or dopamine, but it doesn't last. And it doesn't raise our pressure threshold. Next time, we have to go back for more.

CHAPTER ELEVEN

The What's Next Cycle

The Roots of Perfectionism

My next lesson with Bruce started as it always did, with a porch session. By this time, I had been riding with Lynn for several months. I would get down to Camden occasionally. Every time, I put on my boots and got out my helmet. But I still had not ridden either Marley or Mac. I guess working on my patience was starting to pay off.

On this day, I told him both stories – rowing in the wind and avoiding the truck with Shah. We debriefed the situations through the lens of his method. As I told one story, then the other, he asked questions such as, "What was your number?" "How did you let the situation tell you what to do, when to do, how to do?" "What did you do with your mistakes?" "Where did your muscle memory take over?" "How did you break it down to the smallest frames?" "How did you feel when it was over?"

The part of me aching for a Gold Star (or is it a "Goal Star?") still wanted him to declare me finished. It's a pattern I know well. The inner child shows up when I'm under pressure, craving the voice that says, "Lynn, I approve of you." My Mistake Cycle, fueled by the education and socialization process, will always be there.

I was one of those kids who loved to get A's. Because my dad drilled me on my multiplication tables in fourth grade, I gained a ton of confidence in math of all kinds. It carried me all the way through college and into my accounting and banking career. My parents got used to seeing all A's on my report cards. Anything less led to an interrogation about what happened. Perfection became my goal, not because I had high standards. Perfection fulfilled my Attachment needs. That balancing act between Attachment and Self-Expression/Authenticity always skewed toward approval.

Perfectionism runs rampant in the corporate world. Even in cultures that have the mantra "Done is better than perfect," individuals within that culture often struggle when they make mistakes or see others make mistakes. For many people, being asked to let good enough be good enough is like hearing fingernails on a chalkboard. It goes against the grain.

Even without external pressure, they feel internal pressure to get it perfect. The Perfection Game is essentially a way of life. It's rooted in a similar cycle to my own. We are conditioned to go for the goal. The language we used in banking was "Flawless Execution." It was a great idea for delivering accurate bank statements. However, it did not set the conditions for stretching into something new and different.

Perfectionism carries two ironies. The first is this: Those who are trying to be perfect are getting in their own way WHILE they are trying to do really good work for the organization. The striving itself diverts time, energy, and attention from solving the problem. In the face of complexity and uncertainty, mistakes pave the way to figuring out what does work. A project with no mistakes by definition must be small and risk free. Anyone can copy it. I've learned this in every domain, from art to water skiing to business. Even if perfection WERE achievable, the cost far outweighs the benefits.

The second irony of perfectionism is that it represents the end. When something is perfect, it cannot be improved upon. It is finished. It is over. A better way to say it is this: Perfection is death.

For someone caught in the Perfection Game, not being perfect FEELS like death. Every mistake signals that something is very wrong.

We can accomplish a thousand great things, and it's that one mistake that will eat us alive.

At the end of one of my corporate programs, a participant pulled me aside and "confessed" that his biggest fear was of failure. He spoke in a hushed tone, making sure none of his colleagues were in earshot. He said his normal pattern is to cover up his mistakes. If they get discovered, he goes on the attack to deflect criticism. When we dug a little deeper, it was clear that he is a competent person who is making his normal share of mistakes. The mistakes are not the problem. How he sees them is causing him all kinds of grief.

I so wanted to have a quick answer for him to turn all this around. But I've been there. It's not that straightforward. Fear of mistakes inhabits our very bones.

Mistakes are not the end of the world. They are our leverage points to proficiency.

As an adult, I went back to taking piano lessons. This was not some long-held dream or bucket list item. No, this was more of an accidental way to deal with my lack of patience.

We had an old player piano that was way out of tune. It was something my new husband brought into the marriage against my wishes. When he unloaded it from the truck, I stood at the front door, hoping to provide a blockade in a failed attempt to prevent him from bringing this old dirty thing into the house. It was REALLY old and dusty, and out of tune.

We got it cleaned up and every now and then I would sit down and play, mostly as an exercise in patience. See, Russ was always late. He would keep me waiting well past my patience threshold. Early on, I tried nagging to get him to hurry up. That just led to blow-ups. So, I started playing the piano to keep my hands occupied and distracted from wrapping around his throat.

As a child, my parents forced me to take piano lessons. I could still play a few things, but they sounded terrible on this old thing. What surprised me as an adult was how much I enjoyed playing. Believe me, as a kid, I didn't like to play. Especially when my mom nagged me (and nagged and nagged and nagged) to practice. She had visions of her daughter becoming a concert pianist. My practice was her obligation. Yet here I was as an adult choosing to sit down and play.

One day I decided to call a piano tuner. After he finished getting that old piano as tuned as it could be, he played. And oh, how he played! It was nothing like the classical music that had been forced on me as a child. This was the Blues, and I was in awe.

We started talking and I learned that piano tuning was a side gig for him. In his other life, he was a professional musician and he had played with many well-known people. He also gave piano lessons. He could teach me to play the Blues!

Right then and there, I signed up for lessons. What I dreaded as a child, I chose as an adult. He gave me assignments and I practiced, and practiced, and practiced.

My younger self never played anything perfectly. I didn't care, or truth be told, I didn't want to give my mom the satisfaction. As an adult, now fully formed and steeped in the "value" of perfection, I went for it. When practice was mine to own, I found a joy in hearing the music coming through my fingertips. I set my sights on playing pieces without making a single mistake.

I sought perfection and beat myself up when I didn't get it. Every day, I sat down with high hopes that this would be the day. When I would make a mistake, it interfered with my rhythm and took me out of myself. I would have to start over, more aggravated, but also more determined. I was so proud of myself for trying so hard! My inner world teetered between pride for my effort and shame for my lack of worthiness. These two forces created an equilibrium of sustained misery. None of it was useful. Yet I had no idea what was really going on inside me until years later.

To start with, what I was calling pride in myself was really me trying to please my piano teacher from childhood. As I was playing along, I would miss a note. Instead of continuing to play, I would freeze for a second. It was as if I felt the need to explain why I made the mistake to the ghost sitting off my right shoulder. Then I would get mad at myself. In the absence of my teacher there to weigh in, scolding myself felt like the right thing to do. Then I would start over from the beginning. So, some of my desire to be perfect was an exercise in proving myself to a teacher who had been dead for 20 years.

Difficult passages in the music created an even bigger dilemma. I didn't have the patience to break it down and really learn the notes. I longed to play perfectly; breaking it down into pieces felt like a series of mini failures. Instead, I kept starting over from the beginning, hoping I could somehow magically get through the piece. Of course, that's not how magic happens. After being stymied over and over again, I could barely stand the feeling of failure.

Because of my perfectionism and lack of patience, I limited myself to the easy pieces of music. Rather than learning and improving, I lowered my sights to a domain where I could feel better about myself and perhaps prove myself worthy.

During a lesson one day, I noticed that my new teacher was really pleased with something that wasn't perfect. I told him it wasn't good enough. Ha! Me the student had higher standards than the teacher! I even mentioned that as a professional, he was so much better than me. My assumption? He was perfect when he played. Then he said something that stuck with me. "I've never played a perfect piece in my life and never will. What we professionals have learned how to do is play through the mistakes. Every performance has mistakes. We just don't let our mistakes knock us off our flow."

He went on to say, "I want you to learn to be a better musician, not to be perfect. Music is not about playing all the notes in the right place and at the right time. It's as much about the space between the notes. You can only improve your skills when you are willing to feel your way through the mistakes and keep playing."

I embraced the idea in theory. In my head I could see the value of mistakes and I talked a good game. Truly believing mistakes were OK was another thing, especially when the pressure was high. My education had worked too well. Learning was never really my objective in school. The allure of the perfect report card really drove the show.

Contrast my attitude (and that of the education system) to that of Buckminster Fuller, who said, "If I ran a school, I'd give the average grade to the ones who gave me all the right answers, for being good parrots. I'd give the top grades to those who made a lot of mistakes and told me about them, and then told me what they learned from them."

That quote first came across this parrot's radar screen when I ran Credit Training at the mega-bank. My first reaction to it was horror. *"Of course, I want these students to give me the right answers!"* I thought, *"My job is on the line. They need to get it right every time. We can't afford for them to make mistakes."* Yet when we applied adult learning principles, we saw that the give-and-take of problem-solving, discovery, and an open learning environment developed better bankers and a more satisfying – even joyful – learning experience. Solving difficult problems has its own reward if we allow it.

When I found myself back on Bruce's porch sharing my successes, I thought I was a "mistakes are good" convert. However, the roots of perfectionism run deep. They wind around every part of the psyche, like old growth vines. Those roots wrap themselves around the very core of our being, promising protection from a world fighting its own perfection game.

On this day we would finally saddle Marley and I would come to realize that this "mistake convert" was just beginning to convert.

"On this day we would finally saddle Marley and I would come to realize that this 'mistake convert' was just beginning to convert."

Finding the Middle — Again!

Several times during our porch session, Bruce would say something and my retort would be, "Got it." "Getting it," he corrected me. This phrase hit me right in the solar plexus of my Mistake Button, sending my Negative Pole way up. My conditioning still reflexively treated that electrical jolt as a sign I was making a mistake. The automatic thoughts showed up even though I was now more aware. *"When, oh when, is he going to tell me 'I've got it?'"* I was still trying to be perfect. It wasn't really a conscious thought yet. He explained that he was simply bringing me back to the awareness that I had chosen to play an infinite game; one where there was no perfection. Growing my proficiency meant constantly getting it, never "got it." It was a gentle rewiring of my brain, which presents the choice of going into my Mistake Cycle or the What's Next Cycle. It still didn't take much to set off the Mistake Cycle.

But I was getting it, even though my impatience flared when he had me start with Finding the Middle. Long ago, one of my coaches had said, "Impatience is just your anger at not being able to control the situation." The words "be patient" always grated on my nerves. My goal this time – as it had been many days before – was "riding lessons." My goal would be achieved once I got on Marley. Everything in between was interference.

Not only is patience rare in our hurried world, but it gives us something we've been missing: the space to learn without the guilt and shame. I wasn't labeling the steps as interference, nor was I consciously driven by a need to have someone check the box that I was good enough. We can't label something we don't see. My brain heedlessly focused in on the goal and galloped toward it. The ride wasn't fun. My anger, need for control, and impatience had been exacting a high cost for a long time – and I was oblivious to it. Bruce's picture differed from mine in very important ways. He wanted to help me help myself to unleash the part of me he called "THE You," not some version of me that had a bunch of notches on my belt. Me riding was the least of his worries.

In the same way the Japanese tea-making ceremony is about the care in the steps rather than the end goal of the cup of tea, Bruce was slowing me down and widening my mental lens. Just as the Zen saying goes, "Before enlightenment, chop wood, carry water. After enlightenment, chop wood, carry water." Finding the Middle calibrated my mind, body, and spirit to slow down to create the picture I was here to create.

Modern day cameras can record at an astronomical rate of frames per second, allowing us to see rich pictures and distinctions previously invisible to the naked eye. The clarity is astonishing.

The clarity of Bruce's picture for me was equally astonishing. When my life could be broken into the multiplicity of frames per second, my picture of being (a rider) would be realized. It would be many more moons before I had my true first taste of being one with the horse. Eckhart Tolle said,

> *"Doing is never enough if you neglect Being. The ego knows nothing of being but believes you will eventually be saved by doing. If you are in the grip of the ego, you believe that by doing more and more you will eventually accumulate enough 'doings' to make yourself feel complete at some point in the future. You won't. You will only lose yourself in the doing. The entire civilization is losing itself in 'doing' that is not rooted in Being and thus becomes futile."*

Bruce was helping me work on Being.

This time, I really felt a shift within me as we went through the Finding the Middle exercise. My Negative/Positive Pole consolidated into a salient laser-like signal. The electricity shooting through my body felt less like death and more like the bubble on the spirit level. My job was simply to read the sensation and adjust accordingly.

When I stepped from one side to the other, my Pole told me when I had split the round pen in half. When I moved into the center, my Pole told me when I was getting warmer — or colder. When I finally planted my flag, I was not the one in control. I had allowed the round pen and the process to tell me where the middle was. I was simply the conduit.

Then Bruce used a stern tone and said, "What in the hell makes you think that's the middle?" I felt a huge surge of electricity. The past offered to EnterFear with protective solutions. For a moment, I questioned myself, doubted myself, wanted to defend myself. I was in the Froth. Then I remembered. I said, "I'm comfortable with this." And Bruce replied, "Well done."

His question was designed to flush the doubt and tune me in to the voice of The Me, the one behind the protective fear wall, the one I could trust when the chips were down. Suddenly, the committee in my head that loved to send out messages from the cheap seats, no longer had the power. The cacophony of sports mom messages didn't disappear – but they faded into the background.

The voices would be back. But every time I had a moment in the Froth where I chose to let the situation tell me what to do, when to do, how to do, my pressure threshold ratcheted up another level.

I would need every bit of that space when I got on Marley.

A More Productive Approach

After we went through the Finding the Middle exercise, we went over to saddle Marley.

We had been on the porch for a while, and even though I had enjoyed Finding the Middle, I was anxious to get moving. The clock ticking in my head seemed to scream at me to move faster. My hands revealed my impatience with each jerky movement. Quietly, Bruce said, "Slow down. Take your time. Go step by step." He couldn't miss my hands fumbling, rushing to get to the end goal. Neither could Marley.

Marley felt the "rushy" energy and stepped away. The saddle placement was off and had to be reset. Bruce said, "It takes what it takes. Complete this step before you move to the next step. And breathe!"

Some part of me realized that I was hearing Sports Mom in the cheap seats coming out of Bruce's head. Of course, that was just my wild imagination. When he spoke, it sounded like a needle scratching across vinyl on an old record player. The screech snapped me out of feeling the false pressure and once again, the sports mom voice faded into the background. We started over and with a deep breath, I shut the clock off in my head and focused. Step by step, moment by moment, quiet, and deliberate.

Bruce seemed to have a highly tuned radar to my inner dialogue. When my subconscious thoughts and energy fed me self-doubt, he caught it early and encouraged me to focus only on the next step.

Later, I came to realize that he had a finely developed sense of my Negative/Positive Pole. The analogy of the car battery is more literal than metaphorical. The Pole is energy. When my Negative Pole goes up, the horse feels it because energy is how horses communicate. Bruce could feel it too. When he could clearly see that I was in no danger, but my Negative Pole was rising and my past was EnterFearing, he interrupted the cycle by guiding me to focus on what mattered NOW.

Before I knew it, the saddle was on. Marley was quiet and relaxed. While we didn't have a stopwatch, my sense was that it took less time doing it the "patient way." I had a flash of many moments in my life where I had rushed, only to end up having it take longer. Going back to redo poorly done steps eats time like a piranha.

Thanks to our methodical go-slow-to-go-fast approach, Marley was calm and ready to ride. I was calm and ready to ride. Just a small dose of patience had kept our energies at a simmer. It was a much better place to start.

Interestingly to me (and obviously to Bruce), the Finding the Middle exercise made my shift from Mistake Cycle to What's Next Cycle happen more quickly.

The next step would challenge my What's Next Cycle. Bruce knew I would be feeling the something-feels-off sensation of my Negative/Positive Pole throughout this ride. He wanted me to have many opportunities to send the cycle down this path:

1. Physical Sensation: Something feels off.
2. Conscious Story: What's Next? What is the horse or situation telling me I need to do?
3. Unconscious Story: Don't have to listen to the voices from the past because I'm not the one in control here.
4. Emotion: Curiosity, interest, acceptance.
5. Wish: USE the sensation so I can solve this problem.
6. Action: Keep recalibrating and playing warmer/colder as the solution draws near.

My first challenge: How to get on the horse. Bruce didn't have a mounting block nearby. He suggested I work out how to mount from the bumper of the pickup truck. Lynn on Screen 1 threatened to take over. *"Seriously? What kind of operation is this? A truck?"* Then the second thought. *"Wait, Lynn, come back. Maybe you can do this."* This moment of coming back would become the most essential lesson of all.

Lynn on Screen 2 looked at the situation as a problem to be solved.

Did I mention that once again the saddle was no saddle at all, but a bareback pad with no stirrups? Or that we were out in the open near the road, no fences to contain a runaway horse anywhere? Or that we were about to ride through the woods with this poor excuse for a saddle on the horse? None of that mattered quite yet. First, I had to get Marley to move his feet in the sequence that would put him in a place where I could throw a leg over. I had to work out how to do that while standing on the bumper, feet lined up front to back as if I were on a slalom ski. At least that part felt familiar. So did the current shooting through my body, indicating something was off!

The Froth bubbled up. *"This is not how you get on a horse!" "What if he runs off after you get on?" "What makes you think you can balance well enough to get your leg over?" "What if you fall?"* My hands shook and my thoughts spiraled into my past programming, yet somehow, I stayed in the Froth.

Bruce asked me first to stand on the bumper, Marley's reins in hand. "Can you do that?" Yes – it seemed slightly uncomfortable – but I could do it. Breaking it down to Frames.

"OK, now, where would Marley need to be for you to get on?" Another Frame in the picture. "OK, now, where would he need to move his feet first in order for him to be in that position?" Another Frame. "OK, now, what's next?" Frame by Frame, I applied the amount of pressure that encouraged Marley to move into position. No more, no less. Marley told me how much pressure to apply through his actions. Slowly, my breath returned, my thoughts reconnected to the NOW and my hands steadied.

Marley stood quietly, right where I needed him to be. However, it was a bit of a leap to throw my leg over. Bruce continued, "Whenever you are ready." I summoned just enough freedom to release my leg from the bumper and swing it over his back.

"Slowly, my breath returned, my thoughts reconnected to the NOW and my hands steadied."

I was on.

He took a step or two and I asked him to whoa. Silently, I thanked Lynn for all the lessons on keeping a balanced seat and how to sit so the horse understood "whoa." My muscle memory also understood "whoa." My old fear-based reaction would have sent my energy soaring, made my legs clamp his sides, and my hands grip the reins. In other words, my fear would have created the very thing it was trying to avoid. We would have been running for the nearby road. In this moment, I savored a moment of satisfaction: At this level pressure, I had learned to stop a horse.

More importantly, I had done the What's Next Cycle. I had many more moments to come as I toggled back and forth between the Mistake Cycle and the What's Next Cycle.

The Flywheels

Both the Mistake and What's Next cycles act much like the flywheel made popular by Jim Collins in his book *Good to Great* and in the follow-up *Turning the Flywheel, A Monograph to Accompany Good to Great*. In these two works, he used the flywheel analogy to drive home the point that great companies became great and stayed great because they kept applying energy into a well-designed flywheel that netted excellent business results. Flywheels are essentially energy storage devices. Whether in my car or on my potter's wheel, a flywheel keeps the momentum going smoothly in the physical world. At first, it takes a lot of energy to get a flywheel going. After a few full turns, it gets easier and easier to turn the wheel.

Collins broke down business flywheels into a distinct set of actions that led to consistent replication, if a business were disciplined enough to keep applying energy into a well-designed flywheel. Once the flywheel gets moving, the stored energy keeps it moving with much less effort applied than at the beginning, as long as the business leaders did not get caught in what he called the doom loop.

In the doom loop, business leaders start grasping for something big and new. They over- or under correct. They careen between trying this initiative and that project, hoping something will interrupt the downward spiral. With their lack of discipline, they end up fueling the same bad results over and over again.

While he never called it a flywheel, Bruce was helping me see my own doom loop in my Mistake Cycle and a more effective way to use pressure in my What's Next Cycle. In Collins' work, both the flywheel and doom loop are self-perpetuating cycles. The difference comes down to knowing the steps and discipline to stick with the well-designed flywheel.

The Mistake Cycle and the What's Next Cycle self-perpetuate as well. In my case, The Mistake Cycle had established its own momentum from the energy I unwittingly applied each time I experienced the something-was-off signal.

The perpetuity aspect of the flywheel is its hallmark. Collins explains in the business flywheel that each step, which represents a loop, leads to the next. The energy of the flywheel keeps the momentum going almost without effort, as one loop builds on another as each moment of truth piles on the next.

Here's how I put together the steps of my own Mistake Cycle or in Collins' words, doom loop:

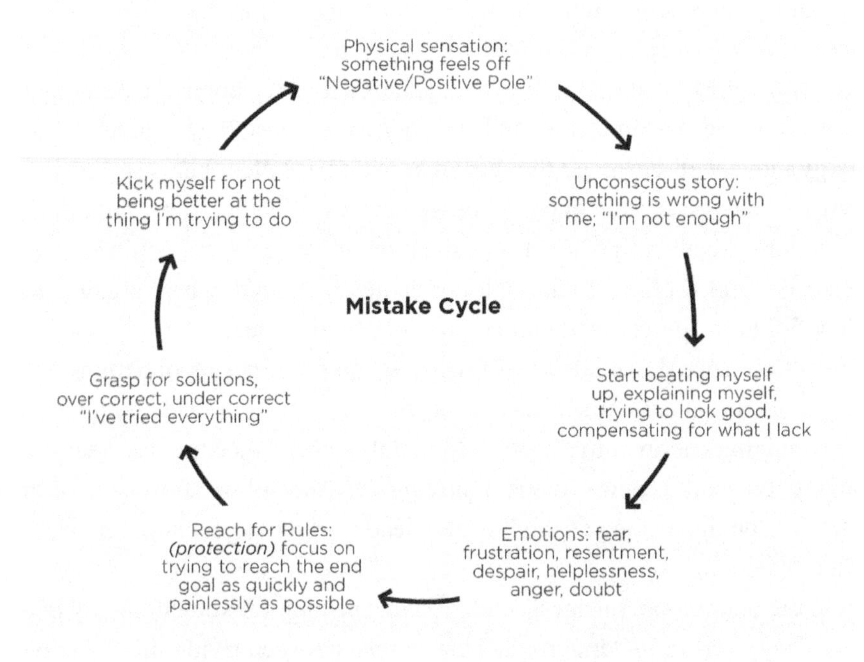

Now, here I was with a fully energized flywheel from a lifetime of practicing my very own personal Mistake Cycle. This thing spun at max speed with little effort. The slightest sensation of something being off sent my mind and my actions into these steps; the little scientist of my childhood had established that THIS was the way to survive in the world. My compensations came in the form of straight A's, being a good little girl, striving for perfection, of proving myself in every venue. I mostly hid the emotions and just got after it to achieve a goal.

So many times, Bruce had pointed out that I had either over- or under corrected. He witnessed me grasp at straws with the unconscious expectation that stopping the sensation would somehow solve the problem. He saw me stuck in my past, focusing more on trying to be good enough rather than in staying with what was happening in the here and now and seeing a different solution.

The What's Next Cycle would need a lot of energy applied to replace the Mistake Cycle. I would need to understand each step and apply it diligently:

Never while I was in the process of mounting Marley did the physical sensations stop. However, with Bruce's guidance, I harnessed the "something-is-off" sensations to break down the process into small steps that I COULD handle. But first, I had to have that moment when I went to Lynn on Screen 1 asking, *"What kind of operation is this?"* The most important moment of all is the interruption, where I pivoted from the old but highly energized Mistake Cycle to the What's Next Cycle. The magic of the interruption comes from not seeing the need to pivot as a Mistake, but as a gateway to raising my Pressure Threshold. The moment on Screen 1 used to be the thing I most wanted to avoid, because I would have to acknowledge

I was not perfect. The next step was naturally to beat myself up, thus giving back the treasure of the momentary opportunity to create something new. Now the moment was my signal to interrupt the old way and chart a new neural pathway.

> "The magic of the interruption comes from not seeing the need to pivot as a Mistake, but as a gateway to raising my Pressure Threshold."

Once I was on and Marley was still and quiet, Bruce said, "Well done." More importantly, I allowed myself to feel the sensation of "well done" before we moved on. After months and months of wanting to ride, I was finally on. And Marley was not just any horse. The little girl who in fourth grade read *The Black Stallion* books was sitting on a bareback pad on the great grandson of Cass Ole, the very horse that played the Black Stallion in the movie.

Holding Space

We would cycle through What's Next many times over the next hour. At each questionable juncture, the Mistake Cycle offered its highly energized support. Bruce interrupted my inner ventures into the land of self-doubt with a question, bringing me back to the moment, where I could reach for skills I already had. Using my "whoa" was just one of the many lessons I had learned that would be applied on this ride.

Some of those lessons came many years before in my facilitator training – but as is often the case, I didn't really get it until more pressure was on the line. Holding space would be the next lesson.

Back in my banking days, I brought in consultants to provide extensive facilitator training for my team and for me. In one particularly difficult session, the teacher said, "One of your jobs as a facilitator is to hold the space for the participants to come to their own conclusions." My initial thought was to stick my finger in my throat in a mock gag reflex. Obviously, this guy had never worked in a bank or in the kind of dog-eat-dog world in which I was operating. Of course, I didn't literally put my finger in my throat, but I did offer to educate him. "We just don't do things like that around here. We tell them what to do and they have to do it."

In that phase of my career, I had yet to learn that leading by fear, intimidation, and force doesn't lead to real change, commitment, or buy-in. Instead, it creates a form of compliance that has the appearance of success. Except, it's merely an illusion. Test it under pressure and it collapses like a pile of cotton candy in a rainstorm.

The teacher was unfazed by my resistance, and lo and behold, in a few months, I was facilitating incredibly difficult, strategic projects full of recalcitrant bankers doing everything in their power to keep the status quo while pretending to buy in to the changes we were making. Holding the space for me had indeed allowed me to learn to hold space for others.

Over the years, holding space became second nature in many of my facilitation projects, both inside the bank and after I started my own company.

It was these lessons with the horses that showed me that my ability to hold space had a clear pressure threshold. Beyond it, I went back to my force and fear methods.

Force and fear were not the way Bruce was teaching me to ride. Learning to listen, hear, and allow the horse to tell me what to do, when to do, how to do was how he was setting the conditions for me to learn to ride in partnership, not domination.

When I stopped Marley after two steps, Bruce said, "Well done. Now let's go take the trail to the pasture next door." Yay! We were finally out of the round pen and walking around on the trails on Bruce's property. I was on Marley! Bruce walked alongside as he asked me questions. "What's your number?" "Left rein, left leg. Move the energy to the side." "Pick a point and ride to it. Keep the Picture of each point clearly in your mind."

Marley's energy was high, sending mine through the treetops. Yet just checking in with it allowed it to drop back to a simmer. Giving it a number gave me the power to change it, simply through awareness. When I settled, so did Marley.

After a short walk through the woods and over a small bridge, we arrived next door at the pasture where several other horses resided, including Marley's dam. Bruce alerted me that the other horses would run along the fence line. When one horse runs, they all want to run. Bruce said, "He's either going to look to you or to them for leadership. Make sure he looks to you." The little girl part of me envisioned the scene in *The Black Stallion* movie, galloping on the beach with my hands in the air. The grown-up version of me thought better of it. I kept a clear picture of "Walk" as we made our way alongside the pasture with the horses, who indeed, did take off, looking so graceful as they ran across the pasture.

We reached the end of the fence line, where Bruce kept the horse feed. My job was to find a comfortable place to stand with Marley while Bruce filled the food and water troughs. The idea was for Marley to stand patiently, and my patience would deeply inform his patience. All this while Marley watched food get doled out to his fellow horses.

Without much space to stand out of the South Carolina July sun, we ended up close enough to the horses on the other side of the fence that Marley wanted to pull his head toward them. I had seen enough horse play to be aware that nuzzling could lead to biting, could lead to kicking, could lead to more running. It was in the best interest of my safety for Marley to keep his head away from the biting power of the other horses.

I could feel the bubble of my spirit level moving off center. The electrical charge running through me risked sending messages to Marley that he should be concerned. The pressure was high enough that I was becoming quite concerned.

At first, every time Marley turned his head toward the other horses, I yanked him back to center. After repeating this a few times, I realized that the horse was much stronger than me and more committed to his game than he was to changing his course of action based on my corrections. Bruce wasn't saying a word about what I should do or not do to solve this problem. He just went about his business, filling water troughs.

It was time to use my Tools. I took a deep breath and relaxed. The horse was showing me how much pressure he needed to stop the unwanted behavior. The problem was that my strength could not match his. I would run out of strength to force the matter long before Marley would.

The typical patterns of Lynn on Screen 1 at a moment like this would be to either go helpless (the child-like victim) or beat myself up (standing in for the overbearing parent). Sometimes I did both. This time, I just kept looking at the problem. Admittedly, I first had a moment where I felt helpless and looked to Bruce to rescue me. Focusing on the problem kept me distracted from feeling out of control. Screen 2 offered solutions if I could just find them.

Finally, I held the reins firmly, rather than allowing him to pull them out of my hand and then trying (and failing) to bring his head back. He could turn his head, but it would be uncomfortable. Pretty quickly, he returned his head to center. He would stand like that for a few seconds and then the temptation would be too much for him.

He turned his head again. I held my position again. No yanking, no correcting. My actions spoke this message, "Here is where I'm holding the reins. You can figure out where you want to hold your head. Up to you."

Within a minute, he was able to stand still, centered, and relaxed.

When I held the space, he made the choice to be comfortable.

The rest of the ride offered more moments. We walked through the woods where there was no trail and where Marley stepped on a rein. We walked alongside a different pasture where the horses were tempting Marley to run. We walked along the boundary between the deep woods and pasture, where the scary things come out at night. I could feel Marley checking in with me at each moment, asking the question, "Are we OK?" I checked in with myself: Negative Pole goes up; pivot from freak out to breathe; pause and solve the problem; reset myself back to center; reassure my horse. Walk on.

As we neared the area where I would dismount, Bruce validated my sense that Marley was checking in with me with an added twist. I had just said out loud "It seems Marley is checking in with me." No sooner than the words had left my mouth, the other horses started creating quite a ruckus. Suddenly, one of them kicked the gate. It sounded like a gun shot. If I had been a horse, I would have taken off running for the hills. My job was to keep the horse under me from doing the same. The chaos was over in a flash, and we were still walking calmly. Bruce said, "Marley did check in with you. He's asking if you are worthy." I came back with, "Worthy of what?" Bruce replied, "Worthy of being his leader."

As we debriefed the many moments, Bruce pointed out that I had survived every one of them. I wondered out loud why he had kept filling water buckets when I struggled keeping Marley away from the other horses. The question itself pointed out that small-child part of me who still wanted him to teach me and tell me what to do. He answered "You were the one feeling what was happening with him. I was not in your position. How could I know what to do when I'm not the one up there?"

While I was holding space for Marley, Bruce was holding space for me. In other words, Bruce chose to take a Power With approach as I solved the problem. He did not choose to do Power Over by having answers, and his approach gave me a chance to step out of Power Under into my own ability to work through the situation. It's the same approach he uses when working with a horse. He allows the horse to work out the answer to the question, which leads both horse and human to a feeling of trusting themselves to handle whatever comes.

With each opportunity to solve a problem by letting the situation tell me what to do –without beating myself up – I ran the flywheel of What's Next and reset my pressure threshold up by a few tiny ratchets.

> **"Bruce chose to take a Power With approach as I solved the problem. He did not choose to do Power Over by having answers, and his approach gave me a chance to step out of Power Under into my own ability to work through the situation."**

The Path is Never Straight

Before long, I had an opportunity to test myself on Scotty. You may remember that Scotty, the finely tuned Ferrari of a horse, belongs to Daryl. She was thrilled that I was choosing to really learn to ride. We both had visions of riding on her trails together, me on Scotty and she on one of her other three highly trained dressage horses. By now, I had learned enough about horses and my reactions when horses did unexpected things to realize that THE horse Mocha was a much simpler horse to ride than Scotty. If Scotty is a race car, Mocha is your average Mom-mobile.

With my success riding Marley, also more race car than not, I decided to try riding Scotty again. By this time, I had come to recognize that the first ride on Scotty a couple of years before had been a warning signal. Everything I was learning had been packed into that one experience. My lack of awareness about riding. My overconfidence in my skills. My inability to read the horse. My proving mindset. My pressure threshold.

We started in the arena, doing a lot of groundwork. We focused on the relationship and helping me learn to connect with him and read when he was not connected to me. The last thing Daryl wanted was for my lack of training to interfere with the impeccable training she had done with Scotty.

After many sessions on the ground, we did a short ride out with just the two of us. Several times during the ride, Daryl had to remind me to relax, sit back, and breathe. While riding, I felt Scotty's energy coming up. Quickly, my mind would call up visions of the accident, envisioning Scotty suddenly running off while my butt was landing on the ground. With this fear in the forefront, I tightened up, leaned forward, and got all clutchy with the reins. But now, thanks to all the work with Bruce and Lynn, with Daryl's reminders, I was able to regain my seat and breathe.

The second time on the trail with Scotty, Daryl's husband David joined us, so we had three horses. Given our success on the first ride, my confidence was high – perhaps a little too high. As we headed out, everything felt the same as the first time. Except not quite.

At the very beginning, I noticed that he didn't really stop when I asked him to a couple of times. Wanting to stay with the pack and "not be a bother," I let it go.

We had crept over my pressure threshold, but I didn't know it yet.

We weaved in and out of the lower trails and things were mostly OK. When we started going up the big trail to go over the mountain, I noticed him aggressively getting up on the other horses, even pinning his ears and nipping butts. Not good.

After a few hundred feet, I asked him to slow down and then to stop. He kept going. We did several full 360 turns. I settled down and he settled down.

He would be OK for a while and then he started with the tailgating and nipping again.

Now my Negative Pole was going up and my adrenaline was going with it. My inner guidance system was telling me something was off, and my adrenaline was telling Scotty that he should be worried.

He got worried.

Scotty is a super-sensitive horse. There was not a lot of room for error.

As we were going up an especially steep hill, I leaned forward to help keep us in balance – probably way too far forward. While my intention was to help him balance, my body position told him, "Let's go fast." He broke into a gait and then a canter. I did NOT want to go fast!

This was my moment of truth. Would the pressure be too great for me to use my Tools? Or would I be able to bring him around and settle him back down?

With some coaching from Daryl, we were able to get him back to a walk and move nicely across the top of the ridge. As we stood there looking at the beautiful views in the distance, we started talking about the plan for the walk down the mountain.

Just the thought of it raised my adrenaline, and of course, Scotty picked up on that right away. He started moving before I asked. Suddenly, something that seemed well within my abilities brought a much higher level of pressure than before.

We were now WAY over my pressure threshold. I was no longer in the Froth. My ability to learn was compromised. It was time to shift from raising my mental Tools to taking steps to lower the pressure.

I dismounted Scotty and we walked together for a few minutes. Given all the groundwork we had done together, we both immediately relaxed. He and I walked down the hill, and at every natural remounting spot, I listened. I gave myself the gift of patience. I breathed. Eventually, we walked into the barn, me still on the ground.

A part of me felt like a failure. But another part saw the wisdom in walking Scotty down the hill instead of riding him.

When debriefing this incident with Bruce, he pointed to the wisdom side of the dilemma. "Did you not read your Negative Pole accurately? Did you not read HIS Negative Pole accurately? Did you not take the correct action to balance your poles? What would have happened if you had decided to let the past interfere, making you choose to prove yourself rather than listen and hear and use your tools? In this case, the pressure was greater than your mental tools. And you responded appropriately. Give yourself credit for that."

There I was, at another moment of truth, another opportunity to dance the tightrope. Scotty and I might have made it down the hill safely. We might have had an accident. How I chose to see it would matter much more than what actually happened. Was it a failure? Or was it invaluable learning?

Choosing to lower the pressure is sometimes the only way through a situation. We cannot always raise our Tools, especially if we are outside of the Froth. I'm not going to say I didn't beat myself up a bit over this. I really wanted to be ready to ride Scotty on the trail.

But wanting and becoming are two different things.

It would be another year before I was ready to be out on the trail with Scotty.

CHAPTER TWELVE

The Froth is My Friend

The Healing Nature of the Heat

Through these different moments of truth, I became aware that the tiny shifts I had been making for the past two and a half years were definitely changing my response to pressure. It's not as if I suddenly was a totally new person. I didn't always reach for my Tools. I still had plenty of moments where I sent my energy to the flywheel of my Rules, seeking to avoid the mistake and prove myself.

However, more of ME was shining through, especially in moments of pressure. "People's world" felt like it had less of a hold on my soul. Mistakes did not trigger me as often or as deeply. When I felt my Negative/Positive Pole fire up, I turned in to the heat, welcoming it as a transformational force.

Fire burns and it also cooks. Fire destroys and it also liberates. Fire transforms wood to ash and ash to soil and soil to plants and plants to food. Fire is death. Fire is life.

Fire became my metaphor for pressure.

We humans have a complex relationship with fire. One of the first survival skills one living off the land must have is the ability to build a fire. The flames and heat not only offer warmth and a means by which to cook a meal; in the wilderness, fire offers protection from visitors in the night who might mean us harm.

On the other hand, fire unleashed decimates everything in its path. We've seen out-of-control forest fires rage through thousands of acres and through towns and neighborhoods. Even then, fire offers a fresh start.

In the early years of the National Park System, fire was deemed universally bad and fire suppression became official policy. Both manmade and fires caused naturally by lightning were put out with the assumption that fire caused only harm. Over the years, the National Park Service began to realize that fire was actually a natural event, and it had a role in clearing underbrush and dead vegetation, opening certain types of seeds, creating a fresh start for many plants and wildlife and otherwise cultivating a healthy forest. Our human reaction to help actually interfered with nature's way.

Changing the understanding of the role of fire in a healthy forest (and planet) changed the response to fire. Official policy changed to account for the need for fire to burn in order for a forest to remain healthy.

Now I was a year into riding lessons and two and a half years past my accident. The horses, with the guidance of Bruce and Lynn, were showing me more distinctions about balance. Much like the National Park Service understanding that man's interference created an imbalance that damaged nature, I was discovering that many of the imbalances within me and around me could be changed. I had more choices than I had seen before.

Ironically, I had an exchange with someone I barely knew somewhere in this time frame. She had heard about my accident and knew I was relearning how to ride. We got around to talking about our work and hobbies and her love of horses, and at some point, she looked at me and said, "Wow, you do a lot. How can you get good at any of those things?"

Her question took me back at first. After all, I'm the coach who tells people that focus is critical. Then something crucial hit me, and I said, "I'm not really doing a bunch of things. … I'm not rowing, or throwing pottery, or coaching, or skiing or riding or painting. I'm doing one thing. I'm working on myself under pressure."

What I didn't say was as important as what I said. I didn't say, "I'm learning to stop a horse," or "I'm learning how to ride without mistakes," or even "I'm learning to deal with my fears."

Looking back on it, this exchange fell into the adage, "Be careful what you wish for. You just may get it."

I didn't know it yet, but I would come to believe the accident was one of best things that ever happened to me. The past two and a half years prepared me for the heat of 2020, as it invited me to a roaring bonfire, with the potential to burn off the underbrush of my old Rules, beliefs and assumptions.

The invitation was NOT engraved.

Nope. This invitation came in the form of pressure from every direction, with lots of opportunities to make mistakes, to fail, to beat myself up, and to otherwise perpetuate my Rules. Or I could reach for my Tools.

The next six to eight months, I faced pressure on every front. Just as the world was about to be shut down with the COVID-19 pandemic, my dad left this Earth for his eternal journey.

While I continued my work with horses, challenges arose in every domain – from family, to my coaching practice to my water skiing and my art. Every type of pressure brought the potential to either crush or elevate me.

One core insight gave me the freedom to welcome the heat.

Pressure is a Catalyst, Not a Test

All the complexity of the past two and a half years boiled down to turning one huge assumption on its head. And like wood blocks in a game of Jenga™, a whole cascade of old assumptions and beliefs came tumbling down after.

Pressure is not a test. Pressure is a catalyst.

Pressure IS the leverage that brings me closer to my true nature.

My old way took me out of the heat as a way to prepare for the heat. Whether in my home or at a retreat, I meditated, journaled, reflected, and worked on my skills. All of these methods are excellent ways to prepare for pressure. However, I've learned something essential on this Pressure Journey: Nothing substitutes for the choices I make while under pressure.

My new way was to turn in to the pressure as the way I would learn, reach for my Tools, and keep recalibrating.

In other words, the heat of pressure offers the opportunity to burn off the armor of my old patterns, beliefs, and assumptions and discover new possibilities. It's not a test to ace. Pressure is the catalyst – for learning, growing, and becoming.

Pressure elevates me if I stay present and choose to welcome it.

However, pressure creates discomfort.

A quote usually attributed to Viktor Frankl says, "Between stimulus and response there is a space. In that space is our power to choose our response. In our response lies our growth and our freedom."

The world of choice happens in that discomforting space – a tiny little moment in time when I can reach for my Tools or revert to the flywheel of my Mistake Cycle. The moment I feel pressure – whether it's a one or a ten on a scale of one to ten, I'm in the Froth. The level of discomfort doesn't matter. My automatic, robotic response is to make the discomfort go away. It's not necessary for me to consciously think "mistake" for the robot to run me.

It takes effort to take the controls from the robot. No longer did I have to think of things happening to me. With this insight, I could see pressure and things not going my way as happening for me. Then the Jenga™ blocks started falling.

The first block to fall was my story about the physical sensation of pressure.

When Bruce said on the very first day, "It's not the horse, it's the pressure created by the horse," I was confused. *"Of course, it's the horse! Can't you see, he's right there, either doing or not doing what I've asked him to do. He can kick me, he can bite me, and he can do nothing when I want him to do something,"* I thought.

Bruce said the same about every kind of pressure.

- It's not the boss, it's the pressure created by the boss.
- It's not the problem, it's the pressure created by the problem.
- It's not the traffic jam, it's the pressure created by the traffic jam.

Now I saw it. No, FELT it differently.

- It's not the horse, it's the feeling I get inside when the horse doesn't do what I asked him to do.
- It's not the boss, it's the feeling I get inside when the boss says, "We need to talk about your performance."
- It's not the problem, it's the feeling I get inside when the problem interferes with things going smoothly.
- It's not the traffic jam, it's the feeling I get inside when the traffic jam makes me late.

The pressures are endless and so are the stories I tell about them. Pressure evokes the emotions that act like glue, holding the past in place. When the old emotions rise to the surface, I can either do the same thing I have always done – or – I can choose a new story, a new action, a different way of being. In other words, pressure is a solvent that loosens the glue of the emotions. It's like pressure opens a portal to my personal change. Pressure creates the opportunity to tell a new story.

The story I had been telling about the feeling was the thing that was off.

The feeling was not a test, it was a signal. When I labeled the feeling as anxiety, avoidance appeared to be my only option. When I labeled the feeling as a signal, it opened my curiosity to listen, discover, reach for my Tools, and ask the pivotal question: What's Next?

Perhaps I was becoming someone who could run into the fire. Firefighters run into the blaze, and they can do so because they have the tools to fight the fire. The firefighters have blankets that shield them from the heat, especially if the fire overtakes them. However, they only deploy the blanket when the heat of the fire is greater than their tools to extinguish the fire. My Rules are like my own personal firefighter blanket, shielding me from the heat. But if I deploy the armor all the time, I lose the benefit of the heat – its ability to transform me. I could let my Rules become the last resort, not the first resort.

The rest of the blocks were simply a shift in my story.

New story: The pressure is the catalyst.
Old story: Pressure is a test.

New story: The feeling means I have something to learn.
Old story: The feeling means I'm making a mistake.

New story: When something happens that looks like a problem or a challenge, I welcome it because the heat will allow me to rewrite the past.
Old story: When something happens that looks like a problem or a challenge, I want it to go away, rush through the steps to get to the end.

New story: I keep the portal open by assuming positive intent. Whatever is happening is happening FOR me, not happening to me.
Old story: I close the portal when I want to prove myself, to make whatever is happening TO me stop.

New story: The source of the pressure can tell me what to do, when to do, how to do in the present moment.

Old story: I have the answers for what to do in the present moment.

New story: Play the game of Warmer/Colder to rebalance my Negative/Positive Pole.

Old story: Over - and underreact to get to the end.

New story: Build trust and connection through listening and give-and-take, seek Power With not Over and Under.

Old story: Command and control, seek either Power Over or Power Under

New story: Break the picture down to smaller and smaller frames, so that IN doing the work, I'm unleashing my Tools.

Old story: Rush to get to the end so I can feel good about myself.

New story: The point of all of this is to build more inner capacity.

Old story: The point of all of this is to allow the end product to define me.

New story: Problems are a gift designed to unleash the true me.

Old story: Problems are to be avoided because they reveal the less-than-perfect parts about me.

New story: Pressure elevates me.

Old story: Pressure crushes me.

Perception may be one of our most powerful Tools. The story I tell about what I observe matters as much, if not more, than the "facts" in front of me. Nothing is personal. Proving myself only builds more armor. If I'm to build more inner capacity, I need to give up the need for certainty, control, and answers.

Rules are Automatic; Tools are Fluid

My opportunity to raise my pressure threshold only happened when things didn't go as planned. Now I see mistakes as a key to open a doorway to another room. I can choose to enter the doorway if I want. I can also choose to stay right where I am.

Michelangelo said, "Beauty is the purgation of superfluities. Every block of stone has a statue inside it, and it is the task of the sculptor to discover it."

So, it is with the Tools. They are unleashed. They are sculpted. They appear when the Rules get in the way. The new dimension offers discomfort, upheaval, and pokes holes in my understanding of the world. It reveals that what I thought to be true might not be true. The new dimension chips away the imposed Rules of my conditioning to unleash my Tools.

Perhaps an even better analogy is how diamonds are formed with heat and pressure. The Tools are unleashed – with heat and pressure.

For some reason, I've always thought of the problems at work as balls. Perhaps it's because of the cliches like; "The ball's in your court," or "Keep your eye on the ball," or "It's a whole different ball game," or my least favorite, "You dropped the ball."

When driving home after my first ride with Marley, I realized I was in a whole different ball game. This was so different; it was like another room – or a doorway to another dimension. Bruce loved adding pressure and throwing problems at me because it was in solving those problems under pressure that I would become. I had always thought that "becoming" happened in practice and the performing under pressure proved it. He turned that idea on its head.

Life is the canvas on which we become through the problems we face.

In keeping with my ball analogy, the new dimension is like living in a world with two different kinds of ball machines.

Just for the sake of this illustration, picture a ball-throwing machine, sending tennis balls, baseballs, and softballs at you. The machine doesn't have many settings, so the balls will come in three sizes and in three speeds, always from the same direction as the machine.

With a little bit of time and practice, you will get very good at catching those balls. When the machine is set on low and a softball shoots out of the machine, you would have an easy time catching it. When the machine is really cranked up and about to send a baseball your way, you might grab a glove to catch it.

Over time, you will know every signal those balls send. The sound of a tennis ball versus a baseball will land on skilled ears. Your fingers will close differently on a softball versus a baseball.

With enough practice, you will be so good at catching those balls that you will be able to do it subconsciously. You've come to know the pattern and have developed your own pattern for success. Catching those balls will become an automatic skill. You will KNOW how to catch them each and every time because you have a learned rule for that.

For the balls that slip by, you have developed a thick skin, sort of like armor. The balls you don't catch never touch you.

You have thousands – if not millions – of Rules that tell you how to automatically deal with the situations that push your buttons. By now, those Rules are unconscious; you just do them, whether they work or not.

Now imagine a world of infinite balls coming at you. Instead of three variations, the types of balls are limitless. Imagine everything from a giant blow-up beach ball to a tiny ball as thin as a bubble machine might make. It's a world of millions of balls and millions of possibilities, and combinations.

In this new world, not only are the types of balls endless, but so are the speeds. They could be coming blindingly fast, or they may float just out of reach. They may change speed in the middle of the path. In fact, they could even change their path.

The balls of this second world can come from anywhere at any time. Because you never know where they are coming from – or when they are coming or how fast they are coming or even whether they will pop if you grab them too hard or hurt if you don't have a glove – you will respond to the balls in this world in a totally new way.

Rather than using your unconscious Rules, you will need to be much more aware. You will have to tune in and pay attention so you can catch the balls you want to catch and allow all the others to drop by the wayside.

In this new world, Tools help you much more than Rules. You will always be learning.

You will drop balls, make mistakes, and face rejection as you shed your Rules. You will fail, and your mistakes and failures will build your Tools and expand your repertoire. The options are unlimited as long as you keep learning.

Rules are automatic; Tools are fluid. When we face pressure, our first choice is whether to react (Rules) or respond (Tools). Rules allow us to react – and sometimes that is exactly what is needed.

Tools allow us to respond in the present moment to precisely what is needed in that moment. Reaching for our Tools opens up our repertoire, giving us something better to do than build more armor.

When unexpected things get thrown at us and uncertainty builds, and things are not going according to plan and people are not behaving in beneficial ways, Rules tend to miss the mark, because they were designed for a different time and circumstance. That's when we need our Tools to solve the problem.

Tools allow you to solve problems you've never seen before and create new solutions for old problems where our Rules have failed us.

CHAPTER THIRTEEN
The Art of Living

Pulling it Together

Working with Bruce's system over the past couple of years offered a maddening paradox. I had answers while at the same time I had no answers. From the minute he started describing his system in the first phone call, I could track with what he described. He was a practical scientist, sharing what he had discovered empirically over the years. So, when he went through the pieces, they lined up with my experience and that of the brain science of dealing with the survival mode of mammals.

Yet my insight that pressure is the catalyst, not a test, did not line up with the experience of the clients I brought to work with Bruce. Time after time, I brought them to Camden for a daylong session outdoors with the horses, excited for them to experience working on fear, being better under pressure, and learning to develop trust and connection. Time after time I left the session hearing Bruce say the same things over and over again. *"When will he ever say something new!?!" Time after time, the clients told me some version of the same thing: "It felt like I was in a test. I can tell there is a system there, and if I could just figure out the system, then I would be able to give him the right answers."*

They wanted definitions of the terms, such as Picture, Frame, Negative/ Positive Pole, Mental Tools, and Conduit. They wanted instructions on how to tie a halter, and work with a lead rope, and understand the inner workings of a lariat.

Initially, I explained away their frustration as part of Bruce's method. I believed it was a one-off, nothing to worry about. However, I recalled a lesson from many years before. The teacher in one of my facilitator training sessions gave some guidance to those of us who were struggling to decipher which feedback we should ignore and accept. He said, "Look, if one person calls you a horse's ass, it's probably about them. If six people call you a horse's ass, it's time to saddle up."

Given that we were up to six clients struggling with the same belief about the pressure test, I realized it was time to saddle up. (Notwithstanding the fact that Bruce would not let me saddle up for the longest time!)
One day, with a client having his first session, we started as always with a porch session. I had brought my iPad and pencil to take notes. Bruce went through the same spiel he had done many times before. Instead of internally bemoaning the repetition, I listened with the ears of a beginner. Soon, my pen started moving, as a picture began to emerge on the tablet. Over the next hour or so, the following drawing came together:

"

Instead of internally bemoaning the repetition, I listened with the ears of a beginner. Soon, my pen started moving, as a picture began to emerge on the tablet. Over the next hour or so, the following drawing came together..."

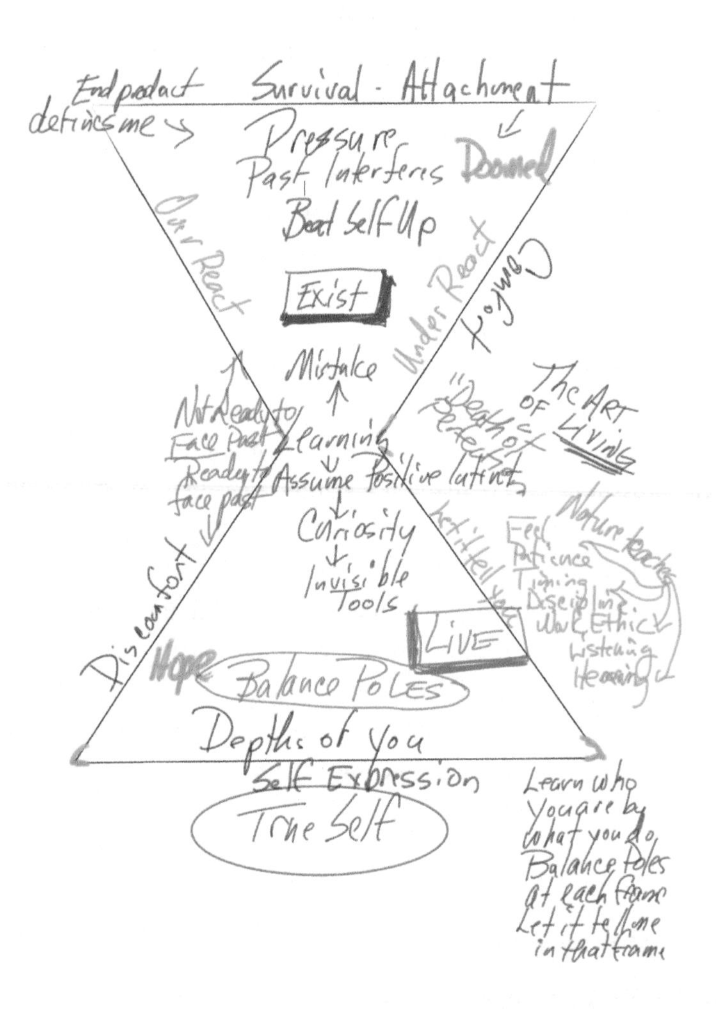

Finally, I had the beginnings of a "picture" of what I had been experiencing in this work. The quest to be "perfect" diagrammed at the top. The point of choice in the middle, offering a moment of truth to exist or live. The bottom depicting me living from my true center. Bruce's method put us through the bottom over and over again. Seeing it on paper made me welcome the agitation all the more.

What really stood out on this drawing were three things: The Art of Living, Exist, Or Live.

"What really stood out on this drawing were three things: The Art of Living, Exist, Or Live."

There it was, drawn by my own hand: the reason

I kept coming back, even though Bruce had been so slow to put me on the horse. I was chasing the option to live. To be fully alive while I was alive.

The Tools are as natural as the air we breathe. Curiosity, feel, timing, patience, discipline, observation, listening, hearing. I can imagine one of my ancestors, living in the pre-modern age. Perhaps he knew how to set a trap to catch dinner or gather fur for a coat. Living off the land, he didn't have Google to tell him where to find the animals. He watched. He waited. He discovered. He learned. He felt.

When his Negative Pole went up, it might have been because he realized the trap had failed. Or he had chosen the wrong place. Or he was being watched. He followed his instincts with a well-developed sense of the subtle cues of nature. He knew how to play the game of Warmer-Colder until he got it right. The same was true for those growing and gathering food. Where did the plants grow the best? When was the right time to plant? What kind of soil was needed? Knowledge of the land and the seasons was passed from one generation to the next and that knowledge was amplified in each generation until dawn of the modern age.

I'm old enough to remember our milk being delivered in glass bottles and our diapers being cloth held together with safety pins. When we left the house in our old cars, our parents usually had no way to contact us until we came back home. We got our news once or twice a day and then went out to play until it got dark.

Dang, I'm starting to sound like an old timer, "Remember the good ole days?" No, I'm not going to say we walked miles and miles to school in deep drifts of snow – but the modern age that was supposed to make our lives simpler and easier has taken us away from our nature.

We've outsourced almost every aspect of daily living that our ancestors did with their own hands. Grocery stores have replaced our gardens and cars have replaced our horses. For the past several thousand years, until about a hundred years ago, horses were the primary form of transportation. A family without a horse suffered huge disadvantages in living, much less surviving daily life.

Living in the natural world offers pressures that are often more consequential than the pressures of modern living. Nature's world demands that we respect it. The ocean, forest, and plains don't care if we are not up to the pressures of waves, weather, and wind. In nature's world, we reach for our Tools or die.

Man's world perverts our natural responses to its own end. Survival mode gets triggered in work settings and our brains at the deepest level don't know the difference between the threat of death and the threat of not getting the next promotion. We do what we must to show others we deserve to be there and quell the Homeless Sequence, which goes something like this: *I need this job. If something happens that threatens this job, I need to do everything in my power to keep this job, because if I lose it, I won't be able to pay my rent or buy food. If I can't pay my rent, I will end up homeless and then they will find me dead on the street in a dark, sad alley*. We feel the pressure and take it the wrong way.

If pressure is a test to show others we are good enough, we are doomed to live at the mercy of those whose approval we seek.

If pressure is a catalyst to unleash our true nature, we can truly live while we are alive.

The chicken scratch drawing eventually evolved into this:

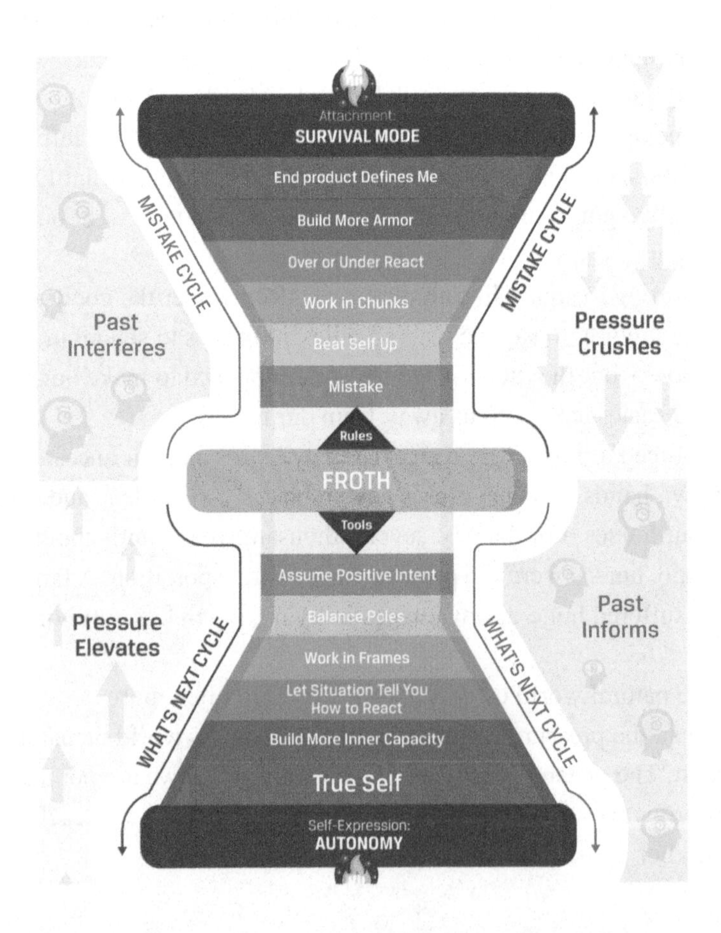

Over the next couple of years, I began to use this drawing with clients, both before and after they worked with Bruce. The simple choice point in the middle offered a clear picture of the challenge they faced when the pressure got high. More importantly, the bottom half showed a path to becoming mentally stronger, rather than mentally "scolded" on the path of the Mistake Cycle.

Research on breaking habits has taught us that stopping a behavior doesn't work. What works is starting a new behavior. I can attest to this practice. When I quit smoking many years ago, I began building model airplanes and needlepointing to give my antsy hands something better to do than reach for a cigarette.

The Mistake Cycle may have bigger consequences than smoking. It consumes the mind with all the ways we are no good, permeating our very being. The What's Next Cycle offers an alternative. We don't have to fix the Mistake Cycle. We simply have to turn in to the agitation of pressure to propel our energy into the What's Next flywheel.

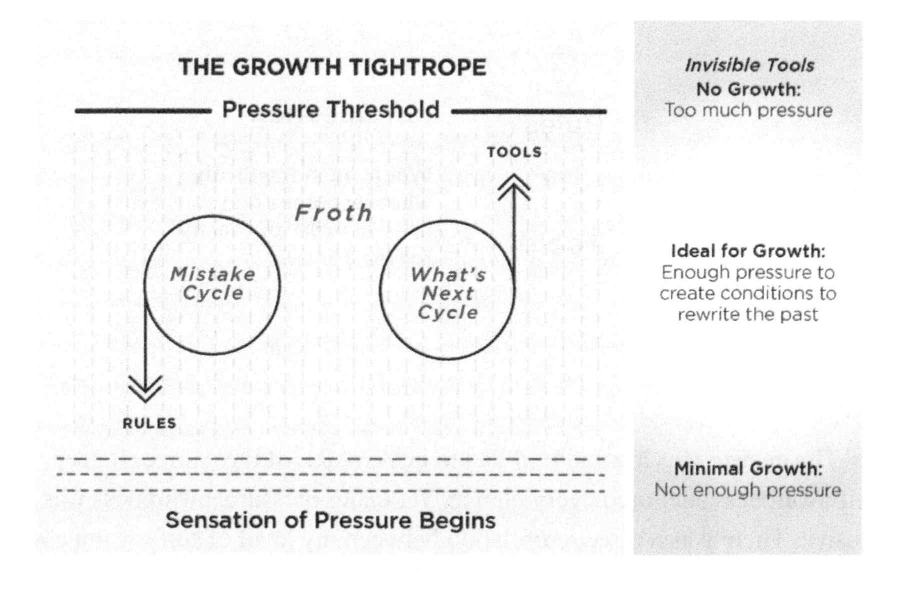

The Five C'S

Navigating the summer of 2020 gave me many chances to turn in to the heat. Having the picture of his method down on paper made a huge difference in being able to reach for my Tools when the pressure was high. The diagram became a central piece in my coaching with clients. I learned more about using pressure as a catalyst as I began bringing these insights to my clients. In doing so, I recognized yet one more missing piece. Or should I say missing pieces. In some ways, the journey had come full circle.

Just because we could clearly see and understand the difference between reaching for Rules versus Tools did not mean we could do it consistently. In that moment of choice, something else was at play.

That something else was tipping the scales in favor of doing things the old way. The Rules still ruled. Something in my Rules weighted the balance in choosing between Tools and Rules, especially when the pressure became greater than my mental tools.

But how? Why?

Rules
???
Tools

KEY QUESTION

When I'm in the Froth, what resources do I need in order to reach for my Tools?

The answer was a paradox. I had to be AWARE of the choice. Indeed, self-awareness anchored every choice. Yet under pressure, awareness was elusive. There was a direct correlation between my level of self-awareness and my ability to reach for my Tools under pressure.

How deep was I willing to dig?

It's one thing to change the story in my conscious mind and quite another to put that story into action when the pressure is intense. Remember, the

Rules are automatic. They live in the subconscious survival brain. The flywheel of the Mistake Cycle spins with a lifetime of stored energy. Making the difficult choice in the heat of the moment requires a higher standard of awareness from me.

Or should I say a deeper standard. If I were to gain more internal fitness and capacity, I had to acknowledge what the horses were showing me about myself.

Just because I was committed to change did not mean anything would truly change. Nope. Commitment may energize me to sign up for gym after my New Year's resolution, but I need much more to stay after it. Commitment is just the first level.

From the first moment I recognized that I need more self-awareness, and in all the wake-up calls I had over the years (remember my first ambulance ride where I thought no one else could do my job?), the question has always been: How deep am I willing to go to find the truth of who I am?

Parsing what is true about me versus what is part of my armor feels scarier than it really is. The Rules are born from fear, and they use fear like a perpetual motion machine. The armor of my Rules is all about protection, and I would argue that some Rules are necessary. Many years ago, when I took flying lessons, the rules of flying kept me safe. There was a checklist for everything from the pre-flight to starting the plane to how to recover from a stall. All those rules were the product of other pilots learning what works and doesn't when operating a vehicle that can fall from the sky. However, just following the rules doesn't make anyone a good pilot. Good judgment plays a critical role. The overconfident pilot who takes a plane up when the conditions are sketchy might discover the adage "It's a whole lot better to be on the ground wishing you were up there than it is to be up there wishing you were on the ground." On the other hand, the underconfident pilot who stays on the ground because of lack of trust in him- or herself to handle the inevitable surprises of flight is no pilot at all.

Unless we challenge the hidden fears in the Rules, we will use those fears to fix the fears, without being aware that we are stuffing those fears in the basement of our inner world. Releasing my armor involves developing self-awareness. No more fear hoarding! Self-awareness involves a constant cycle of going ever deeper to clear the basement of old musty fears that are no longer serving.

Here's where the paradox comes in. Trying to develop self-awareness alone is like standing in a bucket and trying to lift it up. The weight in the bucket and the strength of the person in the bucket offset each other and hold the bucket in place. The protective inner self will offset the seeking self, maintaining a sense of equilibrium, which perpetuates the same old pattern.

We need an outside mirror to help us see the truth of ourselves if we expect to bring our best to the journey.

While I cannot be my own mirror, I can bring a willingness to learn about myself.

Dancing the Tightrope involves developing a fair bit of self-awareness, through five stages of self-awareness.

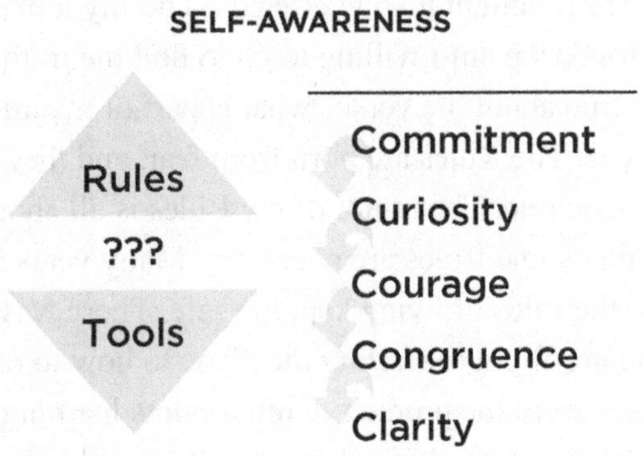

SELF-AWARENESS

Rules
???
Tools

Commitment
Curiosity
Courage
Congruence
Clarity

- **Commitment** – Want the truth. How willing am I to understand more about my inner self and my impact on others? *Chapter 14*
- **Curiosity** – Seek the truth. What's in there? What's out there? *Chapter 15*
- **Courage** – Face the truth. What will it take for me to face what's in there? What's out there? *Chapter 16*
- **Congruence** – Show my truth. What will it take for me to own what's in there? What's out there? *Chapter 17*
- **Clarity** – Live my truth. How can I begin to unleash what's true about me? How can I create the space for others to be true to themselves? *Chapter 18*

We can only allow others as much freedom as we allow ourselves. Armor locks us down. If we are locked down, we will lock down others, whether we mean to or not. We owe it to ourselves and our horses – and others – to open up to a dance where we each have a voice, where we give and take in a rich exchange of trust and connection.

In my story about Diane, I went through all of these levels in short order. Initially, I had committed to the project because it was my job. That kind of commitment is actually compliance. When it became clear that I would have to look at myself, I bailed out. Until Diane committed suicide. The shock of her act – whether it was defiance or premature perfection – energized me to my core. When I told Steve I was back in, it wasn't a small commitment. I was IN. Suddenly, I wanted to know why – curiosity. I was determined to walk through fire to learn what was driving me – courage. I dropped some of my pretenses, acknowledging what I didn't know – congruence. My inner eyes pierced through the opaqueness of my armor to know that Diane's fate would not be my own –clarity.

The many steps in a self-awareness journey take us through these levels over and over again. We can often recognize where we are by simply asking, "Where am I not … Committed … Curious … Courageous … Congruent … Clear?"

These five C's or my "steps into my basement" took me across the summer of 2020 as I dove deeper into getting over my fear of having another accident like the one that set all of this in motion.

CHAPTER FOURTEEN

Commitment

A Source of Energy

Commitment provides an intangible, but very real, source of energy to get something done. In context of a self-awareness journey, we have to first commit to learning things we have kept hidden – either intentionally or unintentionally. How willing am I to understand more about my inner self? How willing am I to understand my impact on others?

As with so many factors, we can either under commit or overcommit. In many companies, I've seen under-commitment in the form of compliance. People are obediently doing their jobs, but without the vitalizing energy that shows they care.

Sometimes, we can get overcommitted. Usually, it happens when we are giving more than the company is giving back in return. As with anything else, there's a balancing act with commitment.

In my deep dive of learning different philosophies of horse training, I saw some trainers who focused almost exclusively on compliance, and others on gaining trust, to the exclusion of asking anything from the horse at all. Both ways are out of balance.

Horsewoman Lee McLean says:

> *"Imagine an old-fashioned scale. In the balance, we'll hang discipline, on the other side, that intangible thing called 'feel.'*

"If this was your scale, which side would out-weigh the other? Most of us, if we are honest, struggle with balancing the two. Based on our inherent personality traits, along with who has mentored us, we will embrace the one mindset, while struggling with its opposing view.

"Those of us who expect obedience seldom have our horses flat-out say no, nor do they ever behave badly. We usually feel safe in the saddle, but we can miss out on a lot of the good stuff. By enforcing rules and concentrating on precision, we sometimes lose our ability to 'give' at just the right moments. Our riding can have a 'taking' quality, while our horses lose their natural flow. We're big on rules!

"Those of us who are all about the connection with our mounts can have the opposite problems. In our quest for 'giving' and 'feel,' we may not send our horses enough leadership. Sometimes our horses can be unreliable or inconsistent without firm boundaries. We may value the concept of peace and harmony above working through underlying problems or times of discord. We're all about the love!

"Often, our horsemanship mirrors our human relationships. For most of us, the challenge comes in trying to find a balance between these two extremes.

"Basic safety demands that my horses go in a disciplined manner ... but the joy in my horsemanship comes from developing the soft feel. I don't necessarily think that one is any better or any worse than the other, for when we live and believe in only one approach, our horses will never rise to be their best. Nor will we.

"Many days, before I swing a leg over, I'll stop and breathe. This is my mantra, particularly on those days I'm fierce and war-like ... or days I'm feeling frail and used.

"Love and rules.

"Love and rules.

"Love and rules." ™

Used with permission.
Lee McLean, Author, Horsewoman
Keystone Equine, Alberta, Canada

McLean directs our attention to the balancing act of the tightrope. Yes, we need to provide safety for the horse. We also need boundaries. We must be prepared to deal with a large animal should he decide he is the one in control, and he has nothing to fear from us.

The same is true in leadership. All too often, we seek "obedience" from those we serve, not recognizing that compliance comes with its own costs. On the other hand, I've seen leaders become doormats – I was one of them – when we become so busy focusing on safety that we forget the dangers of having no boundaries. Leadership is a constant game of give and take, as we ask people to rise to their greatness while at the same time, controlling the heat so they stay in the froth and below their pressure threshold.

Too Much Fear and Too Much Help

On one of my visits to Bruce, I went into the round pen with Mac, a horse who is quite committed to being close to humans. He's a small horse who can tend to act like the annoying little brother, constantly poking his nose into my space. It was Mac in the round pen when the big tree branch fell the year before, and Mac who came running at me full speed, hoping to jump in my lap for safety.

Bruce has a very useful technique to keep a horse out of a human's space. Jumping jacks. The beauty of doing jumping jacks is that the energy created by the movement raises the horse's Negative Pole. Creating a bunch of energy with jumping jacks allows him to build his mental tools, by making the right thing easy and the wrong thing hard. On that day when Mac came running, I did those jumping jacks like my life depended on them, and he chose to stop and figure out how to self-regulate.

On this day, Bruce was sitting in his usual spot outside the round pen, and I was just inside the fence as we were planning our session. Mac was free to graze or walk around or stand next to us. He chose to crowd me. Thankfully – for the sake of this lesson, anyway – I forgot one of my most powerful Tools.

As we were speaking, Bruce ignored my failed attempts to keep Mac from pushing into me. First, I would step back or step aside. That only emboldened the needy little horse. Then I would wave my arm like I was waving off a fly. That worked for a millisecond. Then he would be back, pushing in, threatening to get nippy. In the meantime, I kept trying to keep up the conversation with Bruce. I was like the little man in the Wizard of Oz, frantically moving the levers while yelling, "Pay no attention to the woman flailing and failing to move the horse away."

Now that Bruce had a clear picture of where my Pressure Threshold was, he asked me, "Why are you not raising his Pole up? Why are you not choosing to do jumping jacks? Is he not telling you how much pressure to apply? Be the conduit!" Oh yeah, I had a better way. Jumping jacks were a skill I had learned as a child. Yet in this case, the pressure of the situation was greater than my mental Tools. Under the pressure of Mac's overtures, the simple skill of jumping jacks was not accessible.

With this reminder, I did a couple of jumping jacks and Mac moved away. We continued talking, now about boundaries and how we set them. Even more importantly, how we defend them. Or don't. In this case, I had failed to keep Mac out of the perimeter I had mentally drawn around me. The same often happens with the people in my life as well. It could be a boundary as simple as, "don't be late." Yet I fail to defend the boundary, instead constantly tolerating lateness until we have a blow-up.

While we were talking, the ever-committed Mac crept back in, as if to say, "Are you sure?" This time, rather than doing typical jumping jacks, I jumped forcefully toward him. I was quite proud of myself. My forceful way seemed to be a good way to raise the pressure and tell him in no uncertain terms to back off.

Bruce saw something different. He asked, "What was that? Did you notice what you did there?"

"Well yes, I did, thank-you-very-much! I was very decisive," I thought to myself. Another part of me thought, *"Uh oh. Here we go again. What is it this time?"*

"Yeah, I made damn sure he stayed back," I said.

"Was that really it? Or were you trying to help him too much? And were you a bit angry with him? Why would you not let him make the mistake? Did you not overreact?" Bruce asked.

Now we were getting to the good stuff. These questions led us to a deep conversation about over- and underreacting, especially from the Parent Child dance that is the hallmark of Kid Mode. On the Parent side, I was trying to help too much, and I was angry with him. I was angry that he was making me expend the energy, angry that he might make me look bad, and angry that he didn't get it right the first time. I wanted to save him from having me correct him.

On the Child side, I was aware that he was bigger than me, stronger than me, and could run over me. I did not want him to use his power against me.

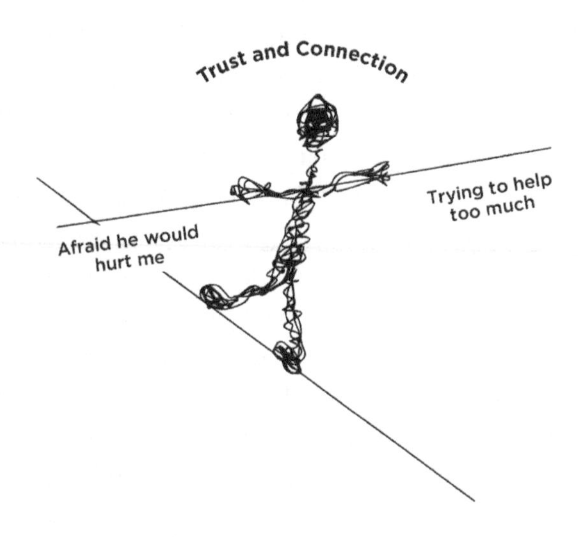

In the grand scheme of things, I wanted him to be perfect.

I wanted me to be perfect.

When I'm caught in the Perfection Game, I'm not being the conduit. I'm not assessing, recalibrating, correcting. I'm caught in the control trap, thinking I know what to do, when to do, how to do. I'm stuck on the Attachment side of the human tightrope, banking my worthiness on the behavior of the horse. I've completely focused on my needs and ignored the needs of Mac. And that's when things start to fall apart.

Bruce asked, "Why would you not give Mac the opportunity to build his mental tools? Does he not need to learn how to survive in the world that we have created? Does he not need to learn how to be OK standing two feet from you instead of all up in your space? How can he learn that if you insist on throwing anger at him, rather than raising up his Negative Pole? You were using pressure to intimidate, instead of using pressure to communicate."

Apparently, my "attack jacks" were not the answer to Bruce's questions.

Bruce was looking for me to be Here. Now. In the mind state he calls

AlphA, where my needs are balanced with Mac's needs. Where Mac is telling me how much pressure to apply. TyranT mindset runs on my past Rules, where I assert either too much Parent or too much Child, and ignores the valuable intel available to me Now. Human Attachment needs are integrated and balanced with Self-Expressive needs. Together, we walk the tightrope where things are just so.

The space is elusive. On this day, Bruce described it as a passing through the line. The picture is more like loops, back and forth across an imaginary line where everything is balanced, if only for a moment.

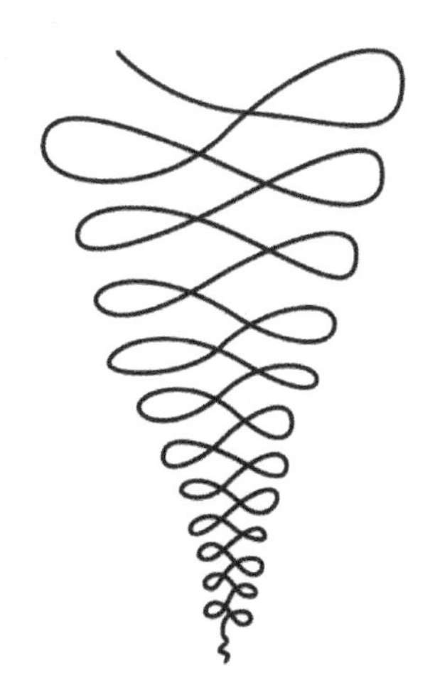

Staying on the tightrope is incredibly difficult, and the real work happens in the recalibration back to center, in both mind and body. We overshoot and correct. We undershoot and correct. With clarity about using our Tools, it's possible for the swings to become smaller and smaller. When our focus moves from thinking imbalance is a mistake and instead transitions to asking what's next, recalibration happens through our Tools, such as patience, timing, feel, discipline, and problem-solving.

Each side of the tightrope offers a different type of over- or under-correction. On the Child side of Power Under, we might lack confidence. We want someone to give us the answer. It's all too easy to feel helpless. Our frustration turns inward, bathing us in the mantra and inertia of, "What's wrong with me? Why is this happening to me? It's not fair!" The Child side of the tightrope screams "victim."

On the other hand, the opposite will throw us out of balance the other way. On the Power Over side of the tightrope, we might get angry. (I've been known to throw a tantrum when I can't make something go my way – as evidenced by my attack jacks with Mac.) Frustration rules our choices. Suddenly, we wield our Power Over by blaming others, seeing them as the problem. Bruce called this "beating yourself up through the other person." Now, instead of being a victim, we become the tyrannical parent with all the answers, or we help too much because we think no one else can handle the situation.

If we are to do anything new, and do it in a meaningful way, we must first commit. It helps to tune in to our tendency to do things out of people-pleasing or to seek approval or not disappoint someone. In those cases, we are complying rather than committing.

True commitment comes from within us. It helps to be curious about what is within us.

CHAPTER FIFTEEN

Curiosity

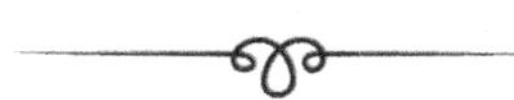

A Super Tool

The gateway to our Tools is curiosity. In some ways, curiosity is like a super-tool, setting the conditions for our mind to listen, hear, solve problems, and feel. If we are not interested in what is happening – either internally or externally – we are not going to be able to make the moves to adjust, nor are we going to learn anything.

The need to be curious often happens right about the time our Mistake button gets hit. If Survival Mode kicks in, we are more likely to be self-protective rather than open to learning. Yet, that's the time when we most need our curiosity. The sooner we can recalibrate back toward center, the better.

Curiosity and experimentation go hand-in-hand. We get to stress-test our assumptions, play Warmer/Colder and seek the balance point. It's always there if we can get out of our own way.

If we double down on showing what we know, we are simply putting off the moment where we are forced to deal with the truth of what's happening.

I once had a coach ask me, "Where do you think that comes from?" referring to one of my intractable patterns. My first answer was "I don't care, and I don't want to know!" In other words, I was not curious about my inner world at all given the tools I had cultivated to that point. My fear of what was in the basement outweighed my desire to know more.

Vulnerability

Over the years, I've coached many executives who were in a variety of transitions, such as joining a new company, taking on a new role in their old company or changing careers altogether. I've also worked with teams that were charged with a new project or responsibility.

The common thread in all transitions is the uncertainty. They are leaving what they know in exchange for what they do not know. Uncertainty puts us in the Froth and breeds all kinds of emotions; anticipation, excitement, dread, self-doubt and caution are just a few.

A lot of high achievers – and I include myself in this group – answer uncertainty with a proving mindset. When I was working in banking, every merger brought with it the hidden questions of uncertainty. *Who will get which jobs? What will happen to me? How will the new leadership team know what I can do? What will I have to do to fit in? Sometimes they voiced these questions. More often than not, they answered with more answers: Here, let me show you what I know. I can do this better than anyone else. See how valuable I am?*

> **"A lot of high achievers... answer uncertainty with a proving mindset."**

When working with leaders taking on a new role in a new company, I remind them that the first 90 days are a free pass to be curious and learn about the organization. The most important thing they can do is listen and learn.

Yet, it can be quite difficult to meet uncertainty with vulnerability. And make no mistake, curiosity and vulnerability are close cousins. We are choosing to open our minds and hearts to something new, something we may not know yet. We are saying, "I don't know. Tell me more." We might discover something that rocks our world. We might find out that what we believed before is not true.

Curiosity asks questions with wonder. I wonder why … I wonder what … I wonder how … I wonder if.

Rocking back and forth to find the middle involves being curious. I wonder – is it better over here – take a few steps – or over here? The game of Warmer/Colder takes us away from the comfortable place and intentionally through the places that don't work, so we can find what does work.

Proving mindset stories come from insecurity. The core question of "Am I enough?" interferes with the desire to learn.

Instead of wondering, we often make up stories based on assumptions from our past. The antidote to assuming we know things is curiosity. My old stories were written to protect me. When I'm living in this moment, my story naturally unfolds with curiosity leading the way. When something happens, I can think to myself, "How fascinating! I wonder what's going on." However, when I'm caught in the past or fearful of the future, my reaction is more likely going to come from a story that doesn't serve the current moment.

In my book *The Elegant Pivot, An Inspired Move for Navigating Corporate Politics*, I share many examples of my early corporate life, where I was the champion of making up stories. Most of the stories involved someone being out to get me or make me look bad in front of the boss. While corporate life does have some dog-eat-dog aspects, making up those stories was on me.

Survival Mode Is About the Fear

In learning about horses, both Bruce and Lynn encouraged me to focus on the behavior happening in front of me, not on some made-up reason the horse was doing something. Early on, I said things like, "He's not respecting me," or "The horse is mad at me," or "Why doesn't he like me?" None of that was true. The horse was behaving in a perfectly logical manner given his history and his survival brain.

My job was to understand the horse, to listen and hear what he was telling me. I could only do that if I chose to open up myself to be curious. But it's difficult to be curious if you are under pressure. No one wants to look bad, and one of my hot buttons is caring what people think of me.

Sometimes, it helps to see it from a distance.

One day on a trail ride, another rider gave me a chance to see from a distance. We had stopped in a busy area where there were lots of other trail riders. Our group decided to get off and have a drink and rest. We saw a small group of riders coming down the trail toward us. One of the horses in the group was backing up, walking crooked, and seemingly refusing to go forward.

As the rider passed us, she looked over at us and said, "He's being such a jerk today!" She said this as she was kicking him to go forward and pulling back hard on the reins as if to stop him. The horse held his head high and we could see the whites of his eyes. We watched as they continued on, the horse jumping side to side and somehow making it down a steep hill nearby. It looked like an accident waiting to happen.

What I saw differed from what the rider expressed. I saw a scared rider riding a scared horse. I saw myself on Mocha the day all hell broke loose. I saw myself in every corporate meeting where I said one thing and meant another.

Survival Mode is not curious. Survival mode is all about fear. There's no room to rock my world. The job of my Survival Mode is to batten down the hatches.

Curiosity is the gateway to being able to reach for our Tools. If we aren't willing to listen, hear and learn, there's nothing to recalibrate. We just simply march on doing what we've always done, wondering why we are not getting different results.

Warwick on my Podcast

In early 2020, I started a podcast. Now that I was giving myself permission to be more curious than ever, I decided it would be fun to record conversations where I could ask all kinds of probing questions. Bruce was my third guest, where he willingly shared his entire method, including his passion for helping horses to be horses in the people's world.

One morning, I was scrolling Facebook when another Warwick Schiller video popped up. As usual, I watched it. Warwick explains things very clearly, and I had learned many practical horse-related skills from watching his videos. However, he was also sharing his personal journey. These days, he was talking about vulnerability, recovering from trauma, and how changing himself had changed his relationship with his horses. Thanks to his engaging presence, I felt like I knew him, even though we had never met.

What struck me most was his willingness to share his journey and to even go so far as to say some of his training methods were wrong. He was evolving right before our eyes, and in ways I could deeply identify with over my journey.

As I read this post, I had a strong urge to invite Warwick on the podcast.

Almost immediately, my Rules tried to kick in, with thoughts like, *"What a crazy idea. What makes you think he will go on the podcast? You don't even know him, and he certainly does not know you!"*

By now, I was much more practiced in recognizing the trap and pivoted to reach for my Tools. Instead, I wondered if … and decided to ask. I made myself a cup of tea and sat down to write him a note on Facebook:

> *Hi Warwick. Lynn Carnes here writing to invite you to be a guest on the Creative Spirits Unleashed podcast — which focuses more on a leadership and corporate audience than a horse audience. They need to hear from you because horses have much to teach us leaders about truly creating partnership, trust, and affiliation. It's time to stop using dominance as the primary tool of leadership in business. I think our planet depends on it. I've watched a ton of your videos and we would have much to talk about ... Since I fell off a horse almost three years ago and got to spend three days in the hospital, I've been on a very steep learning curve to get back on the horse and it's transformed my coaching and leadership practice. I know you mostly focus on people who work with horses directly. Are you willing to share your message with people who need to learn how to develop their presence to work with other people? I really, really hope you will say yes.*

Within minutes, I got his response back, "Yes I would love to." A week later, we had an incredibly memorable conversation, filled with his stories of learning to develop presence. We talked a lot about mind chatter and its impact on our horses and on our own well-being. At one point, he confirmed a question I had asked. "Yes. Horses can read your mind."

Had he said that to me before this Pressure Journey began, I would have dismissed him as a kook. However, I had experienced a horse reading my mind far too many times by this point to doubt his claim.

What kind of chatter was the horse reading in my mind? Early in the podcast, I mentioned my accident and my illusion that trail riding was easy. He said, "Just trail riding is just like jumping out of a plane … as long as nothing goes wrong, it's really, really easy. But you've got to make sure there's quite a bit of preparation for it not to go wrong."

He summed up my whole journey in that one sentence.

So much of that preparation occurs in developing safety for the horse, as I had been learning. On the podcast, Warwick said:

"… What makes horses feel safe is a herd situation … If someone goes and gets a horse out of a herd and leads them away from the herd, the horse a lot of times is whinnying and running around. And you think, what is it that herd of horses provides that I don't? … What I think makes horses feel safe in a herd environment is the awareness of all the other horses."

He went on then to share lots of examples of ways we humans are not present with horses. We may be three seconds ahead or three seconds behind, or we may be thinking about what our teacher in fifth grade said about how we slouch and told us we are not really all that coordinated.

As my journey had shown me, developing my own presence under pressure could have life-threatening consequences. My incident on Shah where the turkey flew under his nose showed me the benefits of being in the moment when it counts. Much of the friendly advice I had received after my accident had nothing to do with being present, or with my energy. It was about improving my skills or learning how to do a one-rein stop or picking a better horse.

It makes sense. In this modern era, we tend to focus on the tangible and provable. We want the push-button answer.

Just as energy and thoughts are invisible, so are our beliefs. If we are brought up in a belief system that says we can fix problems with horses by either controlling the environment or training the horse to be nothing but obedient, then we will reach for the Rules that give us the answers we seek.

Reaching for the Tools of listening and hearing does feel more uncomfortable. So many times in the past three years I had longed for an answer that did not involve me having to own my part in the problem.

Ironically, owning my part gave me the opportunity to change it – if I were willing to work on my own mind.

Warwick had seen plenty of people who held the belief system that wanted tangible proof and avoided anything that felt too "woo-woo." He described what often happens when he asked people if they meditate:

"You know at clinics, … I asked if people have a meditation practice and a lot of people say, no, I don't, or I don't like that, or whatever. And I say, you know, meditating is just controlling what your mind thinks about and when you are around your horse, you need to be able to control what your mind thinks about. So, it's basically practice. It's practicing what you're going to do with your horse when you're not with your horse. And especially if you're out riding, like you were, and that horse runs off. Right then you have to be able to control what your mind thinks about … OK, what have I got to do here? To ensure I survive this thing, I'm going to reach down this rein, put a bend in the horse, and so on. It's controlling what your mind thinks about. And if you can't control what your mind thinks about when nothing's going on, you really can't control what your mind thinks about when you're on the back of an animal that's leaving town."

Horses know if we are not here right now, whether we are living three seconds or thirty years out of the moment. They crave our presence.

We don't always know it, but we crave our own presence too.

We can be present when we have nothing to prove. Choosing to be all-knowing rather than curious leaves us divided. Part of us keeps stuffing emotions and hiding and the other part demands to be heard. The subconscious mind plays a way bigger role in our actions and decision-making than our conscious mind.

It takes courage to see our truth.

"We don't always know it, but we crave our own presence too."

CHAPTER SIXTEEN

Courage

Courage Fuels Confidence

When we see pressure as a test, we use it to build our confidence. When we see pressure as a catalyst, we cultivate courage. And courage is actually the primary nutrient for confidence.

We need courage in order to try something that might or might not work. Whether it's facing up to a difficult boss, making a critical presentation or trying out a new idea, we can't really be confident until we are willing to make a move with an uncertain outcome. I once heard someone say, "Courage is commitment plus doubt." Makes sense, because if you knew without a shadow of a doubt that you could do something, it would not take courage to do it.

Courage is the antidote to our self-doubt and self-criticism. Beating ourselves up may well be the most well-intentioned, useless strategy for self-improvement on the planet. The inner voice that loves to beat us up for not being enough has a way of undermining our shaky confidence with all the ways we haven't measured up before. Courage is the energy that says, "It's worth a try. I would rather make a mistake than regret not trying."

Courage sees us through the moments of the Froth, keeping us focused on this moment, as we navigate through pressure-filled situations. After we have exercised our courage, we earn a different kind of confidence. With practice, our courage expands an inner-fueled awareness that we can handle whatever comes our way.

Much of my journey with the horses has helped me see that I was cultivating my courage.

Three Ways to Prepare

Both horse and human have to be prepared to go into circumstances where anything can happen. And with horses, anything can happen. My desire for control was turned to the outside world. My journey had been preparing me, much like horse trainers prepare their horses.

Let's go back to where Warwick Schiller talks about taking unprepared horses out on the trail. He describes it this way:

"Trail riding is like going out on the freeway with your car. It may be OK to drive around the pasture or paddock at home in a car that's not safe, maybe the brakes are iffy or the steering not so good, but when you get out where you may have to take some evasive action to circumvent situations that are out of control, it's a really good idea to be prepared."

There's a tightrope for helping a horse deal with uncertainty, especially while carrying us on its back. My travels had taken me through many different barns, horse shows, and other settings where horses and humans interact. As I gained awareness about horse training, I saw three different ways people prepared their horses for the unpredictable: Control, desensitizing, and "couraging."

Control and desensitizing fall on either side of the tightrope; couraging walks the tightrope.

On the control side, I've seen people shrink their world. Rather than helping the horse deal with the scary things of the world, they do their best to control the scary things. They never ride on windy days. They create Rules about what can happen around them when they are riding. No tractors or weed eaters allowed. They make sure no plastic bags are floating along anywhere nearby. They don't take the horse out of the arena. The human parallel to this is the person who doesn't start that business for fear of failing, or the employee who doesn't speak up because of the fearful consequences.

On the other side, people take their horse through a process called "desensitizing." They keep after the horse with the scary things until the horse no longer reacts to those things. I liken this method to what my parents used to say when we kids were upset, "You better stop crying or I will give you something to cry about." We learned quickly to swallow whatever was making us upset, which in effect, caused us to shut down and put up an emotional wall of protection. In the corporate world, the equivalent is the boss who doesn't listen to the employee, but instead says, "Just do your job." If you were to write out all the words that can be inferred from such a statement, it goes something like this, "I don't want to hear it. I don't care what you think. Just shut up and do your job or you will not have a job." This is the human version of desensitizing. On the surface, this bravado sort of looks like it works. Things have the appearance of being calm, cool, and collected. The simmering underneath the surface isn't revealed until the pot boils over. Then we wondered what went wrong.

Warwick Schiller tells a story of a woman who asked him to help her with her "crazy horse." She went on to say they would go out on a trail ride and her horse would see a rabbit hopping out of the woods. He might notice it but not do anything. Farther along, another rabbit might run past and again, only a slight reaction from the horse. This would go on throughout the ride. As she said, "We can go past twelve rabbits with no problem, and then on the thirteenth rabbit, he just goes crazy and becomes unmanageable!"

Schiller answered by saying, "Your horse can only hold twelve rabbits worth of worry. In other words, your horse passes the first rabbit and holds on to that worry inside of himself. With each rabbit, he adds a little more worry, because he hasn't had a chance to release the worry of the previous rabbits." Schiller called this "trigger stacking," a term that applies to horse training as well as dog training. It also applies to humans.

Trigger stacking happens when one thing builds on another that builds on another to take us over our pressure threshold. I remember when I was a single mom raising Jen. The morning would start with the coffee not right, then we would get into horrible traffic on the way to work. Something always seemed to make school drop-off more complex than it should be and then I struggled to find a place to park. As soon as I got into the office, my phone started ringing and a stack of messages beckoned me away from the project I was supposed to finish that morning. All the traffic and complexity repeated on the way home and the crazy woman who picked her up at after-school care was far beyond her twelve rabbits worth of worry.

With horses, we are often asking them to go against their nature. It's not natural for them to leave the comfort of the herd, have a predator put a saddle made of another dead animal on their backs and a piece of metal in their mouths. Then we put them in a setting where someone might be mowing in the pasture or a new horse is coming in as we walk them down a trail into the woods, the same place where they watch various wildlife moving all day long. One thing after another, we pile on the triggers without even thinking about it from the eyes of a horse.

With time, I began thinking of Warwick, Lynn, and Bruce's method for dealing with scary things as "couraging." Instead of shrinking, faking, or stuffing, preparing the horse this way builds genuine tools, skills, and capabilities in both horse and human. Couraging raises our pressure threshold, and it raises the horse's pressure threshold. Instead of stacking the triggers, using the Tools gives both horse and human a way to release tension instead of holding on to it until it boils over.

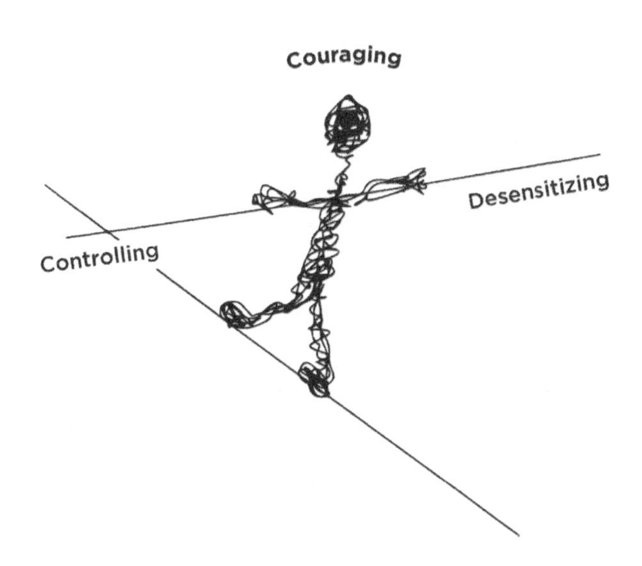

It takes courage to reach for our Tools instead of the self-protective Rules that have proven to work for us, at least in some circumstances. Giving up control takes courage. Becoming the conduit takes courage. Using the Tools of curiosity, listening, hearing, problem-solving, patience, timing, feel, discipline, work ethic and more starts with having the courage to trust myself to wield them effectively under pressure.

Shah Meets the Lawnmower

One day, when I showed up at Lynn's barn for a lesson on Shah, she asked me to help her move the lawnmower up to the back pasture before I started my lesson. After we moved the mower, we went through all the usual steps down at the barn, reading Shah as I groomed and saddled him. By this stage of my journey, I often rode Shah up to the arena if both Lynn and I assessed that he was feeling relaxed and connected to me.

It was never a given that I would ride him from the barn. The path from the barn to the arena goes up a hill through a small forest, past two guest cabins, near another pasture sometimes housing horses, and around a bend. Even though it's a short ride, we had seen all kinds of things happen to offer a chance for "couraging." Sometimes we met families walking on the road. More than once, we encountered dogs along the way. And there were always those pesky turkeys, just waiting to fly up as we passed by.

On this day, Lynn asked me if I were going to ride him or walk him to the arena. I checked in with my Negative/Positive Pole. My number was about a three, which isn't that high. I wasn't able to read why it was anything other than a zero. However, by this time, I had learned to trust this signal. "Nope, I'm going to walk him up. I think it will do both of us good to keep connecting on the way up," I said.

As we walked into the arena, I got to see what some part of me knew all along. We were about to have an opportunity for couraging – as evidenced by what I was witnessing in Shah: Arabian horse fear in its full glory.

Before we got two steps past the gate, Shah stopped, braced and raised his head up high, nostrils flaring and eyes wide. The back pasture abuts the arena. And there on the other side sat the lawnmower that Lynn and I had just moved. For Shah, it wasn't the lawnmower he had seen thousands of times. It was a black and yellow dragon, rising up from the earth, waiting to devour him in its jaws.

We had choices. We could have decided to work somewhere besides the arena. We could have moved the lawnmower. We could have continued on, hoping for the best and scolding Shah for being worried. I've seen people use all of those strategies and more when faced with the thing the horse deems dangerous and we humans see as no big deal.

In this case, we used it as an opportunity to show Shah he could handle it. We listened to what he was telling us. Lynn had me walk him closer and then retreat. As he relaxed, we cycled back and forth, approaching and retreating, releasing pressure as he gained confidence that the mower wasn't coming for him. Rather than force, fear, and intimidation to get him through it, we showed him he could handle the scary thing.

Soon Shah became a curious and willing partner, fueled by trust and connection rather than fear and force. When Shah showed he was relaxed, having released his "twelve rabbits" worth of worry, I got on him. We rode all through the arena with no concern for the lawnmower out in the field. When we rode out of the arena, Shah was as calm and relaxed as he could be.

"Rather than force, fear, and intimidation to get him through it, we showed him he could handle the scary thing."

It was the pressure of the lawnmower that opened the doorway for both Shah and me to develop our Tools. At the moment of maximum pressure, the doorway of learning opens. We had a choice: *Would we walk through the doorway and be present in this moment, or go back to our old ways? Would we choose Tools or Rules? Would we use the situation for couraging or would we grasp for control?*

The first move – for both of us – was to spook. Standing next to a horse with wide eyes, flaring nostrils, and the threat of lashing hooves is scary. My first thought about the lawnmower, tinged with a bit of anger, was, *"We made a mistake to put it next to the arena."* With Lynn's support, my second thought was, *"OK. You can do this. This is an opportunity. Let's work through this."* As a result, both Shah and I raised our pressure threshold another notch. For the sake of contrast, here's another reminder of what this was NOT:

...leading by fear, intimidation, and force doesn't lead to real change, commitment, or buy-in. Instead, it creates a form of compliance that has the appearance of success. Except, it's merely an illusion. Test it under pressure and it collapses like a pile of cotton candy in a rainstorm.

Shah and I developed courage under pressure. As I helped him with the lawnmower, he gave himself over to my direction, offering his full commitment to go where I asked. We moved as one, his legs becoming my legs, our spirits intertwined as we walked out on the trail.

Shah was not prey; I was not predator. We were partners.

Who we are as humans impacts the horse whether we want it to or not.

Who and how we are as humans decides the truth of our leadership.

Over these past couple of years, Bruce and Lynn had frequently reminded me of my responsibility to be the horse's leader – not his slave master. When we were returning on Marley after his first ride, Bruce subtly reminded me of what he had said:

"Marley did check in with you. He's asking if you are worthy." I came back with, *"Worthy of what?"* Bruce replied, *"Worthy of being his leader."*

In that moment, Marley wanted to know if I heard him. Shah wanted to know the same in the moment of facing the lawnmower. They are reading my energy. If they could talk in human words, it's as if they are asking, "Are we good? Can I trust you?" I've learned they can only trust my reassurances if I first show them I am aware of what they are facing.

This applies to true leadership. When we lead with safety and presence, we produce a rich exchange of give and take that builds trust and connection.

Putting the Tools To Practice

Coaching client Maria worked in a volatile industry, and she was at the forefront of leading change. Her business had many problems to solve if it was to survive as an important player in the industry. She frequently found herself in the Froth, and she had asked me to help her operate with a clear head, rather than getting caught in her fear. I asked her an important question. "What might it look like if you were to tell a different story about the electrical charge?"

Problems she had never seen before came at her like fastballs out of a pitching machine. As is often the case, the industry was growing out from under her company. However, most of the people in her company were deeply invested in continuing to do things the way they had always done them. She had been charged with bringing a new, more consolidated approach that would create a single point of contact with her company's customers. On the surface, it looked like she was responsible for a new product; instead, she was actually responsible for comprehensive change management. She needed a lot of cultural buy-in to deliver on the strategy. She had an opportunity to create that buy-in at the next quarterly review with the CEO. She asked me to help her prepare both the messaging and her mindset.

We set aside a whole coaching session to prepare her for this critical presentation, one of her first at this level in the organization. During our meeting, Maria said, "The guy in the sister division is painting a very rosy picture of all the good things and ignoring the bad things. Do you think I would be better off stripping some of the bad news out of my presentation?"

The dilemma she faced was bigger than just a decision about how to tell a balanced story about what was really happening in her division. Under that question was this one, "What if I end up looking bad in comparison to him? What if I look bad compared to all the other presenters?"

Worrying about looking bad is one step removed from the survival question of, "What if they kick me out of the tribe?"

In the dilemma with Maria, both sides of the tightrope lead to undesirable outcomes. Paint too rosy a picture and the resources she needs end up diverted to a different area. Paint too dire a picture and questions arise about her deployment of the resources she has been managing. She needed to walk that fine line that both highlighted the problem and inspired confidence in her ability to be a part of the solution.

To complicate matters, the presentation would be over video conference, a screen full of talking heads. Time blocks were granted, with each minute handed out like gold coins. Most presenters would read their bullets on the screen, ignoring the fact that everyone else has already read them. The safe path. Boring. Do what everyone else is doing. Stick to the script. Take no chances.

This session was a moment of truth. After years of navigating the minefield of the organization, on this day, Maria would finally have the ear of the CEO. Playing it safe felt like a capitulation, so it was off the table – or so she thought. She also did not want to be reckless or come off as powerless.

Maria would need a plan and her Tools. In addition to the coaching we had done together; she had also worked with both Bruce and Lynn in leadership sessions. We would draw from many relevant experiences with the horses in our preparation.

We decided it was OK to have a script – just not the one on the PowerPoint. Her journey in the division had been a master course in resilience. The whole division was formed when one of the executives asked the question, "What if we could make our clients' lives easier by creating one point of contact?"

Her preparation had three tracks. First, do the research and build compelling slides. Second, develop a storyline about what the slides were showing. This would be her script. Third, reinforce her Tools so that she could deliver the story with courage and confidence.

The first half of the meeting unfolded as predicted; everyone read their slides and checked their watches. The meeting proceeded in an orderly fashion; no feathers ruffled. When it came to Maria's turn, she felt the froth of the old and the new. *Should I do it the way I always have? I've never presented using a story before. What if I bomb? Reading slides is working for everyone else. Wouldn't that be safer? And then this thought: How will I feel tomorrow if I don't take the chance?*

She chose the courageous path.

After the meeting, she called me. She was ecstatic. At the end of her presentation, it was the CEO who went off script. Instead of marching on, Maria's story prompted the CEO to turn the conversation into a strategy session on how to solve the problems Maria had so clearly laid out.

"Staying on the tightrope had paid off. Maria was beginning to understand that it is IN solving the problems that she grows; wishing for no problems is an ineffective defense against the dangers of the world."

Staying on the tightrope had paid off. Maria was beginning to understand that it is IN solving the problems that she grows; wishing for no problems is an ineffective defense against the dangers of the world. The pressure of the meeting gave her a chance to get just a little bit more in touch with her true nature. This is couraging.

The beautiful thing about welcoming pressure as a catalyst is that we no longer allow the end goal to define us. Winning the game is nice, but it's not the point. The point is the opportunity to cultivate our courage, or perhaps a better word is to unleash our courage.

Bruce would often say "It's not about the horses. It's IN working with horses that we become the true self."

CHAPTER SEVENTEEN

Congruence

The Antidote to Perfectionism

Congruence is the antidote to perfectionism. The more we believe we can achieve perfection, the more we have to hide our imperfections and mistakes. We sometimes go so far as hiding our mistakes from ourselves. At the congruence level of self-awareness, we show our truth. *What will it take for me to own what's in there? What's out there?*

As we begin to own our mistakes, flaws, and weaknesses, we lessen the power they have over us. This is not a popular idea in our modern culture, and especially in the corporate world. In many cultures, mistakes are not well-tolerated, setting off a chain of events that causes people to hide them, deny them, and blame others for what's going wrong. Soon, teams are nothing more than working groups that are on guard against being the one caught making a mistake.

Congruence means to own how we feel about something, without letting our emotions drive our behavior in unhealthy ways. For example, I once worked with a company whose CEO was known to throw things when he was angry over poor performance. The bearers of bad news had learned to either duck or lie. However, the problem wasn't his anger – a perfectly natural human emotion. The problem was the book throwing.

If we haven't learned to feel our emotions and allow them to pass through, we do all kinds of things to avoid them. We stuff them, deny them or act out on them in harmful ways. Yet feeling is exactly what we are meant to do. We were born with this fabulous system for tuning in to what serves us and what doesn't. If the horses showed me anything, it's that sensitivity to the energies around us is the most natural thing in the world. It IS the way of nature, and if we are to be true to ourselves, we must cultivate our feelings, not stuff them. Part of our authenticity comes from honoring our inner knowing and feeling. Being congruent means to feel what we feel and own it. In that way, we create harmony between how we feel and act.

Opportunities, Weaknesses, and Doorways

Somewhere during my tenure at the bank, they quit using the word weaknesses in context of doing performance evaluations. Suddenly, the word "opportunities" became all the rage. There was just one problem with the semantics: They meant the same thing. Trying to make it sound somehow more palatable by using the word "opportunities" felt a bit like a cover-up to me.

Incongruity drains safety and trust.

During that time, I had no words or context to describe the icky feeling I got when faced with someone saying one thing and meaning another. My internal guidance system simply said to me, "Watch out. Something's not right here." Often, I misread the feeling as a signal the person was trying to give me negative feedback or otherwise illuminate my weaknesses. Having them wrap it up in a peanut butter ball of "opportunity" did not help me feel safe. In fact, it did the opposite.

These days, the term psychological safety has entered the corporate lexicon, largely thanks to Google's research on teams. In 2012, Google conducted a study, called Project Aristotle, to understand what made effective teams tick. They were surprised to find that psychological safety ranked number one on factors that lead to teams that outperformed.

The key question in psychological safety is whether or not team members feel safe enough to be vulnerable in front of their teammates, whether admitting mistakes or looking ignorant or foolish.

The need for safety is non-negotiable. In his famous 1943 paper "A Theory of Human Motivation," Abraham Maslow proposed that if certain physiological, safety and belonging needs are not met, the human will feel anxious and tense. Corporate life has a way of wringing all three of those levels out of the equation. The Homeless Sequence makes us feel like we will not eat if we don't have this job. The pressure to fit in, go along, and not rock the boat are all rooted in our core human needs. Much of my corporate life involved me being triggered into Survival Mode, and I wasn't alone.

I remember sitting in my boss's office one day as we commiserated on the latest edict from above. We didn't agree with the decision and knew that the powers that be had not considered many factors when making the call. We saw many potential failure points. We also knew that if we were to push back, we would be faced with force, fear, and intimidation to get us to fall in line. As we talked it through, it was clear that we would go along and reluctantly do our best to make it work. He looked at me and said, "Lynn, this is why you need go-to-hell money."

Back then, I was surprised he took me into his confidence that way. From my inside-out way of looking at things, it appeared to me that I was the only one struggling with navigating corporate politics. The gamesmanship required to survive seemed like a game everyone but me had figured out. It took a long time for me to realize that others struggled as much as I did.

Looking back on it, I see so many assumptions never challenged. Perhaps the most flawed was the Homeless Sequence. Did I really believe that if I didn't have THIS job, I would never have any other job? I also never saw things through the eyes of those who were asking us to get things done on their behalf. They needed our commitment more than our compliance. Did I really believe that if we shared our perspective on better ways to get things done that we would be instantly fired? Most importantly, I didn't take a step back to look at my own capabilities. Did I really not trust myself to handle whatever came my way? Was my fear running me that much?

My Survival Mode eclipsed such logic. Incongruence may drain safety and trust, but it also felt like the only way to survive.

Horses showed me something different. They have a mammalian survival brain, much like ours. They do not have a prefrontal cortex, that plots and plans revenge. Bruce often said, "Horses don't have problems, humans are the problem." I often found myself saying things like, "He's trying to get away with something," or "He doesn't seem to like me," or "He's an awful horse." My Kid Mode perceptions vacillated between feeling like I had no power, to doing my best to forcibly assert my power. Bruce and Lynn were both trying to help me see that horses don't judge humans. They show humans. They reveal their needs through their actions. They tell us when they are hungry (which seems to be all the time). They show us their preference for being among their herd. They reveal their inner state – as well as our inner state – in their responses to us.

With shut-down horses, it is only evident to a knowing eye when a horse doesn't feel safe. Even though they are flight animals, they are masters at freezing, which may look like they are relaxed or uninterested. They can hide their true feelings much like the bunny rabbits I walk up on out in nature. The rabbit sits there looking like a dog waiting to be petted until you make that last move, and they bounce off into the woods. Horses can go into a state of waiting for the other shoe to drop. They stand there quietly, but if you look closely, they are not relaxed. Instead, they are cautious, and have likely shut down their natural reactions. When someone walks up to them, they may lean their head the other way. They may have their feet set in a position like a sprinter, just waiting for the gun to go off. They may be barely breathing, too tense to take a deep breath. They are afraid – and yet they don't always show it in obvious ways. The clues are mostly happening in the unseen realm, where energy makes all the difference.

What to do with all my fear became quite the conundrum for me. No doubt, my adrenaline hits were sending out fearful energy. I couldn't control it, so I fell back on my old corporate rules of pretending, "I've got this."

I was creating the same kind of incongruence, an unseen force of energy, that made me feel unsafe.

Congruence Versus Hiding Fear

My daughter Jen and I got a master class in reading the unseen when we went to ride with Lynn one day. We went to catch the horses and bring them into the barn. Lynn had a couple of guest horses in the stalls next to where we would brush and saddle the horses. Jen had ridden a couple of times with Lynn but was still quite nervous on the ground with the big animals, especially in the close quarters of the barn. Of course, being the ever-observant mother, I was oblivious to her anxiousness. Phoenix was not.

Lynn went to speak with someone doing work on the farm as Jen and I entered the barn. Both Shah and Phoenix were more nervous than usual, clearly aware of the new horses in the stalls.

Shah calmed down nicely, as I used everything I remembered from my early days of training with Lynn and Phoenix. I continued grooming Shah, assuming that Jen was fine. When Lynn entered the barn, she noticed that Jen had stepped out briefly and was looking at her phone. She said, "Be sure to focus on your horse, not your phone." Jen came back in and Lynn started giving her guidance on how to handle Phoenix, who was having a hard time keeping his feet still. Suddenly, Jen walked out of the barn, apparently in tears. Lynn and I looked at each other and said, "What the hell?" Lynn asked me what was going on. I shrugged and said, "Maybe your comment about the phone hit a Mommy button. I assure you I planted a lot of them. I honestly don't know."

We let Jen be, and in a few minutes, she came back in. She had somewhat gathered herself but was still clearly very emotional. As I stood there trying not to say the wrong thing, Lynn asked some gentle questions. She asked Jen to go stand by Phoenix. To our surprise, Jen told us that she was scared to death. Early in life, she had been admonished at summer camp to stay away from the kicking hooves of horses. As Phoenix moved around the pivot point of his tie-up, she became increasingly fearful that he or Shah would deliver a sudden blow she couldn't dodge. Lynn asked her if she were willing to try and promised that she would be safe, especially if she stood near his head.

Lynn did not ask Jen to cover up her fear, nor did she ask her not to be fearful. In fact, the more Jen owned up to how she was really feeling, the more Phoenix relaxed and let down. The more he relaxed, the more Jen opened up. As she stood there allowing the tears to fall, Phoenix melted. Lynn explained that it was the cover-up that was causing the problem. While the new horses in the barn set off the stream of events, Jen's reaction perpetuated Phoenix's anxiety. Suddenly I remembered that my daughter is a master of hiding her feelings – at least from humans. (She should be a poker player.)

But horses read energy and the subtle gestures of body language. When Jen's inner experience and outer expression of her feelings matched, Phoenix relaxed. It wasn't her fear that was the problem. It was the mixed message. It was the saying one thing and meaning another. It was the incongruence. Once Jen owned her fear, Phoenix relaxed, and her fear dissipated. We ended up having a lovely ride.

It makes sense on many levels. Energy is the horse's main form of communication. With them, we don't get the luxury of saying one thing and meaning another. That kind of incongruence is the energy they detect from a deadly predator right before the sneaky attack.

Congruence disappears when we are not willing to feel or to reveal.

Jen was not wrong to fear the horse's ability to hurt her. That's the big balancing act with horses. We must walk that tightrope of meeting their needs without allowing them to run over us.

Jen's experience with Phoenix reinforced the benefits of creating trust and connection with a horse. Trust and connection with people in the corporate world were beginning to seem more possible.

Culture and Human Needs

It has happened many times in my life. I found myself doing something that felt like everything I had done to that point prepared me for the moment at hand. So it was in the summer of 2020, when COVID was still new, and I was part of The Culture Project. I was riding often – but getting back on Mocha still felt like a leap too far. The Culture Project afforded me a chance to work on my Tools, both with the client (a hospital) and with Bruce, who happens to live a few miles down the road from the hospital.

The Culture Project was unlike any I had done before, yet it called on many things I HAD done before. Surprisingly, it called deeply on two aspects of the work with horses: building trust and connection and raising my pressure threshold. I was looking forward to bringing the new lens my accident had given me.

I had worked with this hospital for ten years. In that time frame, I had coached several executives individually, facilitated many team working sessions and supported the executive team through a CEO transition. When the scope of work exceeded what I could do on my own, I brought in colleague Susan Robertson, one of the best coaches and facilitators of self-awareness that I know.

Susan Robertson is a leadership rock star. She created the pioneering leadership program called the High Impact Leadership Seminar, a program that gave high-achieving corporate leaders such as me a window into the possibilities of living a whole-hearted life while being successful.

I had been a facilitator in the High Impact Leadership Seminar as well for the past several years. We could see that we were making an enormous difference – one leader at a time – and that was fine by me. Not so with Susan. She believed it possible to impact people's lives on a much larger scale, so she started a new company, Linceis Conscious Business, and published her book Real Leadership, Waken to Wisdom. Susan's REAL Leadership Method formed the backbone of the Culture Project, along with a Cultural Fitness Survey rooted in Maslow's hierarchy of needs. In the Culture Project, we were surveying every single employee in this mid-sized hospital to get a read on how well the culture met the core human needs of the people working there. The statements measured by the survey are the kinds of questions many bosses hope will never get asked, like, "My direct supervisors do not play favorites," and "Our work environment is free from retaliation." The questions uncovered the culture down to the root ball of human needs.

Before my accident, I didn't really consider human needs, or horse's needs for that matter. Working with horses the way Lynn and Bruce were teaching me involved meeting the horse's needs and creating a partnership of give and take. In many ways, this was radically different than most horse trainers, where horses were expected to be compliant and obedient. Interesting. I had worked in human cultures that preferred compliant and obedient over trust and connection. The rules of man superseded – or attempted to supersede – the rules of nature. Much like horses were not made for the modern world, neither are humans. We really aren't meant to work in these large organizations where we are expected to blindly trust.

Measuring culture through a survey was an enormous commitment, which mirrored the commitment for this hospital to generate a great culture. The leaders were aware that their rapid growth had set the conditions for people to feel disconnected from the mission and each other. Little did they know all the pressures that would come their way as they began the process of first understanding and then improving their culture.

The COVID-19 pandemic hit a month after we had completed the survey. For several months, the Culture Project was on hold as the hospital handled the surge in patients and navigated the uncertainties of what the pandemic would bring. We were not entirely certain that they would continue with the project. The pandemic offered very good reasons for them to double down on just doing the work – and no one would blame them for choosing to let a project in its infancy drop. However, the same level of commitment that prompted the leaders to start the project in the first place made them realize that walking away would sow seeds of doubt and mistrust among their people. They stayed the course.

They desired a culture that could heal and offer the best possible place to work and do so in a timely and profitable way. In many cultures, efficiency and profits rule the day. In others, relationships and employee satisfaction matter more, to the detriment of tangible metrics. This team knew having both was possible – and that's why they were interested in measuring the quality of their culture.

It was clear to me that this team would be interested in finding a way to walk the tightrope between the "hard stuff" and the "soft stuff." We also needed to find ways to re-sensitize people, rather than de-sensitize them. We needed their best thinking, their creativity, their deep care for their job. All too often, we settle for compliance over commitment. It seems more peaceful that way; however, the opportunity cost is huge. People who are shut down and putting one foot in front of the other are usually operating in Survival Mode. Decisions made from an internal state of self-preservation are often not good. Many a plane crash or workplace accident has occurred because someone was too afraid to rock the boat and speak up. We are leaving what matters on the table. When we shut down – albeit for good reasons – we block our own light.

Like a tangled ball of roots, Rules wind their way into our guidance system, blocking the pathways to our personal truth. The interference makes it very difficult to find our voice. And here's the strangest part of all of this. We are not aware that our Rules are interfering. Because all of these Rules have been with us for so long, they feel like a part of us. As they direct us out of our awareness, our Rules feel as if they ARE us.

We worked together over the next two years as the pandemic oscillated between huge spikes and momentary declines. While the members of this team were tired at times, they were never dispirited. Their mantra of *"Taking care of people is what we do,"* carried them through.

Being congruent is about showing who we are to ourselves as much as it is showing it to others. Much of our early conditioning teaches us to conform to the people who are caring for us. Since we need each other to survive, it's pretty difficult to do anything else.

CHAPTER EIGHTEEN
Clarity

Impeccable Picture

Clarity takes us to a whole new level of depth. Becoming clear on who we really are takes a lifetime of self-awareness exploration. As we learn to live our truth, we ask "How can I begin to unleash what's true about me? How can I create the space for others to be true to themselves?"

This Pressure Journey refined my idea of what the word "vision" really means. Companies create a "vision statement" and share it widely in posters, advertisements, and town hall style meetings. Athletes "visualize" their performance, often seen closing their eyes before they begin their game. Individual leaders describe their vision for their department. Yet sometimes these visions fall short. In my own experience of visualizing my slalom ski runs, I learned that it was critical that I visualize in real time. Before this insight, it would usually take me over a minute to visualize a twenty-second ski pass through the course. Then I would wonder why everything felt so fast when I was doing the real thing.

The answer was lack of clarity.

My mental preparation was more about making me feel comfortable rather than preparing me for the pressure of the speed I would experience when I was on the water. Subconsciously, my desire to be safe interfered with the point of visualization.

When I began to understand the term "impeccable picture," I also began to prefer it as a way to envision a good outcome. In working with a horse, who thinks in pictures, an impeccable picture transmits from my brain to his. At first, the idea of horses being able to understand what I was thinking from simply an image in my mind seemed completely implausible. Mind reading was a step too far for my logical mind. However, time after time, I experienced my thoughts impacting the horse, whether I was on his back or on the ground. In my podcast with Warwick Schiller, I asked him directly "Can horses read our minds?" His answer was a resounding yes, and he's not alone. In her book *Thinking In Pictures, My Life with Autism,* Temple Grandin describes how her thoughts are not verbal, but are instead visualizations, and this is how she has communicated the animal viewpoint in many settings.

Our mental pictures are often muddled with conflicting desires. We confuse the desire for comfort with the desire to achieve our goals. In the name of playing it safe, we create fuzzy pictures. The difference is much like that of an old black-and-white TV from the 1950s, with static and blurred edges versus the high-definition color TVs of today. While we may wish for a life with less pressure, fear and uncertainty, choosing to see ourselves – and the world as it really is affords us the ability to shed our armor and operate from the deeper source within.

What Do You Want?

My first time to have a coach happened through the back door. The company did not offer it; in this case, I had found her through a series of serendipitous events. Since I was hiring her, my interests and hers were completely aligned. Her job was to make me truly better, not to help me become a better cog in the corporate wheel.

In our first meeting, I filled her in on all my challenges, the many ways the world was causing me problems, all the ways I was feeling screwed by the system and how little control I really had.

After hearing my whole sob story, she asked, "What do you want to have happen?"

The question stopped me in my tracks. I stumbled over my words as many thoughts ricocheted around my head. *"What do you mean what do I want?" "You are supposed to help me figure out how to deal with these bastards!" "I want you to tell me what they want me to do." "If you could help me figure out how to get them what they want so I can get promoted, that would be great." "What do I have to do to fit in here?"*

So many questions.

But no answer to the simple query, "What do you want?"

I didn't dare tap into what really mattered to me. Without the word survival ever being involved, I knew at my core that my survival was at stake. At least, that's how it appeared at the time.

Thirty years later, I've asked that same question of hundreds of clients and participants in my programs. Most have exactly the same frantic internal response, with their own personal set of "What do you mean?" questions.

With some gentle probing and with me holding up a metaphorical mirror, they begin to untangle the confusion. We review the operating Rules of their life and the biography of those Rules. They begin to see the moments they gave away their heart's desire in order to be responsible or safe.

Jack quit playing music as soon as he got married. He knew that the life of a musician would probably not support his wife and kids.

Jenna put down the paintbrush and took a job in marketing, hoping it would fill her creative well. She soon learned that marketing is a game of numbers more than it is of colors.

Richard became a doctor so he didn't have to go into the family business. He hated medicine as much as the family business, but he had a wife and two kids by the time he graduated, and it was time to start his practice.

Kerry became an engineer at the encouragement of both parents and landed a coveted job at a global technology firm. She was proud of her skills and yet in her late twenties, was already counting the days to retirement when she would be able to enjoy her life rather than having her every decision revolve around her job.

As we dove deeper, the balancing act between Attachment and Self-Expression usually emerged.

The Attachment side of the tightrope involves being responsible by taking care of self and family, keeping food on the table, a roof overhead, making sure everyone fits in, and having enough. All those Rules mattered because they prescribed how to win at the game called life. Having enough trumped being enough.

In my case, after responsibility came the shackles. Instead of using the newfound freedom that goes with having earning power to get more of what

I really wanted, I loaded up my life with more responsibility.

Gaining more money became more important than empowering my purpose.

Money is such a concrete measure, it quickly gained precedence over more meaningful, yet intangible marks of living a good life.

I traded peace of mind for the chase for more – more money, more accolades, more approval, more prestige, and that bigger bonus that would allow me finally to have enough money in the bank to have peace of mind.

Economic Servitude

Money is one of the inventions of the modern age that we can't live without. Just try losing your wallet on a road trip and see how far you get! In some ways, we also can't live with it, as money has a perverse way of taking us away from ourselves.

After one of my sessions in a multi-day leadership program, one of the men in the room pulled me aside and asked me about a dilemma he was facing. Everything in his body language said he was facing a crisis of his conscience. As James' story unfolded, it became clear that he had been living with the awareness for some time that he had been accepting otherwise unacceptable behavior. He had been making tradeoffs to please his bosses that he knew in his heart were wrong. He had been compromising his personal values and it was eating him alive from the inside out. Furthermore, he knew the right thing to do. He had known it for a long time. Maybe even years. So, I asked him the obvious question: "Why haven't you done it (the right thing) yet?"

His body slumped and he let out a sigh. He cast his eyes downward. He said, almost shamefully, "I can't. They pay me so much money."

In that moment, I knew he had forgotten his worth. He had forgotten who he really was. His fear was palpable. All he could see was what he had to lose.

Here was a guy who had made it. James was the first in his family to go to college. Never in his wildest dreams did he think he would be a senior vice president in a prestigious Fortune 500 company, and yet here he was, attending the most senior leader's roundtable. People in the room cared what he thought. He had a seat at the table!

He and his wife had a beautiful home in the suburbs. His kids attended one of the prestigious schools in his community. They took the kind of vacations that showed they had made it. They had the right cars – you know the ones, right? Along with his glorious salary, he had a long list of payments and obligations to feed the insatiable beast of his lifestyle. He had appearances to keep up.

Along with his seat at the table, he had started to understand the unseen yet very real deal that he and his co-workers had made. The culture went something like this in his company, "We want you to tell us what you think – as long as it agrees with us. We want alignment. That means staying between the lines, you get that, right? The only bad news we want to hear is about your kid losing the soccer match this weekend. Your job is to make your numbers. If you help us keep making money, you will keep making money. We will help you feed the insatiable beast."

I have to pause here and say this does not make this or any other company bad. In order to get a bunch of people to work together in far larger groups than we have done over the centuries, it's necessary to do all kinds of artificial things, like getting people aligned. Money is such a compelling motivator. Of course, they are going to use it. The point of this story is to remind you that it's not all about the money. Now back to the story.

When he said, "But they pay me so much money," his internal fear said so much more. The fear said, *"If I do the right thing, they will hate me. I will be ostracized and shunned. They will find someone to tell them what they want to hear. They might decide I'm not worth having around if I cause too much trouble. I cannot imagine anyone else paying me this kind of money. If I lose this job, I can't keep up with all my payments and obligations. I will lose the house. I will lose the cars. I will have to put my kids in public school. I will lose my status. I might even be homeless."*

He said none of this out loud – but I've heard this sequence of doomsday thoughts a thousand times. I've been in this sequence myself. I've made these compromises. I've had to feed the insatiable beast. I have felt the shackles of keeping my money and my status.

He didn't love it when my answer to his money comment was, "What does that say about what you will do for money?" It was a sincere question. I wanted him to see, hear, and feel the consequences of his mindset. I wanted it to hurt a little bit.

He looked down and then back at me. I saw the pain in his eyes. All I had done was voice the same question he had been asking himself for years. "What am I doing for money?" "What does it make me when I compromise who I am to get a paycheck?" "How have I let them gain so much power over me?"

And most importantly, "How do I get out of this dilemma?"

When we make money our god, money will happily make us its slave.

Recognizing the difference between our human needs – and in the modern world, money helps us survive – and our transcendent needs provides much deeper clarity into what drives our choices and how we feel about ourselves.

Scott Barry Kaufman's book *Transcend, The New Science of Self Actualization* provides a lovely picture of the dichotomy of Attachment and Self Expression. A sailboat.

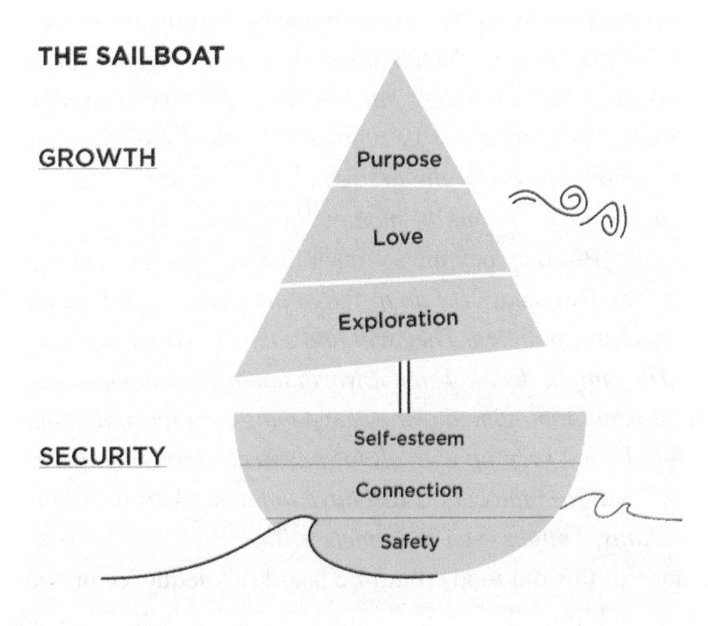

Adapted from Scott Barry Kaufman, Transcend, The New Science of Self Actualization, 2020

The boat is like the Attachment side of Maté's needs framework. Kaufman calls that side Security. Just like letting the water into a boat will cause it to sink, letting in the wrong things into our personal boat – or under our skin – can cause us to sink. We need to keep the boat in good working order. On the other hand, a boat with no wind in its sails is in the doldrums. We need the sail to propel us forward. The sail represents the Self-Expression side of Maté's needs framework. Kaufman calls this side Growth.

The sailboat metaphor more closely represents my experience in understanding my own human needs. The survival stuff, including psychological safety, plus the fact that we humans are wired for relationship and connection, make up the boat. If the boat is not solid, free of holes, and is in poor working order, it will not sail. We need to keep our boat in good order.

We also want to go somewhere. When the conditions are right, we can unfurl our sails and catch the wind. When we feel secure, we have the internal freedom to love unconditionally. We have the innate sense of security to remain present in the moment. How we sail our own boat is unique to each of us.

The simplicity of the sailboat metaphor gave me an easy way to orient myself. When I am working with a horse, I can quickly assess: Does he feel safe and secure? How's his health? Has he had enough water, food, rest? All these questions come from the idea of checking in on his "boat."

I can also quickly assess the other side of the balancing act. "Am I giving the horse choices?" "Is he being challenged?" "How much am I allowing him to own his part of this ride?" In other words, does the horse get a chance to sail? (Funny picture, right?)

The boat and the sail each represent a side of the tightrope. Are the two core needs of Attachment/Security/Survival and Self-Expression/Growth in balance? Which side of the tightrope do I need to work on right now? What is off, and which way do I move to make a correction toward the balance point?

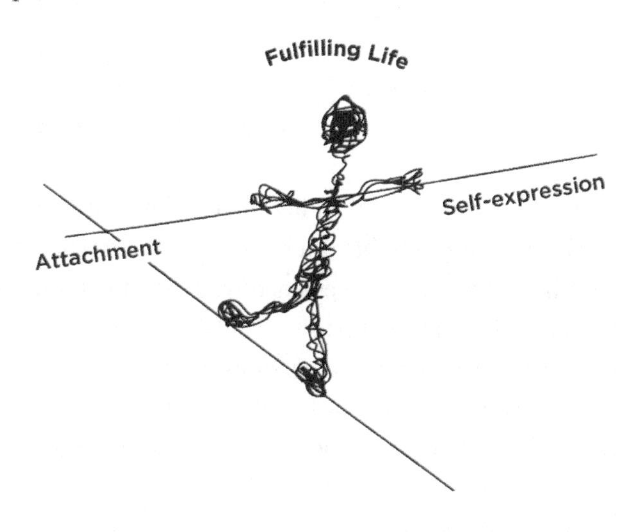

Security/Survival always comes first. Just like the sails are useless without a sound boat, no horse (or human) will do its best work with a leaky boat. We often have a leaky boat.

Bruce would often say, "The horse is here to help you build THE you." I loved the idea – but couldn't quite get it at first. Eventually, I realized that our sessions in the round pen were helping me repair my leaky boat.

Back to Nature

The modern world may need money, but real humans are from nature's world. Except the modern world has a way of making us afraid of our nature.

While I grew up spending most of my time in nature, my adult life had brought me decidedly indoors. By the time I was 45, my body was growing soft and matronly, and my mind was growing ever more fearful of the great outdoors. This version of Lynn was very different than the lean, muscular athletic body with an attitude that welcomed adventure of my youth. I was not consciously aware of this change until I was in a leadership program that focused on deep self-awareness. We were in rural Florida at a Catholic retreat center. Our class of mostly non-religious business folks ate meals in the same dining hall as the priests.

On the last evening, we met after dinner for what I expected to be a short session, after which I would return to my spartan room with the tiny towels, skinny twin mattress, and anything-but-luxurious bathroom. They didn't even provide a hair dryer! I was already looking forward to escaping this hellhole of simple living that had no cell phone service when Barry, one of the retreat leaders, announced that we would all be going outside for an evening meditation. We had done many group meditations during the week, and I was over it. But that's not what freaked me out. What caused me to flip my lid was the next instruction.

"You are going to do an individual meditation. Over in that corner of the room are portable chairs and flashlights. Pick out a chair and flashlight, and then go find a place along the trail that speaks to you. Set up your chair, turn off your flashlight and sit in your meditation," said Barry.

I'm sure Barry gave more specific instructions on the point of the meditation and how we were to do it, but I couldn't tell you what he said to save my life. His voice couldn't reach my ears through the buzzing sound of fear.

My mind started racing. *"It's pitch dark out there. There's no way they are asking us to do this. What a terrible idea! I'm not doing it."*

I spoke up and tried to sound very logical and corporate. "Isn't that kind of dangerous?" I asked.

Barry asked, "How so?"

"Well, if I'm out there all alone, can't somebody or some animal come kill me?" I retorted.

Barry said, "Well, I guess they could. But it's not likely. It's not like there are people hiding in the woods waiting for you all to go out there and get caught. And there will be other people in the area meditating as well."

I was so disappointed that Barry could be in denial like this. He seemed smart and all, but I felt like I was addressing a real problem and he was simply not willing to see the truth of the matter.

I tried one more time to help him see the error of his ways. "Look, you guys run this program every few months. Anyone that wants to can find out when the program happens. And those same people can quickly figure out that you send out unwitting people into the darkness to be sitting ducks. It's always on Thursday night. They are probably out there, lying in wait as we speak!"

Barry and his wife and co-facilitator Susan both chimed in with as much encouragement as they needed to get me moving. It took a lot. Eventually, I did make my way out to the trail, angry and shaking with fear all the way.

Looking back on it, I laugh at my perfectly logical fear. As Aristotle said, "The things you see, you are." When all I saw was danger, Survival Mode was my primary state of being. Self-Expression is impossible when we are locked in fear.

Nature has a beautiful way of providing clarity. We both stand in awe and see our powerlessness at the same time. The four seasons mirror our own existence. When we stop and notice, almost all answers come from watching how nature does things, from how airplanes are designed to how to dress for the cold. On the other side of the tightrope, the modern world has a way of interfering with the truth of our existence. The horses showed me many of the flaws of the modern world. Our obsession with time and deadlines. Our need to succeed at any cost. Our mixed messages. Our striving for perfection. Our fear of being out of control. Our disconnection from the earth that feeds us and the spirit that fortifies us.

Now Bruce's word made so much more sense. "I'm helping the horse to help himself survive in the world we have created." Bruce was showing me how to let the horse be a horse in people's world. And the horses were reconnecting me to nature's world. They were showing me my nature. On one side of my tightrope was "people's world." On the other side was "nature's world."

Clarity starts with removing that which does not belong. Whether creating a simple picture for how my day is going to go or a picture for the horse on a trail or a vision for my life, the art of subtraction makes room for what is real and true. I can only afford to remove my protective armor when I've come to own my true inner strength and acknowledged my true nature. We really live in two worlds. First, the world we have made — i.e., the modern world. Second, and more importantly, we live in the world for which we are made. We are made for the pressure of being in harmony with forces of nature.

"Clarity starts with removing that which does not belong."

When this insight clicked, I was ready to complete the circle.

CHAPTER NINETEEN

Back on THE Horse

Going Home in A Car

Three years after the accident, I returned to the barn at Babs' place for the first time. As I drove over the hill, I spotted the place where the ambulance met us that day a little over three years before. I waited for a wave of emotion, for some sort of visceral fear to arise. All I felt was a sort of settled excitement.

As I walked to the barn, I reflected on the difference between this time and the day of the incident.

On the day of the accident, I had one focus: Get on the horse. I was there to go on a trail ride. Except for sporadic vacation rides, it had been forty years since I had the opportunity to have the magical experience I remembered as a child.

In that state of mind, only one thing mattered: my goal of getting ON the horse. Everything leading up to the moment of mounting was just an impediment. I rushed through grooming. I never connected with the horse. I focused on the mechanics of the saddle and bridle, just wanting to show I could do it by myself. Once he was saddled, I did not take the time to walk with him on the ground. It was all a blur of tedious action awaiting the big moment. Once I was up there, I pulled out my phone and took a picture. Looking back on it, my modern, disconnected mind was almost laughable.

What I didn't know – couldn't know – was that every mindless action sowed the seeds for the disaster awaiting me.

On this day, I was soaking in everything. Babs greeted us with a huge smile. She was so thrilled that I was back. The minute I walked into the barn; I noticed the expression on each horse's face.

Daryl had been working with me and Scotty through this whole time. A couple of weeks before, she had seen me gain more and more clarity and said "You are ready." On this day, she joined us for moral support. We decided for this ride, I would ride Cody and we would follow THE horse, Mocha. He preferred to lead, and I was not quite ready to be on the horse in front. Daryl would ride Mocha.

When it was time to brush the horses, I took the time to recognize which spots Cody enjoyed being scratched, and which ones to avoid. I asked for help with saddling and bridling, wanting to be sure the saddle was in the proper place. Once he was saddled, we walked around on the ground to give him a chance to breathe and for us to connect. Breaking things down step by step, Frame by Frame, listening to and balancing my Negative/Positive Pole, I felt no urgency. In fact, taking things Frame by Frame had become pure joy. Listening, hearing, observing, waiting, breathing, dancing through the give and take as we took our time.

Once mounted and on the trail, I expected to feel that hit of adrenaline I had felt so many times before. In the early trail rides following the accident, every hill or unexpected move by the horse sent so much adrenaline through me, it was almost intolerable. After three years of soaking in my lessons, all I felt was a quiet excitement to finally be there, unaware but ready for what might come on the trail.

During the past three years, I had come to realize that every trail ride brings the potential for an opportunity to raise my pressure threshold. My many rides at Cedar Creek had shown me that even horses that take people of all levels of experience can have moments. Horses are not motorbikes. They have a keenly tuned survival brain. The horse in front keeps an eye out for danger and their scan can go as far as a mile. The horse in the rear tunes in to danger coming from behind. The horses in the middle are counting on those in the front and rear to alert them to trouble on the trail.

Putting me in the middle was a deliberate strategy to make things as controlled and safe as possible for my first time back to the scene. Ironically, as I was walking Cody around after putting the saddle on, I realized that I had ridden many, many more times since I started riding two years ago than I had in my entire sixty-two years of life. In preparing to get back on the horse,

I had ridden more than twenty-five horses in different settings.

What started as a mission to overcome trauma had offered me a new way of being with fear and danger.

We planned the ride to avoid any steep downhill traverses. In our debriefing after the accident, we recognized that a good part of my fear was triggered by the steep hill and Mocha's big, rocking gait. When my Negative Pole went up and I had no skills or Tools to address the feeling, I gave myself over to it. With every grippy, fearful action, I had communicated to the horse, "We need to GO. FAST. NOW."

While I was confident I could now walk a horse down a hill without adrenaline coursing uncontrollably through my body, we were determined to set the conditions for a calm and easy ride.

But you never know what you are going to find on 2,100 acres of mostly preserved wilderness. We had been riding for a while, talking casually, when suddenly a deer exploded out of the woods in front of Mocha. The deer was gone as quickly as she arrived. Now the question was how would she affect the horses? In this case, nothing happened with the horses, and we moved on with relief. This first opportunity only confirmed that my pressure threshold was higher. Rather than automatically be in fear, I tuned in to how the horses were feeling.

The deer sparked a conversation on each horse's unique reaction to being startled. Cody, the horse I was on, does a sudden jump to the side. Good to know.

Just after we crossed a leaf-covered bridge, Daryl and Mocha stopped. "We have a situation. Snake on the trail." We all stopped and waited for a few moments, hoping the snake would move on. Perhaps he was hoping to stay invisible or avoid being trampled by the twelve giant hoofs looming near him. Either way, he wasn't going anywhere.

As we started to move past him, the snake decided it was time to skedaddle. We heard leaves rustling as he tried to slither up the hill, falling, regaining, and falling again as we walked past. Suddenly, Cody caught sight of him and in a microsecond, all four of his feet levitated to the left as the snake went by to our right. Fortunately, I stayed balanced. I quickly reassured Cody that all was well, and we walked on. Second opportunity to reconfirm my pressure threshold.

We arrived back at the barn, all in one piece. I was able to drive away in my own car, not the ambulance. Just as had been the case in many rides over the past two years, I survived.

There really was no question about my survival. I had built a much stronger foundation in both my skills and more importantly, in raising my pressure threshold.

The only thing left was to get back on THE horse, Mocha. But first, I had the opportunity to discover just how far I had come – and a chance to move through pressures I had never been able to withstand.

The Heights of Fear

It was almost inconceivable that I had been on this quest for three years. What would it mean for me to finally achieve the goal of getting back on Mocha? While just a mere few months before, the goal seemed way out of reach. After the ride with Cody, I realized that riding Mocha was within reach. Ironically, I started thinking it could be a letdown, because I had treated it like the Holy Grail.

It was quite strange to consider that riding Mocha could be any sort of letdown. After all, it had not been that long ago that Bruce had asked, "Are you ever planning to get back on THE horse?" My answer at that moment was a yes, but with the same level of confidence as if he had asked, "Do you think you will ever book a trip to outer space?" It sounded great in theory – but only because it was so far out of the realm of possibility at the time.

Now the day was near. *What would it mean to check off this box? Would I quit riding lessons? Would I somehow declare myself complete? Would I treat it as a test rather than allowing the experience to help me burn off the old ways? Would I go back to my previous life without horses? In what ways had this quest truly changed me?*

The answer to the last question came in a surprising way that had nothing to do with horses, and everything to do with perhaps my greatest fear of all: heights.

If our most core human need of all is to be safe, it is second only to a mother's need for her child to be safe. When my mom was pregnant with me, she had a dream that would color the rest of my existence. She and my dad were vacationing at the Grand Canyon. I was a toddler. In her dream, I ran toward the edge and disappeared. She woke in terror as little Lynn, who was not even born yet, fell off the cliff. Even though she quickly recognized it was a dream, she treated it as a premonition.

For the rest of my life, five words were echoed – no screamed – in my ear, "Don't go near the edge!" She meant it literally and figuratively. Don't go near anything where I could fall off. Don't go near anything where I could be hurt. Don't go near anything at the edge of a belief, rule, or principle. In her world, I needed to stay far away from any kind of risk that could lead to death, falling, or being judged.

"If our most core human need of all is to be safe, it is second only to a mother's need for her child to be safe."

My mom just wanted me to be safe. What happened mostly was that I developed a debilitating fear of heights.

My history of dealing with high places was littered with experiences where I lost my composure. Yet here I was, married to Russ, a man who loves high-adrenaline adventures involving going near frightening edges. The better part of me probably chose him to help me work through my fear so that I could enjoy life.

For most of our marriage, my fearful, fretful inner child gave him no chance to help me.

Instead, I embarrassed him with a primal scream when he took me rock climbing. I slapped his hand away when he tried to comfort me on the stairs of the Statue of Liberty. I quivered and shook in every steep place we ever visited, including the deck on my own mountainside home. On more than one hike along a cliffside route, I balked and then melted in a puddle of tears. My fear of heights even freaked me out while scuba diving. I went under, took one look at the edge of the Cayman Wall dropping into oblivion – in the ocean, mind you – and levitated out of the water. To say I had a fear of heights is an understatement.

Eventually, he gave up on doing most extreme activities. In the meantime, I somehow managed to learn to ride a snow ski lift without holding a death grip from bottom to top. We settled into occasional, safe, middle-of-the-road vacations like our parents took.

None of this was on my mind when I booked a trip for four to go to the zip line down the road at one of the local attractions known as The Gorge. Ironically, we were going with our friends David and Daryl. The same woman who had introduced me to Bruce and was teaching me to ride Scotty might get to see my fear of heights in all its Texas-sized glory. Little did I know at the time that this was the fastest, steepest zip line in North America. I learned that fun fact while they were strapping us into the harness. It wasn't until that moment I remembered; I was afraid of heights. What the hell was I doing here? And why had I booked it? Our friends had mentioned it would be fun and, being the "camp director" style organizer, I just made the reservation.

Now sitting on the edge of the deck at the Gorge while getting strapped into my harness, I checked in for the usual syrup of fearful sensations that would start coursing through my body at these moments. Interesting. I felt something, but this was different than the usual pre-meltdown sensation. My Negative Pole was barely registering. If I had to give it a number, it was a three. Instead of Jell-O® legs, feeling locked down in fear, I was excited.

As they took us through the preflight routine, I checked in with myself again. Interesting. I found myself curious if the sensation would be like water skiing. Was it as fast? But would my curiosity last? What would I do when it was time to step off the edge? Should I wait until the end just in case I needed to bail out and let everyone else go have their fun?

That choice was taken from me rather quickly. They hooked us to the line in the sequence we would go, and it would be complicated to reset. So, I went with the flow.

When it came my turn, I walked to the edge of the platform and then the guide had me step up on a tree stump that doubled as a mounting block. That was another clue that this time was different. I was able to step up with firm, non-wobbly legs as he hooked me to the zip line. Then he gave me the "all clear" to step off. And I did. Off I went, flying at breakneck speed, holding on to the tiny little handle.

It was exhilarating!

The zip ended with a hard stop, the kind of jolt that felt sort of like a car accident. Such a hit formerly would have sent me spiraling into freak-out land. Indeed, there was a moment of surprise. But then again, this time was different. The guide pulled me in and once again, I easily stepped up onto the bench as he unhooked me and asked me to step onto the small platform surrounding the tree. We continued in this manner for several more zips. At every stop, we were standing on a platform built around a tree very high off the ground. I was fine. Until we reached the tree with no zip line out. Wait. What? Now that I had mastered flying on the zip line, I eagerly looked for the next ride.

Instead, this time we would exit the tree by first walking across a swinging bridge and then going down on a rappel line. I've never been a fan of swinging bridges, especially ones hanging way up high in the trees. There were only two choices at this point. Walk the bridge or have the guide lower me down on a rope. I had no interest in going straight down!

The bridge was not fun, but at least my feet had something to step on. During this traverse, I was just happy to keep one foot moving in front of the other. Once we reached the next tree, we were back to the same choices, only this time, there really wasn't a choice. I could rappel of my own accord or let the trip guide lower me using his special rope. Same way out. One the drop of shame and the other the glide of victory.

As the guide demonstrated the method we would use, it was a veritable house of horrors to the old me who feared heights. The guide asked if anyone had ever rappelled before. "Yes," I said, "I've been down a few feet in a rock-climbing gym." (What I didn't say was doing so was a single frame in a twenty-year journey that only ended in a rappel because I was too tired to climb my way back down.) Then she said, "Well, this is nothing like that. This is more like a free fall – but controlled." Grrrreeeeaaat. The guide showed us how to walk to the edge, where she said we needed to hang all ten toes off the platform. Then she said, "Trust the sit" and disappeared into oblivion.

Toes. Hanging off the platform. In other words, the opposite of "Don't go near the edge."

For the first time that day, echoes of my fearful past started rattling around in my brain. Lynn on Screen 1 knocked on the door of my psyche, promising a better answer to "Trust the sit."

Here's where it got interesting. Yes, I could feel the sensations of a potential freak-out start to stir. Lynn on Screen 1 pummeled me with thoughts, like, *"Is this woman crazy? How do you ever think I'm going to step off this ledge?"* My Negative Pole was now a solid five, registering the highest number of the day.

However, when I checked in with myself, I realized that the fear, while present, would not drive me. While definitely in the Froth, I wasn't over my Pressure Threshold. I had the power to shift to my Tools. My old Rules would not run me. Lynn on Screen 2 had managed the sculling boat in the wind. Lynn on Screen 2 had dealt with dozens of horse incidents scarier than the original trauma. Lynn on Screen 2 had learned to be the conduit,

> "I wasn't over my Pressure Threshold. I had the power to shift to my Tools."

take things Frame by Frame, shed mistakes, and shift into the What's Next Cycle. It was time for Lynn on Screen 2 to step up. Or to be precise, step off.

My turn came. I was a bit incredulous as I stepped to the edge because this time actually FELT markedly different than any other time in my life. My body was not filled with the sensations from an overwhelming adrenaline hit. My mind had set aside the screaming thoughts driven by fear. My legs functioned like real legs rather than feeling like liquefying Jell-O®.

So, I stepped up to the edge. The guide took the slack out of the rope and just like that, I stepped off the platform.

All day long, Russ marveled that I was managing the zip lines. When I dropped off the rappel – which turned out to be the first of three similar dismounts from the trees, he was thrilled beyond words.

My recovery from falling off the horse had given me so much more than horseback riding skills. I had not just changed around the edges. I was fundamentally different. In getting back on the horse, I had unleashed my Tools.

Mocha

A week after I rode Cody, Daryl and I returned to the barn. We had been working on the ground with Scotty, as I continued to learn to develop trust and connection with horses. Working with Scotty had helped me see the subtle signals and shifts that horses are always sending.

In the intervening three years, I had often wondered about the signals I had missed from Mocha. That day when I saddled him, it never dawned on me to check in with him. If he was standing still, I assumed he was fine, and I went about my business.

My reflections also took me to the people in my life. I wondered how many hundreds of people I had worked with where I might have missed the subtle signals they were sending. How often had I just gone about my business, not noticing whether the person I was with was sending signals that they were uncomfortable?

The incident with Jen in the barn with Phoenix had brought this lesson home to me. Jen is both incredibly sensitive in a tuned-in kind of way and is also a master of not showing how she feels. Often, the most sensitive horses are the ones that are the best at hiding how they feel. Which was Mocha?

On this day, I knew everything would be different from the time we started. I took my time brushing him and checking his feet. Rather than rushing through to get the saddle on so I could get on, my mind stayed with each task. Mocha happily stood there from start to finish, without so much as a halter.

Step by step, Frame by Frame, I went through each task. After I had him saddled and bridled, I asked Babs to make sure everything was in the right place. While I would not have been surprised to feel anxious as I stepped on the mounting block, it just felt normal. I had raised my pressure threshold by this point so that even a return to the scene did not trigger a trauma response.

Once we started out, I felt confident to be in the lead. Unlike the first time I rode him, I could feel his responsiveness to my every request. Until we got to the first intersection where we could either go back to the barn or keep going out.

At that point, Mocha just stopped. No amount of urging on my part would move him. Daryl rode calmly past on Cody and Mocha then decided he could go along with the plan. The rest of the ride was as uneventful as a trail ride can be.

Perhaps the most drama we had was taking on a steep downhill. Babs had watched during the ride and could see that Mocha and I were doing well together. She knew it would be a confidence builder for both me and Mocha. As we neared the top of the hill, Babs reminded me to do large S-turns with him on the way down and trust him to find his footing. This hill was actually much longer and steeper than the one where I had the accident. When we reached the bottom, I was both thrilled and aware that I had crossed another threshold.

Many months later, we took a turn down another steep hill. As we reached the bottom, Babs said, "We call this trail collarbone alley." My first thought was *"They had someone else break a collarbone here?"* Before I could voice it, she said, "This is where you had your accident."

All I could say was "Really? It was here?" Nothing had come up for me. It did not look like I remembered at all. In fact, my first instinct was to question whether she had the right place. Then I realized that Babs had designed the trail system. She directed her husband to find us that day. She had passed the site many times in the intervening three years. Yeah, she might know better than me where my accident occurred.

While I had been saying for some time I could tell that my sessions with Bruce were rewiring my brain, revisiting the place sealed the deal.

The accident was behind me.

Time after time, I had chosen a Tools response while under pressure. Every choice led to a new set of neural pathways in my brain. The old pathways became like an untended trail in the woods, grown over with vegetation while the new pathways were opening like a superhighway.

After many months of riding Mocha regularly, I came to realize that he is the ultimate trail horse. He stands quietly to be groomed and tacked without being tied up. He likes to be in the lead for good reason. Deer crashing through the woods don't faze him. Snakes barely register a glance. We have faced it all together and more.

Looking back on the accident, I can see clearly now that Mocha did nothing wrong. He was simply trying to figure out what I wanted. What I wanted was not clear — to me or to him. On that day, I was way over my pressure threshold. I didn't even know I had a Pressure Threshold. I believed that skills were all that mattered and mine were lacking.

Returning to ride him was uneventful because I had significantly raised my Pressure Threshold and I had gained skills.

With my new eyes, I now recognized that riding Scotty was the next opportunity to raise my Pressure Threshold.

An Even Bigger Moment

Daryl and I made Friday mornings a regular thing. Before we went back to face the pressures on the trail with Scotty, she wanted me to be extremely comfortable moving him through a lot of transitions, from walk to slow walk to forward walk to working pace. This made a lot of sense. Based on my handful of experiences with him to date, my greatest fear was of him running away with me. Learning transitions would give me the confidence that going fast was not a one-way street.

The most important transition was into his gait and then back to walk. Scotty doesn't trot; he gaits. It's a fast, shuffle-like movement that is as smooth as silk. I was super excited to learn how to do it with him.

First, Daryl demonstrated as I stood in the arena. From what I could tell, she did nothing and simply said, "gait." Scotty then moved from a forward walk into his beautiful gait. It looked so easy – until I tried it.

I had ridden Scotty enough to realize how finely tuned he is. He responds to the slightest aid and is always happy to go faster. As I walked around the arena, Daryl guided me to maintain a loose rein as I asked him to go faster and slower and finally, she said, "Just say the word 'gait.' Change nothing else."

Well, I said the word gait, and Scotty cantered off, much like he did the very first time I ever rode him three months before my accident. Cantering was definitely NOT the Picture we had for this moment. Even though my inner little girl wanted to run like the wind, my more sensible adult self knew better. Always lurking in the background was the fear that he would run, and I would not be able to stop him.

So, I would bring him around and try again.

It was in these moments that both Daryl and I were aware that this time, things were different. Rather than finding my body flooded with adrenaline, I was able to calmly bring him around to a stop. Then we would try again.

In the past, it was often my terrified fear response that sent Scotty running. With three years of working with Bruce under my belt, I had raised my Pressure Threshold to the point that I could stay relaxed and present when Scotty cantered off. However, we still had not solved the problem.

In these moments, I could feel myself at a choice point between Screen 1 (the Mistake Cycle) and Screen 2 (the What's Next Cycle). It was so tempting to beat myself up for not being able to get it. In the far recesses of my mind, I could hear the little voice trying to say, *"What is wrong with me? Why can't I do this?"* Now, I was seeing that temptation for what it was: a new coating of self-protective armor to take me away from the discomfort of the Froth. I knew the What's Next Cycle was the better choice. Choosing the path of Screen 2 allowed me to remember my Negative Pole for the tuning fork that it was.

Since Daryl introduced me to Bruce, we had shared language around balancing my Poles. As an extremely experienced horse trainer, she also recognized that I would need more skill in order to effectively ride this highly trained horse.

She studied the arena video, which captured what was really happening. She could see something in my form that I couldn't feel. When I asked for the gait, I subtly shifted my weight forward in preparation for the unknown. While Daryl knew from many years of experience that it would not feel that much faster, my subconscious mind was not convinced. Whether I meant to or not, Scotty heard my movement as a request to canter. That's how he was trained. The problem was me; it was going to take many, many repetitions of me doing the wrong thing to get it right. In the meantime, Scotty would be cantering off on my subtle moves, thinking he was doing the right thing.

Rather than confuse the horse, Daryl decided to take another path.

Over the next several weeks, she taught me to ride with contact, which involves riding with a much shorter rein, sort of like holding hands with the horse. The key to contact is presence and feel. Unbeknownst to me at the time, it's one of the most difficult riding skills to learn. Do it either too hard or too soft and the horse can develop a hard mouth or become very confused about what the rider is asking. Once again, I was dancing the tightrope between too much and too little. The only way to find my balance was to feel my way through it.

Slowly but surely, week by week, Frame by Frame, we built my skills. The path we were on now fit into the category of, go slow to go fast. We broke things down even more to the Frames within the Frames. Every now and then, I could feel my impatience rise, trying to send me into the Mistake Cycle. This time, those far-away voices tried to say things like, *"This is remedial training. You should be advancing more quickly!"* Inevitably, the question at the root of the Mistake Cycle, *"What is wrong with me?"* presented itself.

When my mind ventured into Mistake territory, I gently brought it back. I remembered that the comfort found in armor might shield me from the angst, but it also kept me small and fearful. Daryl reminded me that this was advanced training, not remedial training.

Also behind those questions was the awareness that horses can spook and run off and jump in weird directions. By now, I was riding many different horses on many different trails, including Mocha. I had been through many, many situations far scarier than the one that caused my accident.

Where I had once chosen to avoid situations that had proven themselves dangerous, now I was recognizing that I could instead choose to build my mental Tools. Not only was I building skills, but I also raised my Pressure Threshold every time I chose the What's Next Cycle on Screen 2.

> **"Where I had once chosen to avoid situations that had proven themselves dangerous, now I was recognizing that I could instead choose to build my mental Tools."**

After a few sessions, Daryl decided Scotty and I were ready to try the gait again. She guided us through several upward and downward transitions through different speeds. Then she said the magic words, "Forward walk – but this time go to the edge!" As we walked, she encouraged me with the words "go to the edge, go to the edge, go to the edge!"

The irony was not lost on me. For all those early years, my mom had yelled, "Don't go near the edge!" Much of my adult life had been spent unwinding that old programming – without much success. Yet now, with a new understanding of how to raise my Pressure Threshold, build my mental Tools and take things Frame by Frame, I welcomed the words.

I went to the edge.

Scotty gaited.

Then he slowed down when I asked.

Then he gaited again.

Then he slowed down.

Then we went back on the trail.

Things could not have been more different. When I changed, Scotty changed.

> **"I had changed. When I saw the world with new eyes, everything changed."**

One of my favorite quotes of all time is, "The real voyage of discovery consists, not in seeking new landscapes, but in having new eyes," by Marcel Proust.

In the past three years, I had changed. When I saw the world with new eyes, everything changed.

CHAPTER TWENTY

Conclusion

The Other Side of Fear

Fear may be one of the most essential, yet potentially damaging human emotions. Without enough of it, we will die. With too much of it, we fail to live. As with anything that matters, it's not the thing itself; it's finding the right balance with the thing that matters. Water is essential to life. Yet water can kill. Salt is essential to life. Yet too much salt can kill. Fire can consume and destroy. Fire also offers lifesaving heat.

There are countless theories of how we humans should treat fear. The ideas range from completely getting rid of fear to putting fear in the driver's seat.

Fear loves to be in the driver's seat. Left to its own devices, fear sends the message, "I'm here to help. Let me tell you what to do, when to do, how to do."

Fear also loves to be hidden in the shadows. Behind the scenes, fear says, "Tell no one about me. You've completely gotten rid of me. You are amazing. Now, do only that which you KNOW you can do. Take no chances, lest you die."

Since most of us don't want to listen to fear in either extreme, it's common to put that voice on other people. When I was in the process of choosing to leave my banking career and enter the start-up world of entrepreneurship, fear said to me, *"What about the risk? What about all the money you are leaving on the table? Are you sure you want to blow up a twenty-year career? What about health insurance? What about your retirement plan?"* The voice of fear didn't come to me in the form of a scary voice on high or a sneaky voice in the shadows. Nope. The voice of fear sounded like my dad. In fact, it sounded so much like my dad that I spent six months agonizing over how to tell him what I was considering. That voice caused me to overreact, taking extreme measures to leave myself a backdoor into the organization I was leaving, just in case I failed. That voice almost caused me to miss the opportunity.

On the day I finally had to tell my dad, because I had submitted my resignation, I picked up the phone and found my hands shaking. I expected to hear him say the exact words that had been rolling around in my head. Living with him for eighteen years assured me that I was the expert on his every thought and feeling. As a result, I had prepared myself with every explanation. My armor strong, defenses up, I finally spat out my decision.

Then I got the shock of my life.

Dad didn't say anything out loud that even remotely sounded like what he had been spouting in my head. In fact, it was the opposite. He said something along the lines of, "That sounds amazing. I'm so proud of you and excited to see where this goes." He went on to ask questions about what I would be doing, how I found the opportunity and what I was most looking forward to doing. Wow. Part of me thought, *"Who are you and what have you done with my dad?"*

After we hung up, I took a moment to reflect on what had happened, and what I had missed. Then I remembered some key things about my dad. His profession was finding oil. He was the classic wildcatter, gambling on finding energy hidden deep in the Earth. His gambling spirit ran a mile wide. Had I used my Tools to listen and hear who he really was and what he really thought, my fear would not have appeared as a dad apparition. Instead, what I heard in my head was not my dad, but my construct of him, created by my fear.

When I was able to own my fear as mine and mine alone, not something put on me by someone else, I was able to address it in a balanced way. Yes, I did need to consider all the factors in taking the leap from steady corporate treadmill to a roller coaster driven by me.

Operating in this mindset, fear was behind me, informing me, alerting me to danger, not running me like a robot.

This incident gave me a glimpse of the other side of fear, where it had a role, but it didn't have to run me. Parents, schools, and society impose all kinds of rules on children to keep them safe. On the Attachment side of the balancing act, we are seeking belonging, relationships, and more importantly, certainty. Humans don't survive in isolation. We need each other and we need the rules that bring us together – as long as we don't overuse them. On the Self-Expression side of the balancing act, we long to shine our own light. We sense the spark that is unique to us. We owe it to ourselves and others to bring to the world that which only we can bring. Just as artists use their tools in ways only they can, the Tools we bring – our perceptions, curiosity, discipline, problem-solving – fuel our ability and our very presence. The heat of pressure shapes us much like it forms diamonds. Yes, it's dangerous. We risk rejection and it's not comfortable. If we reject the process, we get stuck in the endless loop of beating ourselves into oblivion. When we embrace it, we unleash our Tools and become truer to ourselves with each tiny moment.

> **"Operating in this mindset, fear was behind me, informing me, alerting me to danger, not running me like a robot."**

In this Pressure Journey over the past three years, I had more and more glimpses to the other side of that wall. Working with the survival brain of horses gave me a whole new repertoire to work with my own survival brain. Pressure is not going away; how I respond to pressure can either crush me or elevate me.

The modern era has created a strange dichotomy in our minds. On the one hand, it's taken us away from our nature, and away from nature. We no longer spend most of our time in nature managing our food and shelter needs. On the other hand, our natural survival brain still runs us, whether we truly need it or not. The amygdala still sends adrenaline for everything we needed it for in the old days. Thus, we end up caught in the Homeless Sequence and filled with anxiety over things that won't actually kill us. Or we end up being wildly successful at a lucrative job we hate, and we feel trapped because the modern world tells us money and status matter more than anything else.

I'm not saying there is no place for Rules. When I was learning to fly private airplanes in my late twenties, it was essential that I follow checklists, the proper flight pattern, emergency procedures and many, many more "rules." They were necessary for my safety and for the safety of my fellow pilots (and unwitting people on the ground). Flying is just one example where Rules have a place. What I AM saying is that our Rules can get out of balance, just as so many other aspects of our lives can get out of balance. Reaching for our Tools in the right place and time helps restore that balance.

Reaching for our Tools offers freedom.

When I went into the round pen with a horse, I found myself tuning in. The first Tool I needed to reach for was curiosity. My brain – the TyranT Lynn on Screen – screamed for me to know something, control something, finish the goal. My true nature – AlphA Lynn on Screen 2 – listened and waited. The horse would show me where he was. I did not need to know everything to do. I simply needed to know the next thing to do.

We don't control nature; we dance with it.

Taking a snow ski lesson one day in the early part of this latest Pressure Journey, I found myself struggling at the end of a ski run with an instructor. He looked at me and said, "Lynn, you are trying to control the skis. You need to let the skis do what they do. They are made to turn."

"But I feel so out of control," I argued.

"You are going to feel that – especially at first. Snow skiing is a dance with the mountain. Gravity always wins. You have to shift in every moment to be in harmony with the mountain. Let yourself feel the balance point as it moves," he said.

"The teachers and pressures of this journey simply showed me the missing pieces to get in touch with my natural gifts—the gifts we all were given. We do not have to keep reliving our past traumas and fears."

Notice that he didn't tell me what to do. He didn't say to "move your weight here" or "turn the ski on edge for a sharper turn." He painted a mental picture for me of what was really happening on the mountain.

His guidance reflects my intention for the readers of this book. It's not about having a formula, answers, hacks or "rules" for living. My journey is now uncovering the Tools that came with me at birth. The teachers and pressures of this journey simply showed me the missing pieces to get in touch with my natural gifts – the gifts we all were given. We do not have to keep reliving our past traumas and fears. We can rewrite the past if we choose to "embrace the suck" by feeling our feelings. It's uncomfortable. But so is spending energy to stuff our feelings, hiding from reality and beating ourselves up. Living life this way – by welcoming the solvent of pressure, reaching for our Tools, being the conduit, using our Negative/Positive Pole to guide us and breaking the Picture into the smallest possible frames – unleashes the true spirit hiding underneath our armor. It makes us a little freer than we were before.

With this mindset, having the perfect job, perfect spouse, perfect hobbies no longer matter. What matters more is IN doing our job, negotiating marriage, practicing our hobbies, we become.

On that ski trip, I had moments of dancing with the mountain. They were fleeting, exquisite and elusive. Yet through my fear, I felt it. A little more of me shined through as I rewrote my past fear of falling.

The fear isn't going away.

So, what are we to do about the fear?

We can stuff it, be overwhelmed by it, or we can choose something more life affirming.

We can dance the tightrope.

Appendix

WHAT I HOPE READERS GAIN FROM THIS BOOK

Some Practicalities to Apply My Lessons

Telling a story and teaching someone else to take the lessons from my stories are two different mindsets and activities. My greatest wish for this book is for people who have fallen off their horse — either literally or figuratively — to get back on by dancing with their fear. Overcoming fear is not the name of the game. Fear will always win. We dance with our fear when we do something we've never done before.

... If you find yourself doubting or second-guessing yourself over anything, remember that you are not the problem to solve. The problem is the problem to solve.

... If you find yourself striving for perfection, remember that there is nothing on the other side of perfection. You don't want to go there yet. Perfection is death. Mistakes are the stepping stones to living as your true self.

... If you beat yourself up over and over again, remember that it's the most well-intentioned, useless strategy on the planet. Turn your energy instead to asking, "What's next?"

... If you find yourself stuck, justifying what isn't working or pretending that everything is fine, chances are you are over your Pressure Threshold. Lower the pressure and be kind to yourself.

... If most of the pressure you deal with comes from within you, hurray! You have the power. Have a talk with your mean boss (you) and negotiate for better working terms. Remind him or her that being hard on ourselves only hardens us.

... If you find yourself in people-pleasing mode, make a list of all the people you are trying to impress or gain their approval. Rank them from most important to least important. Then focus on impressing only the top one or two.

... If you find the feelings and sensations **of doing something wrong** intolerable, play the game Warmer/Colder around different ideas to solve the source of the sensation. Pick the action that makes you feel your Negative/Positive Pole is balanced.

... If you keep trying to reach for your Tools and your automatic Rules keep kicking in, take yourself through the Five C's. Do an honest assessment. Are you really committed? Can you tap into your curiosity? Can you feel a teeny, tiny bit of courage? Can you show one person how you really feel about something? Can you write down one thing you really want to have happen?

A SUMMARY OF

The "Method"

After the book was completed, my editor Tina Wolfe saw the idea of Dancing the Tightrope in a new way. She sent me the drawing we now call The Froth. Immediately I said, "This is the whole book on one page without all the false starts, dead ends and repetitions."

The things I learned along this journey are not easily learned from a book. The benefits I experienced were hard won because they were experienced, not intellectualized. What mattered most happened in unseen territory. For a reader of the book to really gain from my experience, you must try it for yourself. Perhaps this drawing and accompanying explanation can give you a road map to start your own journey. Just remember…

"The Map is Not the Territory." - Alfred Korzybski

Our choice point when we feel pressure starts in the Froth. It's that unsettled feeling of disequilibrium and agitation. The gateway to learning – or unlearning – is now open. We can be balanced on the tightrope if we remember we have Tools as well as Rules, which represent our conditioning and the way we've always done it under pressure.

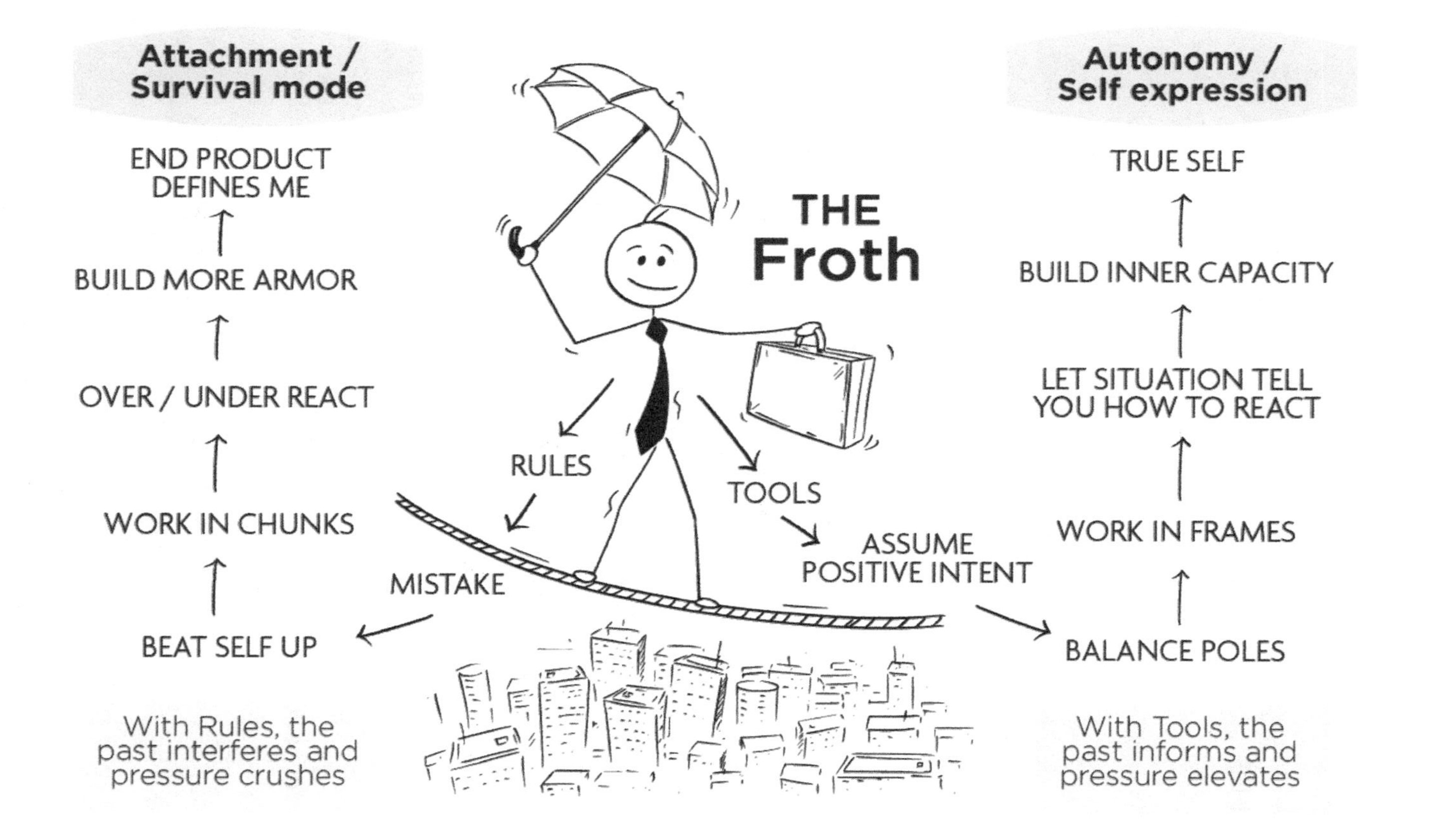
Attachment / Survival mode
END PRODUCT DEFINES ME
BUILD MORE ARMOR
OVER / UNDER REACT
WORK IN CHUNKS
BEAT SELF UP
With Rules, the past interferes and pressure crushes
THE Froth
RULES
MISTAKE
TOOLS
ASSUME POSITIVE INTENT
Autonomy / Self expression
TRUE SELF
BUILD INNER CAPACITY
LET SITUATION TELL YOU HOW TO REACT
WORK IN FRAMES
BALANCE POLES
With Tools, the past informs and pressure elevates

Let's work each side of the tightrope.

RULES

Rules	On the Rules side, think of this as the influence of the modern world. The Rules are mostly about safety, including following the rules of the group so we stay included.
Mistake	The first place we go when we feel the pressure of the Froth is the story of "mistake." We have an automatic response to the feeling of making a mistake.
Beat Self Up	Most of the time *-not always-* think of it as something happening TO us. Then we beat ourselves up. It could look like frustration, panic, self-doubt or a critical inner dialogue. Sometimes we beat up the other person, which looks like blaming, judging and resentment. This is really beating ourselves up through the other person.
Work in Chunks	We collapse the steps to do the thing into chunks. For example, imagine getting out of your car with a lot of things to carry. Working in chunks would look like trying to grab everything at once while standing up to get out of the car.
Over / Under react	Then, as we are doing the thing and something doesn't go quite right, we might overreact or underreact. In the car example, we feel the eggs sliding off the top of the pile of things in our arms. We quickly reach to stop them from falling, but we move TOO quickly, so the ceramic coffee mug crashes to the concrete floor. Or we fail to react altogether and the eggs end up on the floor.

Build More Armor	Our Mistake cycle serves a purpose. It provides a sense of safety, albeit a somewhat false one. When we vacillate between over - and underreacting, we keep the cycle going, thus further building armor. In the end, it looks like frustration, self-doubt and critical inner dialogue that we can't seem to stop from happening.
End Product Defines Me	We are focused on the end goal, so when we do finally succeed, we let that success tell us whether we are good enough or not. Or if we fail, we let the failure define us, thus perpetuating a fear of failure and a desire to be perfect.
Attachment / Survival Mode	Working from the Rules side of the tightrope, we lean towards Attachment because as humans, we are hardwired for relationship. We need each other to survive. Because of the survival component, the Attachment side tends to get overused.

On the Tools side, the past informs and pressure elevates

TOOLS

Tools	On the Tools side, the purpose is to unleash the inner abilities that were with you at birth. These abilities, such as listening, patience, feel, timing, problem-solving, discipline, work ethic, commitment, curiosity, courage, congruence, and clarity were with you at birth. The conditioning in our modern world shuts these down. In other words, the Tools do not require you to change who you are. Instead, the Tools UNLEASH who you are.
Assume Positive Intent	When we assume positive intent, we interrupt the typical reaction that makes us beat ourselves up, or beat up the other person. We can think "This is happening FOR me." We can treat the pressure of the Froth as a catalyst, where the conditions are right for us to open up, release old ways, rewire our brains and be the conduit.
Balance Poles	The Negative/Positive Pole can be a signal, or it can be noise, depending on the story we tell about it. Here, we learn to feel and properly calibrate what the signal is telling us, so that we can take the next best step.
Work in Frames	Working in frames means to break tasks down to steps, or the smaller pictures that make up the whole picture. In the example of gathering things when getting out of the car, first look at the big picture. Is it possible to carry everything? Then decide what goes in which hand. Then begin to pick up one item at a time, in an order that allows you to hold everything securely. Then step out of the car.

Let Situation Tell You How to React	Your job is to hold the picture. Then the people or horses or dogs or others can tell you what to do, when to do, how to do. The idea is to be the conduit, through listening, hearing, patience, timing, feel, etc. For example, in getting out of the car with packages, the number of packages, their weight, the ability to hold them firmly, and how fragile they are might tell you what to do, when to do, how to do. In the case of a horse, notice what he is telling you with his body language and other signals. In leading a company or team, the leader may have the picture. The team has the answers for HOW to complete the picture. Then as things get out of equilibrium, you can react based on what is really happening, rather than over - or underreacting.
Build Inner Capacity	Every time you reach for your Tools, you open up a little more inner capacity to handle difficult situations from within yourself. Conflict and danger are still conflict and danger, but instead of avoiding them, you are able to address them as they are.
True Self	How you handle the pressure that comes your way defines and unleashes who you are. Using our tools allows us to live while we are alive.
Autonomy / Self expression	Working from the Tools side of the tightrope, we begin to unleash our true selves. We operate from the top of Maslow's Hierarchy of needs.

From Rules to Tools

Learning to reach for your Tools is easier said than done. And then there is the question of how it looks in real life. I outlined the following distinctions for a coaching client; it became a useful resource for both of us, so I'm sharing it here as a resource for my readers.

Element	**FROM RULES** *Mistake Cycle*	**TO TOOLS** *What's Next Cycle*
Pressure *(on the front end)*	Test; Dread it	Catalyst; Welcome it
Core Human Need	Attachment; Survival	Self-Expression; Autonomy
FROTH: Something is off; Negative/ Positive Pole	Feeling means "mistake;" problems are to be avoided	Feeling means "assume positive intent;" problems are gifts to be welcomed
Emotions	Seen as good or bad; avoid, suppress, repress. Eventually flatline	As natural as the ocean waves. Seen as indicators of what matters; signals of the human experience
Story about froth and emotions	Depression, anxiety, something is wrong with me	Negative/Positive Pole; use the physical sensation as a tuning fork (or spirit level)
Mindset	I don't want to make a mistake; want to prove self as worthy	Welcome the heat; burn off old assumptions; improving mindset
Self-talk	Beat self up; self-doubt and criticism	Ask the question "What's next? How do I balance my Negative / Positive Pole?"

Element	FROM RULES *Mistake Cycle*	TO TOOLS *What's Next Cycle*
Picture (Vision/Goal)	I create picture AND decide how to create it; OR I try to figure out your picture and think I should know how to create it	I create picture; those involved tell me what to do, when to do, how to do
Frames	Blend the steps together; rush things; jump to the end	Break the picture into the smallest frames possible; take each step mindfully; allow the picture to emerge
Presence	Either ahead of or behind the moment	In the moment, frame by frame
Balance	Static alignment; rigid and not flexible	Dynamic alignment; fluid; adaptable
Energy	Pressure drains me; feels like weight; a burden	Use the energy of the pressure; gather and deploy; recovery *(learning in the down cycle)*
Calibration of actions	React; I have to have the answer; I decide how to react; think I "know" the answer	Respond; I am the conduit; play the game of warmer/colder; recalibrate based on what's happening
Focus of judgment	Based on "right and wrong"	Based on "what will this lead to?"
Process	Rush to get to the end; end defines me; builds more armor	Create a clear and impeccable picture of what "good" looks like; process unleashes true me; creates more inner capacity

Element	FROM RULES *Mistake Cycle*	TO TOOLS *What's Next Cycle*
Rewards	Achieving the end goal; fleeting and empty	Dopamine and endorphins (along with adrenaline). Natural and useful only if we claim it and allow ourselves to feel it.
Consequences	Blaming, guilt, self-doubt, denial, justification	Ownership, responsibility, continual correction toward picture
Quality of personal relationships	Based on power over/under; command and control or placate and suck it up; sense of being better than the other; exploit	Based on power with; trust and connection, give and take; sense of equality; empower
Pressure threshold (on the back end)	Crushes me; have to lower the pressure in order to perform	Elevates me; raises my pressure threshold (i.e., strengthens my mental tools to be greater than this level of pressure)
How we end up feeling	Locked up; more of the feeling of not being enough; "impostor syndrome"	Free; more of the feeling of being good enough; feeling like my True Self
Relationship to nature	Man's World; the world we have made	Nature's World; the world we were made for
Relationship to self	It's in the quality of the finished product that decides who I am	It's IN doing—through the pressures—that I become truer to myself

Acknowledgments

When the words "I'm going to write a book" came out of my mouth in April 2018 at the breakfast table with my dad Peyton Carnes and his wife of six years, Jane, I had only an inkling of what was yet to come. When I was a young child, I said "I'm going to write a book" every time my mother Sally gave me a new pad of paper and a blue felt-tip pen. All of those blue scribbles are long lost in the trash bins of time. On this morning, after an engaging conversation about self-awareness, Jane said "you should write a book" and I answered with words that carried the energy of conviction. A book would be written, some way somehow. Not only did Jane, a brilliant artist and writer herself, offer the creative spark that started this journey, she also offered beautifully candid feedback that made it so much better. All of my readers can thank her for thoughtful contributions.

On the day Babs Strickland invited me over for a trail ride on Mocha, I was completely oblivious to the amount of trust it takes to offer a horse to another rider. Any reader of this book is well aware by now of my lack of knowledge or awareness about all things involving horses. After my accident, she would have been well within good judgment to never make such an offer again. Yet she enthusiastically followed my progress through the journey I share in this book and trusted me once again to ride Mocha, who is now one of my most trusted mounts. I am so grateful to both of them!

From the very beginning of this journey, Daryl Nelms took me under her wing, sharing her wealth of knowledge in working with horses. When she first saw me on Scotty, she could have dropped the idea given how far I had to go. Instead, she helped me start over at the beginning. Her patience, guidance and high standards are unparalleled. She offered her wisdom and encouragement over and over again as I rebuilt my confidence. She is also the one who suggested I contact Bruce Anderson, with whom she had worked with one of her horses.

I have wondered more than once what would have happened if I had never gone back after the first day of working with Bruce Anderson. Luckily for me, I will never know. Not only did Bruce help me see horses with new eyes, he also helped me see pressure with new eyes. Once I saw both the inevitability and value of pressure, it was like entering a parallel universe on Earth. Things that used to scare me became worthy challenges. The mistakes I used to avoid became stepping-stones to something better. And the horses showed me a pathway to trust and connection in human relationships. I'm deeply grateful to Bruce for honoring his commitment to help the horse to survive in the world we have created, for it's helping me do the same. I'm also grateful for his partner Julianne Neal of JA Media Productions for her work in film and other media to share the message broadly. I'm grateful in the way words cannot express to Marley, Trini, Mac and the pony, all of whom gave of themselves so I could learn about myself.

Bruce was not the only person offering a bridge between horses and humans. Lynn Brown came across my radar screen right about the time I realized I would be wise to take regular riding lessons closer to home. Where Bruce started with my mindset in relating to horses, Lynn started by teaching me the horse's mindset. She held me to the high standard of discipline that I needed to break through my old assumptions about how horses behave and how my leadership mattered. I cannot imagine being successful on this journey without her guidance in reading the subtle signals of the horses so that I could develop a true relationship with them. Of course, I also have to thank horses Phoenix and Shahlik for their honesty in showing me a true reflection of myself.

In learning anything, practice matters most of all, and Cedar Creek Stables offered me saddle time. From the first time Howard

Redmon said with a twinkle in his eye that I would ride Ben, he welcomed me as I came back time and time again to ride different horses. At first, he made sure I had the horses that would bring me confidence. Eventually, he started asking "Are you ready to ride Stella?" – the mule famous for challenging her riders with off-road adventures and insistence on stopping for a long graze. As my confidence grew, so did his willingness to put me on horses that were still learning their way in a new home. Eventually, we agreed it was time for me to ride Ben, who turned out to be another delightful and steady horse. In many ways, Howard, Lois and his whole team of dedicated horse lovers have been and continue to be my consistent cheerleaders as I've navigated this journey.

When I started my riding lessons, friend Tammy Tappan often called and asked if I would like to go on a trail ride on her horse Drifter. He's a tall quarter horse who requires a confident rider. Usually, my answer was a strong "No way." One day, she suggested I come over and meet him and walk him around on the pasture. Even on the ground, Drifter could see that I wasn't ready to be his leader and he led me around. Once again, a good friend persisted and believed in me as I raised my Pressure Threshold bit by bit. It would be well over a year before I was ready to go out on the trail with Tammy, her horse Hondo, and the horse I rode named Drifter. We eventually had many fun rides together. In the past year while I was finishing this book, she trusted me enough to care for both horses for six months while she was invited to be an artist-in-residence at the Celebration of Arts in Scottsdale, Arizona. So not only must I thank Tammy for her trust, I also am incredibly grateful to Hondo and Drifter for all they taught me.

While I was writing this book, I started a podcast called Creative Spirits Unleashed. It was an opportunity to have the kind of conversations that enliven my world. I did not expect it to inform my journey, yet the podcast became an integral part of my learning. Just twelve episodes in, I invited Warwick Schiller to be a guest. This was before he started his own blockbuster podcast called The Journey On Podcast. In one of Warwick's early episodes, he spoke with Nahshon Cook. Soon thereafter, I reached out to Nahshon, who blew me away with his wisdom and kind heart. I found Nikki Porter by listening to her interview with Warwick Schiller. She helped me see that my passion for horses was perfectly "normal." I found Robyn Schiller (Warwick's wife and business partner) when I got to meet both in person at a reining show in 2021. My latest guest, Lee McLean, was as eloquent in person as she is in her thoughtful writings on Facebook. Every conversation I had influenced me in ways that are still unfolding. I'm incredibly grateful to each, not only for saying "yes," but for the way they informed my horsemanship – and human – journey.

When I started this book, my intention was to write about the role of self-awareness in the corporate world. I wrote a lot of words before I realized this book was going to be much more difficult to write than I first envisioned. I started and stopped over and over again, seeking clarity on what exactly this book was going to be. In the Spring of 2020, I joined a group of writers called Writing in Community. We were in the COVID-19 lockdown and it seemed like a good time to really focus on my book. Writing in Community offered an online forum to meet other writers, get honest feedback on the work and to learn the ins and outs of book writing, editing and publishing. As I took in all that I was learning and hearing in the Community, I realized that this book would be about my journey to get back on the horse. There were so many fellow travelers to thank, although too numerous to mention by name.

However, one group I must give a huge shoutout is the Writers Salon. A few of us started meeting weekly to share our progress in publishing our books: Kira Higgs, author of *Winnowing, A Memoir;* Terri Tomoff, author of *The Focused Fight, A Childhood Cancer Journey: From Mayhem to Miracles;* Katy Dalgleish, author of *Dear Democracy, You need us to survive. Sincerely, Public Schools*; Julie Rains, author of *Growing Wealth: Essential Money Lessons from My Garden to Yours*; Kymberly Dakin, author of *The Listening Coach: Head Heart & Hands Listening in Coach Practice.* Writing a book can be a lonely endeavor. The fellow travelers of my Writers

Salon offered every kind of encouragement, feedback and support imaginable.

Once again, I am ever grateful for my editor Tina Wolfe. She too has traveled alongside me, from early days, when the book was a mash of unrelated stories, to its current state. Throughout, she had confidence that the book would share something different than all the other books out there. The challenge was finding and organizing the words that mattered. We knew we had the title the day she said "It's like you are describing a tightrope. It's like dancing a tightrope." She also made the cover and graphics so much better than their original form.

A book in finished form is not really complete until it has been through the eagle eyes of a professional copy editor and proofreader. Marjo Rankin is one of the best one could ever hope to find, and I found her at the lake. Not only is she a fantastic copy editor, she is also a phenomenal water skier and ski partner. I'm so grateful to have her on my team. Any errors you find in this book are because of something I did after it left her capable hands.

One of the early readers of almost everything I wrote was my daughter Jen Maneely. Not only did she participate in many of the stories in this book, she offered gentle feedback when my writing and my intention did not line up. She went so far in one of the early drafts as to print the whole book and rearrange it to help me find a line through the stories. No one had to endure more of my questions, frustration and moments of joy than she did. The book is so much better thanks to her ever-patient ear and support.

I'm also incredibly grateful to my husband Russ Pitts, who provides many opportunities for me to face pressure. There was a time when I tried to avoid it at all costs; today we enjoy many activities together, such as flying, rowing, and ziplining, because I now welcome the pressure like a long-time best friend.

Connect With The Author

Lynn Carnes is the author of *The Delicate Art, Learn to Say "No" and Unleash Your Performance* and *The Elegant Pivot: An Inspired Move for Navigating Corporate Politics.* Her TEDx talk "From Raging Bitch to Engaging Coach, The Power of Positive Intent" amassed thousands of views. While her official title is Executive Coach, a better name for what she does is Professional "Unleasher". After twenty-plus years in Corporate America, she decided to wrap work around her life and started her own leadership consulting firm. She has worked with thousands of senior leaders across a variety of industries. The leaders who work with her reclaim their peace of mind while making big things happen. She is an avid water skier, watercolor artist, potter, rower, horsewoman and loves all things outdoors. Including the snakes and spiders.

Other books by Lynn Carnes

The Delicate Art, Learn to Say "No" and Unleash Your Performance, 2019

The Elegant Pivot: An Inspired Move for Navigating Corporate Politics, 2021

Companion Workbook for The Elegant Pivot: An Inspired Move for Navigating Corporate Politics, 2022

How to Stay in Touch

As you have probably guessed by reading this book, my experiments, learning and failures continue to this day. You can keep up with my "adventures" through The Coaching Digest, a weekly newsletter, as well as my podcast titled Creative Spirits Unleashed. I interview some very interesting people, including business people, athletes and horse trainers. Many of the people mentioned in this book have been on the podcast. It's the best way for my readers to get access to my incredible network of coaches and teachers.

Most importantly, with a subscription to The Coaching Digest, you get something available only to subscribers: unlimited access to the first six months of my executive coaching program. It's loaded with tools, practices, recorded meditations, videos and exercises. Sign up at www.lynncarnes.com.

You can also follow me on LinkedIn *(Lynn Carnes)*, Instagram *@creativespiritsunleashed* and Facebook *(Creative Spirits Unleashed)*. You can find a link to my TEDx talk titled From Raging Bitch to Engaging Coach at www.lynncarnes.com.

Made in the USA
Coppell, TX
07 April 2023